Lecture Notes in Artificial Intelligence   10341

Subseries of Lecture Notes in Computer Science

LNAI Series Editors

Randy Goebel
  University of Alberta, Edmonton, Canada
Yuzuru Tanaka
  Hokkaido University, Sapporo, Japan
Wolfgang Wahlster
  DFKI and Saarland University, Saarbrücken, Germany

LNAI Founding Series Editor

Joerg Siekmann
  DFKI and Saarland University, Saarbrücken, Germany

More information about this series at http://www.springer.com/series/1244

José F. Quesada · Francisco J. Martín Mateos
Teresa López-Soto (Eds.)

Future and Emerging Trends in Language Technology

Machine Learning and Big Data

Second International Workshop, FETLT 2016
Seville, Spain, November 30 – December 2, 2016
Revised Selected Papers

 Springer

Editors
José F. Quesada (iD)
University of Seville
Seville
Spain

Francisco J. Martín Mateos (iD)
University of Seville
Seville
Spain

Teresa López-Soto
University of Seville
Seville
Spain

ISSN 0302-9743   ISSN 1611-3349   (electronic)
Lecture Notes in Artificial Intelligence
ISBN 978-3-319-69364-4   ISBN 978-3-319-69365-1   (eBook)
https://doi.org/10.1007/978-3-319-69365-1

Library of Congress Control Number: 2017956774

LNCS Sublibrary: SL7 – Artificial Intelligence

Printed on acid-free paper

This Springer imprint is published by Springer Nature
The registered company is Springer International Publishing AG
The registered company address is: Gewerbestrasse 11, 6330 Cham, Switzerland

Preface

Without any doubt, the interest in different techniques, tools, and models of the field traditionally known as artificial intelligence has exploded during the past few years. With more than 60 years of history, and a clearly interdisciplinary approach, artificial intelligence integrates as a discipline different approaches that try to simulate or reproduce behaviors or models that we call intelligent, cognitive, or rational. Among them, we can highlight functions like learning, reasoning, or language understanding.

Among the many areas of work that integrate the field of artificial intelligence, machine learning and natural language processing play an especially relevant role. Gartner recently published (October 2016) a report on the Top 10 Technology Trends for 2017. Within the list of key trends, "AI and Advanced Machine Learning" occupies the first place. It is worth noting that the main adjective used to describe these trends is intelligent: "AI and machine learning have reached a critical tipping point and will increasingly augment and extend virtually every technology enabled service, thing or application. Creating intelligent systems that learn, adapt and potentially act autonomously rather than simply execute predefined instructions is the primary battleground for technology vendors throughout at least 2020."

Intelligent Apps (including virtual personal assistants) and intelligent things (robots, drones and autonomous vehicles) occupy positions number 2 and 3, respectively. Curiously enough, trend number 7 is for conversational systems: "… systems [that] shift from a model where people adapt to computers to one where the computer hears and adapts to a person's desired outcome."

At the European level, our multilinguality represents both a challenge and an opportunity. An outstanding group of researchers and industry leaders have promoted the "Strategic Research and Innovation Agenda for the Multilingual Digital Single Market": "*The integration of the unified and connected Digital Single Market must address our languages: The Digital Single Market is a multilingual challenge! Our treasured multilingualism, one of the cultural cornerstones of Europe and what it means to be and to feel European, is also one of the main obstacles of a truly connected, language-crossing Digital Single Market. The European Language Technology community –including research, development, innovation and other relevant stakeholders– is committed to provide the technologies to achieve this goal.*"

As a representative outcome of this trend, the Spanish government has implemented a plan to promote language technologies with an estimated investment of over 70 million euros.

In conclusion, language technologies are playing a crucial role inside a complex and complete technological ecosystem that integrates fields like cloud computing, Internet of Things, data science and big data, business intelligence, machine learning, and many other subfields in artificial intelligence.

In 2015, a group of professors and researchers at the University of Seville faced the challenge to convene a workshop where experts from different countries could meet to analyze emerging trends in the field of language technology so that they could also envision the pace for the future.

The event took place under the name First Workshop on the Future and Emerging Trends in Language Technology (FETLT 2015). This workshop was organized around a series of keynote speakers: Steve Young (University of Cambridge), Sebastian Möller (TU Berlin), Pierre-Paul Sondag (European Commission). Four coordinators of active European-funded research projects gave specialized presentations: Núria Bel (Pompeu Fabra University), Asunción Gómez-Pérez (Technical University of Madrid), Giuseppe Riccardi (University of Trento), and Steve Renals (University of Edinburgh).

Several other researchers could also share their results in a peer-reviewed process that resulted in 10 papers been presented at the workshop. All conferences and papers are published by Springer in the series *Lecture Notes in Artificial Intelligence*, volume 9577.

After the organization of the first edition of FETLT 2015 the Workshop "Future and Emerging Trends in Language Technology, Machine Learning and Big Data 2016" became a reality.

The strategic objectives of the 2016 edition were to facilitate the dynamics between research groups through the presentation of several keynote speakers, the organization of a specific workshop on the key areas of future research, and the development and innovation priorities in language technology, with special attention to machine learning and big data. The workshop hosted the presentation of peer-reviewed items. The event had a scientific committee of more than 60 experts, worldwide experts from both academia and private industry. The Andalusian Agency of Knowledge also showed interest in the event and in the organization of a specific session to guide researchers on the preparation of grant proposals and the presentation of different funding possibilities at national and international levels. This volume includes the articles presented by the keynote speakers as well as the contributed papers accepted by the scientific committee.

As conference chair, I would like to thank all the attendees of the workshop, the authors of the papers, and the keynote speakers for their participation in this event. And finally, the Scientific and Organizing Committees played the crucial role of making this conference a nice opportunity to meet and network in a highly motivating environment.

December 2016   José F. Quesada

Organization

FETLT 2016, Future and Emerging Trends in Language Technology, was held at the University of Seville, Seville, from November 30 to December 2, 2016. It was organized by the Department of Computer Science and Artificial Intelligence (University of Seville), the Research Group in Logic, Language and Information, and the Research Group in Multimodal and Spoken Dialogue Systems.

General Chair

José F. Quesada   University of Seville, Spain

Program and Advisory Committees

Joseba Abaitua	Deusto University, Spain
Alex Acero	Apple
Roberto Basili	University of Rome, Italy
Núria Bel	Pompeu Fabra University, Spain
Nate Blaylock	Nuance Communications
Joaquín Borrego	University of Seville, Spain
Wauter Bosma	Netherlands Forensic Institute, The Netherlands
Malek Boualem	Orange Labs
Zoraida Callejas	University of Granada, Spain
Nicoletta Calzolari	CNR-ILC
Montserrat Civit-Torruella	.
Thierry Declerck	DFKI, Germany
Christian Dugast	DFKI, Germany
Juan Fernández Fernández	Séntisis Analytics
Raquel Fernández	University of Amsterdam, The Netherlands
Antonio Ferrández	University of Alicante, Spain
Björn Gambäck	Norwegian University of Science and Technology, Norway
Ana García-Serrano	UNED
Jesús Giménez	Nuance Communications
Xavier Gómez-Guinovart	University of Vigo, Spain
David Griol	Carlos III University, Spain
José Carlos Gonzalez	MeaningCloud
Julio Gonzalo	UNED
Gregory Grefenstette	Inria, France
Helen Hastie	Heriot-Watt University, UK
Veronique Hoste	University of Ghent, Belgium
Eduard Hovy	Carnegie Mellon University, USA

Rebecca Jonson	Artificial Solutions
Dietrich Klakow	University of Saarland, Germany
Staffan Larsson	University of Gothenburg, Sweden
Alon Lavie	Carnegie Mellon University, USA
Marc Liberman	University of Pennsylvania/LDC, USA
Ramón López-Cózar	University of Granada, Spain
Teresa Lopez-Soto	University of Seville, Spain
Joseph Mariani	LIMSI-CNRS and IMMI
M. Antonia Martí	University of Barcelona, Spain
Patricio Martínez-Barco	University of Alicante, Spain
Mike McTear	University of Ulster, UK
George Mikros	National and Kapodistrian University of Athens, Greece
Ruslan Mitkov	University of Wolverhampton, UK
Antonio Moreno-Sandoval	Autonomous University of Madrid, Spain
José M. Pardo	Technical University of Madrid, Spain
Mirko Plitt	Modula Language Automation
Andrei Popescu-Belis	Idiap Research Institute
James Pustejovsky	Brandeis University, USA
José F. Quesada	University of Seville, Spain
Manny Rayner	University of Geneva, Switzerland
Steve Renals	University of Edinburg, UK
Antonio Reyes	Language Technology Lab ISIT
Giuseppe Riccardi	University of Trento, Italy
German Rigau	University of the Basque Country, Spain
Carlos Rodríguez	AIA, GLICOM-UPF
Jesús Romero-Trillo	Autonomous University of Madrid, Spain
Francisco J. Salguero	University of Seville, Spain
Javier Sastre	Ateknea Solutions
Richard Sproat	Google
Gerard Steen	University of Amsterdam, The Netherlands
Dan Stefanescu	Audible Inc.
David Suendermann-Oeft	ETS
Maite Taboada	Simon Fraser University, Canada
António J. Teixeira	University of Aveiro, Portugal
Alice ter Meulen	University of Geneva, Switzerland
Doroteo Torre Toledano	Autonomous University of Madrid, Spain
Khiet Truong	University of Twente, The Netherlands
Alfonso Ureña	University of Jaén, Spain
Paul Vogt	Tilburg University, The Netherlands
Piek Vosen	University of Amsterdam, The Netherlands
Jason D. Williams	Microsoft Research
Hendrik Zender	Nuance Communications

Organizing Committee

Joaquín Borrego-Díaz	University of Seville, Spain
Juan Galán-Páez	University of Seville, Spain
Diego Jiménez-Palmero	University of Seville, Spain
Teresa Lopez-Soto	University of Seville, Spain
Francisco J. Martín Mateos	University of Seville, Spain
Ángel Nepomuceno	University of Seville, Spain
José L. Pro-Martín	University of Seville, Spain
José F. Quesada	University of Seville, Spain
Francisco J. Salguero	University of Seville, Spain

Contents

Position Papers

With or Without Meaning? Hype Cycles in Language Technology and What We Can Learn from Them

António Branco[(✉)]

Department of Informatics, Faculty of Sciences,
University of Lisbon, Lisbon, Portugal
Antonio.Branco@di.fc.ul.pt

Abstract. Despite its relatively short period of existence as a scientific area, natural language processing has gone through a succession of diverse mainstream research paradigms. How similar are these inflection moments in the history of the research on language technology? What can we learn from that similarity, if any, about the overall shape of the evolution of this field? And importantly, what can we anticipate from this shape, if any, about the future and emerging trends in language technology? — which is the topic of the workshop where this paper was presented.

The result of this study is meant to be of help to organize research agendas of centers, laboratories and individual researchers and innovators, as well as to guide informed institutional funding and support for research and innovation in language technology.

Keywords: Hype cycles · Scientific progress · Future and emerging trends · Natural language processing · Language technology · Computational linguistics

1 Introduction

The Association for Computational Linguistics (ACL) is a leading organization of researchers and professionals in natural language processing, a field whose object of research is the computational mapping between linguistic form and meaning and the language processing applications that such mapping can support. This association organizes an annual meeting in a different country across the globe every year. An important moment of these conferences is the plenary session with the presidential address, in which the president typically shares his views about the mission of the association and the emerging challenges and opportunities for this area.

In contrast to the conference programs of previous meetings, the program for the 2015 conference, which was held in July in Beijing, looked like having been flooded by papers resorting to, supported or inspired by deep learning techniques. The president of ACL at the time, Chris Manning, Professor at

© Springer International Publishing AG 2017
J.F. Quesada et al. (Eds.): FETLT 2016, LNAI 10341, pp. 3–19, 2017.
https://doi.org/10.1007/978-3-319-69365-1_1

Stanford University and a leading researcher in the area, though he had been exploring deep learning for language technology in his own work for some time, seems to have been impressed by what this might represent as a tectonic change in the direction that the field might be taking — so much so that he devoted his presidential address (Fig. 1) to share what he understood that was and could be the relation between natural language processing (NLP) and connectionist techniques.

In a nutshell, he argued that, given the nature of natural language, the application of deep learning techniques to its processing should not be expected to lead to the high level of gains that were obtained in their application to other domains, such as vision or speech processing, where the state of the art performance more than doubled. His talk might have been motivated by the greatly increased weight of deep learning papers in that year's conference program, but it was also seen as a reaction to the big wave of immoderate optimism which was both being motivated and ridden by the promise of deep learning for the unlimited progress of any domain where it might be applied to.

Fig. 1. Picture of the President of ACL in the opening address at the 2015 ACL meeting, Beijing.

In that year of 2015, a few months before that conference in Beijing, in one of its May issues, the *Nature* journal included a dissemination paper with the title "Deep Learning" by leading researchers in that area [1]. Defending the superiority of (unsupervised) deep learning, they stated that:

"Human learning is largely unsupervised: we discover the structure of the world by observing it, not by being told the name of every object."

While it may be indeed not correct that humans discover the structure of the world just by being told the name of every object, that sensible acknowledgment by itself, however, does not make it correct, in turn, that humans discover the structure of the world just by observing it — as centuries of research on the theory of knowledge and human learning have helped us to understand. But rather than being taken as a key contribution for the theory of human learning, this statement helps to illustrate how optimism and a certain ideological reductionism may go hand in hand, and emerge even in the ranks of skillful scientists.

Interestingly, ideological reductionism backing the concentration of research efforts into a given technique or methodology — represented by the above quotation —, and eliciting exercises of devising upper bounds for the success of that technique by its mere analytical inspection — illustrated by the plenary talk referred to above — induces a déjà vu feeling. Though with a different methodology and players, the same type of jolt was experienced in the area of language technology (LT) around two decades ago, with the advent of statistical approaches to natural language processing.

This apparent analogy, together with the questions that it elicits, is driving the analytical exercise of the present paper: How similar are these two moments in the history of the research on language technology? What can we learn from that similarity, if any, about the evolution shape of this field? And importantly, what can we anticipate from this shape, if any, about the future and emerging trends in language technology? — which is the theme of the workshop where the invited plenary talk corresponding to this paper was presented.

In the next Sect. 2, we elaborate on what may be the basic elements that can be found as driving the evolution of research on language technology.

Section 3 will be devoted to represent the effect of those drivers along a timeline covering the history of this field, which will support the exercise of identifying hype cycles and their respective triggers.

In Sect. 4, we ponder on the attractors and deflectors of these hype cycles in language technology, which are supported by the research on cognition at large, while in the following Sect. 5, we ponder in turn on the enablers of scalable language technology solutions, which are supported by innovation in information technology in general.

On the basis of the materials and evidence collected in the sections preceding it, in Sect. 6 we discuss what we consider to be the emerging enabler and the ultimate attractor of language technology, which may help to devise the direction of future trends in this field.

In the last Sect. 7, we close the paper and its prospective study with an indication of what, in our view, follows from the analysis undertaken along the paper as the emerging trend for the area of natural language processing.

The outcome of this prospective analysis is meant to be of help to organize research agendas of centers, laboratories and individual researchers and innovators, as well as to guide informed institutional funding and support for research and innovation in language technology.

2   Swinging Back and Forth Between Form and Meaning

Let us start with the first question put forward above.

The advent of statistical approaches (statistical NLP) and later on, the advent of connectionist approaches (neural NLP) are two salient moments of accelerated change in the research on natural language processing. As in many respects they are inducing a somewhat déjà vu feeling among practitioners who participated in both, what can be motivating that feeling? How similar are these two moments in what they represent to the history of the research on language technology?

As made evident by the quotation above in Sect. 1, the perceived key advantage of neural NLP is to be able to do without supervised training. As supervised training relies critically on linguistically interpreted and annotated data sets (e.g. syntactic treebanks, semantically annotated corpora, etc.) — which approximates in different degrees a representation of the meaning conveyed —, the perceived supreme advantage of neural NLP is thus to rely only on input raw linguistic forms to be fully operative, thus dispensing with linguistic analysis and ultimately with the need of prepared linguistic features and specifically designed linguistic and semantic representations.

Dispensing with linguistic analysis, and a fortiori with a representation of meaning, was also the promise that prompted the enthusiastic optimism around statistical NLP in its initial days. At those times, the research work that had been carried out on meaning representation and processing was termed as symbolic NLP. That was the "old school" with respect to which statistical NLP was initially seen as bringing superior advantages by focusing on raw linguistic forms, and thus by allowing for a more streamlined and directly accessible research field, liberated from the cumbersome intermediation of linguistic generalizations and meaning representations.

Analogously, neural NLP is exercising its initial attraction by distancing itself from distributional NLP with its focus on designing and obtaining the representations of the meaning of natural language words and expressions.

In both occasions there seems to be a movement of swinging away from the representation of meaning, and towards focusing on raw linguistic forms. Of course, the repetition of this movement was possible because in-between there has been a pendular change, from statistical NLP to distributional NLP, where the representation of meaning regained its momentum again (Fig. 2).

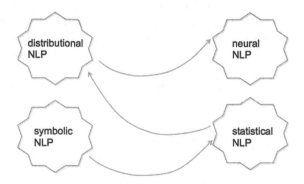

Fig. 2. Sequence of mainstream NLP paradigms.

Given these considerations, we should turn to the second question put forward in the previous section: What can we learn from these similarities about the shape of the evolution of the language technology field?

Breaking free? One possible interpretation could be that this circumstance indicates that this field is advancing by successive superior paradigms that successively replace previous, inferior ones.

But that is not the only possible analysis.

Encircled? A less positive view is that this putting into perspective of different moments of the research on language technology allows to bring to light that this field is actually not making substantial progress after all, as it may be stagnated with competing paradigms that oppose each other, with no essential advancement.

Some publications could be brought in support of this view. For instance, in their paper on "Improving Distributional Similarity with Lessons from Word Embeddings", Levy et al. report on an exercise of systematic and controlled comparison of statistical and connectionist approaches to similarity under distributional semantics [2], concluding that:

> "... we observe mostly local or insignificant performance differences between the methods, with **no global advantage to any single app-roach** over the others"

Spiraling forward? Yet another view could be that the language technology area is actually advancing, but by new paradigms extending previous ones rather than by replacing them. An example of a paper that could support this view is "A Study on Similarity and Relatedness Using Distributional and WordNet-based approaches", whose experiments by Agirre et al. [3] indicate:

> "that distributional similarities can perform as well as the knowledge-based approaches, and a **combination of the two can exceed the performance of results previously reported** on the same datasets"

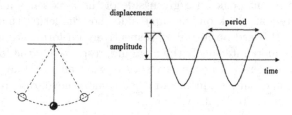

Fig. 3. Representations of oscillatory motion. (Credits: https://en.wikibooks.org)

As it often happens in science, changing the representation of a state of affairs may be crucial for a novel insight into its key ingredients and thus for gaining a more thorough understanding of it. In what concerns for instance an object in physical oscillatory motion, this movement can be captured by representing the points where the object may be along its trajectory (Fig. 3, left), or by bringing also time into the representation and thus by recording its displacement with respect to the central position along the time in a two-axis graphic (Fig. 3, right).

As noted above, language technology has evolved in a pendular fashion, with stronger foci either on the representations and processing of linguistic meaning or on the processing of linguistic forms. Taking inspiration from the figures above, it may be serendipitous to depict those transitions along a timeline represented in the x-axis, with the y-axis representing the predominant emphasis of the approach, either on the side of form or on the side of linguistic meaning (Fig. 4).

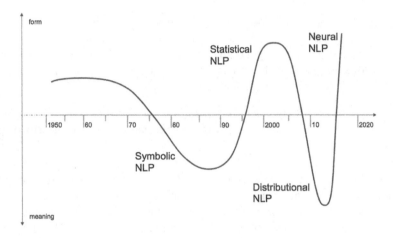

Fig. 4. Hype cycles in language technology.

There has been more than one phase in the research on language technology where the mainstream focus was on the meaning or on the form. That is rendered by there being more than one peak both above and below the x-axis.

Also, a more recent peak on a given side of the x-axis has a higher amplitude than the previous peak on same side thus rendering that more recent approaches to NLP based on meaning, respectively on form, are more sophisticated and explore more intensively the meaning, respectively the form, relations.

Additionally, more recent peaks have shorter wavelengths than previous ones. This reflects the increasing frequency of the advent of novel research approaches in the field of language technology.

3   Hype Cycles in LT and Their Emblematic MT Triggers

Our third driving question is about what can be anticipated from this shape concerning the future and emerging trends in language technology. In order to get a better vantage point to address this issue, it is worth having first a more informed understanding of the context and triggers of the hype cycles underlying that shape.

It is common wisdom among practitioners of language technology that machine translation (MT) is a most demanding application in natural language processing, deemed to be its quintessential challenge as it virtually calls for the articulation of a whole range of partial results and processing tasks in this domain. Very interestingly, key inflection points shaping the hype cycles in language technology can be traced back to key papers that introduced novel MT paradigms (Fig. 5).

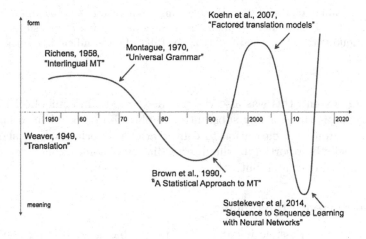

Fig. 5. Hype cycles in language technology and their emblematic machine translation triggers.

3.1 Meaning Transfer

The proposal towards an MT whose crucial step is based on the transfer of meaning representations dates back at least to the four page seminal paper of Richens from 1958, "Interlingual Machine Translation" [4]. But it would be the article "Universal Grammar" from 1970 by Montague [5] that may be better seen as one of the emblematic triggers of a consistent trend towards meaning oriented MT, and away from previous approaches based on some version of word-into-word replacement.

For any sentence of a fragment of English, this paper showed how it was possible to algorithmically obtain its translation into a logical language. As the resulting logical formulas allow to model key semantic relations, these were thus primary candidates of representations of meaning that are independent of particular natural languages. Hence, this represented a major encouragement for the exploration of the MT model based on the transfer of meaning, or at least in some abstract enough representation of its linguistic properties along the so-called Vauquois triangle (Fig. 6).

$\langle h0, \{h1 : every(x, h2, h3), h4 : dog(x), h5 : probably(h6), h7 : chase(x, y),$
$h8 : some(y, h9, h10), h11 : white(y), h11 : cat(y)\},$
$\{h0 =_q h5, h2 =_q h4, h6 =_q h7, h9 =_q h11\}\rangle$

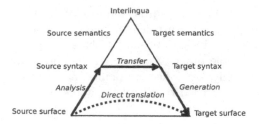

Fig. 6. Top: Meaning representation of the example sentence *Every dog probably chases some white cat* in the Minimal Recursion Semantics description formalism [6], p. 302. Bottom: Vauquois triangle. (Credits: http://mttalks.ufal.ms.mff.cuni.cz/images/f/f1/ Pyramid.png)

To a large extent, this was also the pervasive model in symbolic NLP. The key assumption is that for any substantive application or problem in language technology — from summarization to conversational interfaces —, it should be addressed ideally by resorting to the intermediation of some explicit representation of the meaning of its input.

3.2 Co-occurrence Inferencing

MT envisaged as a possible instance of some stochastic model may be traced back at least to 1949, when Weaver wrote his memorandum titled "Translation" [7]. But it would be the article by Brown et al., "A Statistical Approach to MT", from 1990 [8], which would become an emblematic inflection point and set in motion a consistent and increasing interest in exploring MT under this paradigm that focuses on the linguistic form and moves away from the previous emphasis on the representation of meaning.

Under this paradigm, the noisy-channel is the basic underlying model, which is used in speech recognition and that had its origin in Shannon's work in 1948 about correcting errors in the communication of messages [9]. The motivating goal is to recover a string that got distorted as a consequence of its transmission through a noisy communication channel: This recovering is undertaken on the basis of the combination of stochastic models of the language to which the string belongs (supporting the prediction of what string components follow each other) and of the communication channel (supporting the prediction of what string components might have been erased, inserted or replaced) (Fig. 7, top).

In an MT set up, the language model concerns the language targeted by the translation process and the channel model concerns the translation model based on possible replacements, and respective probabilities, between the source language and the target language words (Fig. 7, bottom).

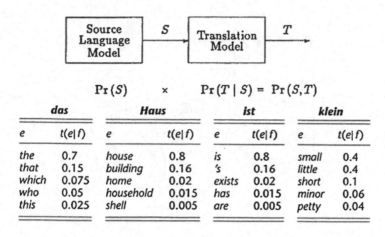

Fig. 7. Top: Diagram of noisy-channel model applied to machine translation, from [8] p. 80. Bottom: Examples of possible lexical translation probabilities in a translation model, from [10] p. 84.

This paradigm shift in MT inspired the application of stochastic inferencing techniques to language technology, which eventually induced the advent of statistical NLP. Ultimately relying on frequencies of co-occurrences of linguistic forms in collections of utterances, this approach brings the emphasis to handling forms and their surface quantitative relations in detriment of language processing intermediated by some degree of meaning representation.

3.3 Linguistic Factors

The mainstream approach to MT and NLP eventually found an inflection point with the inclusion into the stochastic models of quantitative information on more linguistic features and generalizations that were increasingly more abstracted away from raw linguistic forms. This hybridization of statistical and symbolic approaches eventually encompassed the representation of meaning.

The processing of meaning and its possible representation gained thus a revival, this time adding a new angle to it, namely under the perspective of distributional semantics (Fig. 8 (b)), where the meaning of expressions and their semantic relations are based on high dimension vectors ultimately relying on frequencies of some co-occurrences.

As in previous changes of focus in mainstream language technology research, this inflection point may be traced back to some emblematic trigger related to MT, like the paper in 2007 by Koehn et al., "Factored Translation Models" [12]. The log-linear model for MT proposed in this publication (Fig. 8 (a)) introduced a new paradigm for MT, where the impact of linguistic factors can be integrated into the translation procedure, including highly abstract linguistic information on underlying syntactic and semantic features.

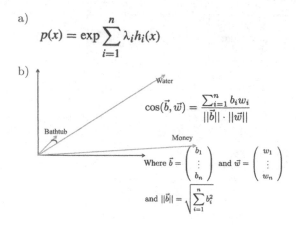

a)
$$p(x) = \exp \sum_{i=1}^{n} \lambda_i h_i(x)$$

b)

$$\cos(\vec{b}, \vec{w}) = \frac{\sum_{i=1}^{n} b_i w_i}{||\vec{b}|| \cdot ||\vec{w}||}$$

Where $\vec{b} = \begin{pmatrix} b_1 \\ \vdots \\ b_n \end{pmatrix}$ and $\vec{w} = \begin{pmatrix} w_1 \\ \vdots \\ w_n \end{pmatrix}$

and $||\vec{b}|| = \sqrt{\sum_{i=1}^{n} b_i^2}$

Fig. 8. (a) Log-linear model structure, where x is the random variable, λ_i are weights, and h_i feature functions that can be instantiated with language and translation models as well as with models for relevant "linguistic factors", from [10] p. 138. (b) Computing similarity between vectors representing the meaning of example words as the cosine of the angle between them, from [11] p. 636.

3.4   Encoding-Decoding

As the mainstream direction of research on natural language processing became oriented towards resorting to some form of intermediary meaning representation, the oscillatory pattern that seems to underlie the research in this field became again apparent. A turning point redirected once again the focus of interest, this time towards approaches based on linguistic forms and their mere surface relations, and dispensing with specifically designed representations of linguistic meaning.

Such inflection eventually emerged and once again a key contribution came from the MT area, in this case by an emblematic paper in 2014 by Sustekever et al., "Sequence to Sequence Learning with Neural Networks" [13], whose title emphasizes the focus on the modeling of the relations between the forms (source and target "sequences"), circumventing the need of handling some linguistic representation.

For each expression of a sequence of input to be translated, the recurrent neural network computes an internal interim output that takes into account that expression and the previous interim output, where in the last step, concerning the last expression in the input sequence, a word of the output sequence is also output. From that point onwards, the model computes the next step by taking the last internal interim output and last expression emitted into account. The sequence of expressions emitted constitutes the proposed translation of the initial input sequence (Fig. 9).

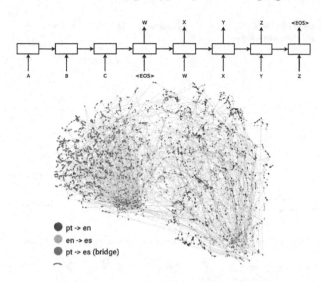

Fig. 9. Top: Schematic diagram of a translation model as a recurrent neural network, where A-C stand for expressions in sequence of the input sentence in the source language, and W-Z are expressions of the output sentence in the target language, from [13] p. 3105. Bottom: Two-dimension projection of high-dimensional vectors where each point represents a single decoding step during the translation process and where points that represent steps for a given sentence are connected by line segments, from [14] p. 10.

4 Cognition at Large: LT Attractors and Deflectors

Following the considerations above, it is enticing to associate the evolution of the research direction of language technology to emblematic publications on MT. Since MT is considered a quintessential NLP application, it is only natural that new paradigms for MT would set the example for new kinds of approaches, and thus be important drivers of change, for the whole field of language technology.

While there may be such a triggering or driving effect by new paradigms for MT, it is nevertheless also worth noting that these novelties are themselves triggered or enhanced by much broader underlying changes that occur outside the language technology (LT) area proper, namely in the broader and encompassing area of cognition technology at large. Accordingly, in as much as the LT inflection points may be fostered by new MT paradigms, like what happens with the emergence of the latter, such LT inflection points appear also strongly influenced by broader changes and successes in cognition technology at large (Fig. 10).

In this connection, it is worth noting that the advances and successes in neighboring areas, like speech or vision processing, have certainly acted as important attractors helping in the inflection of the direction of mainstream language technology.

The success of statistical methods in speech processing stimulated research seeking similar success in applying such methods first to MT and then in a generalized way to the whole field of language technology. The inflection towards

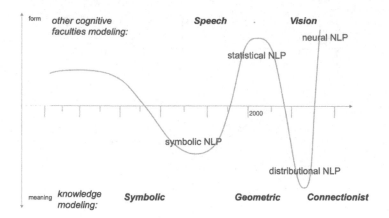

Fig. 10. Hype cycles in language technology and attractors from other areas in cognition technology.

statistical NLP in the 1990's was greatly influenced by that attempt of emulating the success achieved in speech processing with statistical approaches.

Some two decades later, in the 2010's, further advances in speech processing, where accuracy was doubled with the application of a neural networks approach, would act again as an important attractor, now towards neural NLP. This time that effect was compounded with concomitant success in vision processing, as also in this area the advent of deep learning permitted important advances.

Interestingly, while the modeling of other neighboring cognitive faculties — speech and vision — and its success pushed the focus of NLP towards linguistic form, knowledge modeling and the advent of its diverse paradigms, in turn, acted as attractors towards mainstream NLP based more on linguistic meaning.

Until the 1990's, when the focus in language technology started being displaced to linguistic form, the mainstream approach to knowledge modeling was based on symbolic methods and this was concomitant with the emergence of symbolic NLP.

When the pendular oscillation brought again linguistic meaning into central focus in the 2000's, with distributional NLP, the geometric approach to knowledge modeling might have played also an important inspirational role.

5   Information Technology at Large: Enablers of Scalable LT

As language is a core cognitive faculty and language technology is a central area in the realm of cognitive technology, it is thus natural that the advances and successes of research in neighboring cognitive faculties and respective research areas — such as speech and vision processing and knowledge modeling — and the methodological innovations underpinning them have influenced the direction of language technology research, and thus played the role of attractors, or deflectors, in what emerges as its pendular shape of development, leaning to giving primacy, in alternation, either to form or to meaning.

While there certainly is such an influence by new approaches from other cognitive technologies, it is nevertheless also worth noting that these novelties are themselves enabled by much broader underlying changes that occur outside the cognitive technology realm proper (Fig. 11).

In this connection, it is worth noting that for the consolidation of statistical NLP started in the 1990's, the advent and generalization of the internet played a crucial role as this permitted the accumulation and availability of increasingly larger and richer language datasets, without which statistical approaches for language technology could not have matured.

By the same token, it is the advent and generalization of computational devices with increasingly large storage capacity and more processing speed that enabled the viability of distributional NLP, since the 2000's, and currently of the emergence of neural NLP, which are both based on data and time intensive computational procedures.

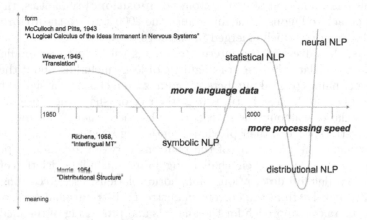

Fig. 11. Hype cycles in language technology and enablers from information technology for seminal proposals of different NLP paradigms.

That these developments in Information Technology at large have had a crucial enabling role for scalable language technology is as more salient as the key methodological insights for distributional and neural NLP had been published long time before, namely more than half a century before.

The key insight for distributional NLP can be traced back at least to 1954, to the paper "Distributional Structure" by Harris [15]. And in the case of neural NLP, as for the whole connectionist endeavor, the seminal ideas from 1943 by McCulloch and Pitts, published in the paper "A Logical Calculus of the Ideas Immanent in Nervous Systems" [16], are a landmark.

6 Emerging Enabler and Ultimate Attractor

As the objective of the present paper is to contribute to the reflection on the future and emerging trends in language technology, the discussion expanded in the previous sections concerns the analysis of previous development in language technology and is thus instrumental to address this objective.

The previous sections helped to make evident the oscillatory shape, between form and meaning, of the focus of the research on natural language processing, and that such shape is influenced by enabling factors from information technology and by attraction factors from cognitive technology. Accordingly, in order to pursue our objective, it is worth pondering on the possible forthcoming enablers and attractors.

In our view, the strongest candidate to be the **forthcoming key enabler** for language technology, contributed from information technology at large, is the advent of the internet of things (Fig. 12).

The advent of the internet helped to accumulate ever larger amounts of linguistic data. This has enhanced the processing of the relations among linguistic expressions and permitted to evolve from **compositional** semantics, the mainstream approach to linguistic meaning until the 2000's, to **distributional** compositional semantics, which emerged in the 2010's.

Likewise, the advent of the internet of things will help to accumulate ever larger amounts of data about extra-linguistic objects, including about their individual proper names (e.g. id numbers, IP addresses, nicknames assigned by their owners or users, etc.), their features (e.g. their color, shape, age, use, etc.) and about the relations among them (e.g. their location, their proximity to each other and to the speakers, their previous mentioning together, etc.). Expectedly, this will enhance the processing of the relations between linguistic expressions and their referents, in all their challenging forms, including deictic reference, contextualized definite descriptions, anaphoric relations, etc. Accordingly, this will permit to evolve from the current mainstream distributional compositional semantics, to a novel approach for the analysis and processing of the meaning of natural language, namely to **referential** distributional compositional semantics.

As for the **forthcoming key attractor** for language technology, contributed from cognitive technology at large, in our view this will result from the ongoing efforts and eventual achievements in the area of knowledge modeling of coming up with **unified cognitive models**, which will amplify the strengths and mitigate the drawbacks of the symbolic, geometric and connectionist contributions.

The impact of the internet of things, as the forthcoming information technology enabler, and of the unified cognitive models, as the forthcoming attractor from cognitive technology, will be convergent in bending the direction of the development of language technology back to be centered around the representation and processing of meaning.

7 LT: Spiraling Forward with Cross Hybridization

The considerations expanded above in Sects. 2 to 5 concern the analysis of previous development in language technology and are instrumental in reflecting about the future trends in language technology, the central objective of this paper. In the previous section, those considerations were instrumental in making evident the recurrent influence of enablers and attractors that are **external** to language technology, and thus in looking for the eventual emergence of forthcoming enablers and attractors and their anticipated impact.

Likewise, those considerations will be instrumental also in making evident the modulation that is **intrinsic** to language technology in terms of the evolving direction of the research in this area, which should also be explored to ponder on its future trend.

Shorter periods. Mainstream approaches to natural language processing have alternated between a stronger focus either on the form or on the meaning of linguistic expressions. As can be more easily observed from its graphical representation (Fig. 12), the pace of this oscillation has not been constant. The changes of paradigm have been succeeding at a faster pace along the decades, with these oscillations happening at an increasingly shorter period. It is likely that this trend continues into the future.

Wider amplitude. Language technology has been driven more than once by a stronger focus on form, respectively on meaning. Interestingly, a revival of a stronger focus on form, respectively on meaning, does not mean a mere return to previously explored solutions but a leap forward with denser relations in form, respectively in meaning, being captured and explored. This trend receives a graphical representation by means of oscillations with wider amplitude and should also continue into the future.

Increased integration. The curve in the plot is an abstraction deemed to represent the direction of mainstream natural language processing. While at any

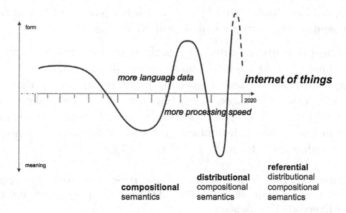

Fig. 12. Hype cycles in language technology, emerging enabler and future trend.

time interval the mainstream focus of interest is represented as moving away from a certain type of approach (and towards another type of approach), it is not the case that the previous results happen to be abandoned altogether. The inflection movements are associated with inherent latencies, which lead to temporal overlaps of different foci and approaches, and importantly, which allow for their hybridization.

Hence, increasingly shorter periods and wider amplitude in the evolution shape of language technology indicate a trend, to be intensified into the future, of an increasing and accelerating integration between the diverse aspects related to the representation and processing of form and meaning, and an increasing and accelerating cross-fertilization among the diverse paradigms.

This can be illustrated by a few recent emblematic examples of hybridizations in MT. For instance, the paper by Devlin et al. in 2014 is an exercise on combining statistical and neural approaches [17]; in 2016, Dong and Lapata, in turn, pave the way for articulating transfer and neural solutions [18]; and Gaudio et al. in 2016 report on advances on hybridization of transfer and statistical based methods [19].

More powerful semantics. The above discussion and analysis helps to understand that the hype cycles in language technology — oscillating between form and meaning — are likely the manifestation of an underlying long term trend of spiraling forward with cross hybridization of approaches and results that are advancing the representation and processing of the relation between linguistic form and meaning, which is the ultimate cornerstone of natural language processing.

Taking into account this intrinsic longstanding evolutive shape, its current direction of progress, and the anticipated impact of forthcoming external enablers and attractors, the future trend in language technology would likely direct its development to be based on a deeper meaning representation more densely anchored in linguistic form.

This more powerful semantics should result from the hybridization between sentential and compositional semantics, evolving from symbolic NLP, lexical and conceptual semantics, contributed by distributional NLP, and future referential and situated semantics, supported by neural NLP.

Better on-the-go applications. The performance of diverse types of NLP applications should benefit from this more powerful semantics.

It is likely that some of them eventually enjoy remarkable progress or even gain a new twist, especially those whose functionality is more related or dependent on a situated usage. That will be likely the case of conversational interfaces, in particular in on-the-go environments and with autonomous agents, be they artificial or human, especially in multilingual settings.

Acknowledgments. The work reported in this paper was partially supported by P2020 Program under the grant 08/SI/2015/3279 for the project ASSET-Intelligent Assistance for Everyone Everywhere.

References

1. LeCun, Y., Bengio, Y., Hinton, G.: Deep learning. Nature **521**, 436–444 (2015)
2. Levy, O., Goldberg, Y., Dagan, I.: Improving distributional similarity with lessons learned from word embeddings. Trans. Assoc. Comput. Linguist. **3**, 211–225 (2015)
3. Agirre, E., Alfonseca, E., Hall, K., Kravalova, J., Pas, M., Soroa, A.: A study on similarity and relatedness using distributional and WordNet-based approaches. In: Proceedings of Human Language Technologies: 2009 Annual Conference of the North American Chapter of the ACL, Boulder, pp. 19–27, June 2009
4. Richens, R.: Interlingual machine translation. Comput. J. **1**(3), 144–147 (1958)
5. Montague, R.: Universal grammar. Theoria **36**(3), 373–398 (1970)
6. Copestake, A., Flickinger, D., Pollard, C., Sag, I.: Minimal recursion: an introduction. J. Res. Lang. Comput. **3**(4), 281–332 (2005)
7. Weaver, W.: Translation. The Rockefeller Foundation (1949)
8. Brown, P., Cocke, J., Pietra, S.D., Pietra, V.D., Jelinek, F., Lafferty, J., Mercer, R., Roossin, P.: A statistical approach to MT. Comput. Linguist. **16**(2), 79–85 (1990)
9. Shannon, C.: A mathematical theory of communication. Bell Syst. Tech. J. **27**(3), 379–423 (1948)
10. Koehn, P.: Statistical Machine Translation. Cambridge University Press, Cambridge (2010)
11. Erk, K.: Vector space models of word meaning and phrase meaning: a survey. Lang. Linguist. Compass **6**(10), 635–653 (2012)
12. Koehn, P., Hong, H.: Factored translation models. In: Proceedings of the Joint Conference on Empirical Methods in Natural Language Processing and Computational Natural Language Learning, Prague, pp. 868–876, June 2007
13. Sustekever, I., Vinyals, O., Lee, Q.: Sequence to sequence learning with neural networks. In: Proceedings of the 27th International Conference on Neural Information Processing Systems (NIPS 2014), Montreal, 8–13 December 2014, pp. 3104–3112 (2014)
14. Johnson, M., Schuster, M., Le, Q., Krikun, M., Yonghui, W., Chen, Z., Thorat, N.: Google's multilingual neural machine translation system: Enabling zero-shot translation (2016). arXiv:1611.04558v1
15. Harris, Z.: Distributional structure. Word **10**(2–3), 146–162 (1954)
16. McCulloch, W., Pitts, W.: A logical calculus of the ideas immanent in nervous systems. Bull. Math. Biophys. **5**, 115–133 (1943)
17. Devlin, J., Zbib, R., Huang, Z., Lamar, T., Schwartz, R., Makhoul, J.: Fast and robust neural network joint models for statistical machine translation. In: Proceedings of the 52nd Annual Meeting of the Association for Computational Linguistics, Baltimore, 23–25 June 2014, pp. 1370–1380 (2014)
18. Dong, L., Lapata, M.: Language to logical form with neural attention. In: Proceedings of the 54th Annual Meeting of the Association for Computational Linguistics, Berlin, 7–12 August 2016, pp. 33–43 (2016)
19. Del Gaudio, R., Labaka, G., Agirre, E., Osenova, P., Simov, K., Popel, M., Oele, D., van Noord, G., Gomes, L., Rodrigues, J.A., Neale, S., Silva, J., Querido, A., Rendeiro, N., Branco, A.: SMT and hybrid systems of the QTLeap project in the WMT16 IT-task. In: Proceedings of the ACL 2016 First Conference on Machine Translation (WMT 2016), Association for Computational Linguistics, Berlin, 11–12 August 2016, pp. 435–441 (2016)

Observatory for Language Resources and Machine Translation in Europe – LT_Observatory

Bente Maegaard[1], Claus Povlsen[1], Sussi Olsen[1], Lina Henriksen[1],
Margaretha Mazura[2], Vesna Lusicky[2], Gerhard Budin[3], Blanca Rodríguez[4(✉)],
and Mª Luz Esparza[4]

[1] University of Copenhagen, Copenhagen, Denmark
{bmaegaard,cpovlsen,saolsen,linah}@hum.ku.dk
[2] EMF, Brussels, Belgium
mm@emfs.eu, vesna.lusicky@univie.ac.at
[3] University of Vienna, Vienna, Austria
gerhard.budin@univie.ac.at
[4] ZABALA Innovation Consulting, S.A., Mutilva, Spain
{brodriguez,mlesparza}@zabala.es

Abstract. The European Digital Single Market, one of the main goals of Europe 2020, is still fragmented due to language barriers. Language technologies (LT), like Machine Translation (MT) solutions, are key elements for solving this fragmentation. Nevertheless, it is necessary to compile, benchmark the quality and facilitate the access to Language Resources to build successful MT solutions. With these aims, the LT_Observatory project has been developed (2014–2016). The project was funded by the European Commission through the H2020 programme. This article describes the main outputs:
  - An on-line catalogue of language resources in existing pools and other national resources based on pre-identified user needs.
  - Methodologies for improving the quality and usability of language resources.
  - National and regional language strategies, policies and funding sources to support language technologies.
  - An EcoGuide that aims to adapt the findings of the LT_Observatory project for various stakeholder groups providing practical information for operational usability of LRs and tools for MT application, funding opportunities, and recommendations geared at European, national and regional policy and decision makers.
This project has been carried out by a team of five EU partners with complementary expertise: ZABALA (EU project management and community engagement), EMF (European Multimedia Forum with experience in outreach/social media, and funding, e.g. ESIF and combined funding), LT Innovate (the Language Technology Industry Association), CLARIN ERIC (LT resources and infrastructure, including a Virtual Language Observatory), and University of Vienna/InfoTerm (international information centre for terminology).

All the authors contributed equally to this work.

J.F. Quesada et al. (Eds.): FETLT 2016, LNAI 10341, pp. 20–37, 2017.
https://doi.org/10.1007/978-3-319-69365-1_2

Keywords: Language resources · Parallel corpus or corpora · Machine translation · Language technologies · Observatory · Public funding · Language policies · Digital Single Market · Catalogue · Guide

1   Introduction

Languages are a sensitive issue as they determine a people's culture, tradition and behaviour. At the same time, languages are of considerable economic relevance. Only 15% of European SMEs sell online – and of that 15%, fewer than a half, do so across borders. SMEs that sell their products and services internationally exhibit 7% job growth and 26% innovation in their offering – compared to a job growth of 1% and 8% innovation for SMEs that do not sell their products and services internationally[1]. More and more commercial transactions are being done online and there are more consumers using the Web that do not speak English than those who do. Recent e-commerce statistics indicate that two out of three EU customers buy only in their own language. This suggests that language is a significant barrier to a truly Europe-wide Digital Single Market. Of course, language barriers do not only impact on e-commerce activities, but also on access to virtually all online content and services. Content exists in all possible languages and translation is necessary to communicate/exploit it. High costs of translation and translation tools are inhibitors for all content/data markets. Consequently, languages are barriers to building the Digital Single Market. Therefore, the use of machine translation could be the key for promoting a real Multilingual Digital Single Market. Nevertheless, for providing successful solutions based on machine translation technologies, high quality and accessible language resources in different languages and domains are required. Where are Language Resources (LRs)? How can I access them? What is their quality? The LT_Observatory project analysed current barriers with MT stakeholders, identified and valorised LRs for use by SMEs, and created on-line support for the community of stakeholders: Main results as described in the following three sections are:

– Language Resources for Machine Translation (MT): LR Catalogue.
– Language Strategies and National/Regional Funding.
– Navigating the MT Ecosystem in Europe: MT EcoGuide.

2   Language Resources for Machine Translation – LT_Observatory Catalogue

Practitioners in Machine Translation (MT), be it providers of MT systems or language service providers, are faced with the lack of relevant language resources

---

[1] http://www.cracking-the-language-barrier.eu/wp-content/uploads/SRIA-V0. 9-final-online.pdf.

(LR) every day [1]. The main purpose of the LT_Observatory is to collect information about LRs available for MT (in particular Statistical Machine Translation - SMT) and similar purposes, and to make it publicly available in a one-stop access point, the LT_Observatory Catalogue [2]. In this section, we first describe efforts to identify LRs in accordance with user requirements. In line with a discussion of LR quality issues, it is outlined how we recommend optimization of LR quality. We describe how tools can contribute to creation of new resources, and finally some recommendations for the future are given.

2.1   User Requirements and Methodology

The LR situation is that even if LRs may be available for research, there is very little available for commercial use. When investigating users' needs, we also see that not only is very little available, but users often need very specific types of LRs, e.g. when they work in a particular domain, they need text and terminology from that exact domain, and for the language of their task.

Building on experience from earlier projects and from user contacts, a methodology and selection criteria for the identification of useful LRs were made. The selection criteria were the following: Availability, Languages covered, Longevity, Validation, Modality, Ease of download. E.g. if a resource is not available for commercial use, then it cannot be selected for our catalogue.

2.2   Quality Assurance

During our meetings with LR users it was frequently mentioned that the quality of LRs is generally too low. Yet subsequent discussions of how to define high quality corpora clearly showed just how obscure the notion of quality is in relation to corpora. Firstly, the perception of what constitutes a high quality corpus is often different from one organization, user or task to another. Secondly, there are different aspects of a resource that can be evaluated; and different aspects of a resource are important in different contexts. The actual corpus text however cannot and should not be an object of an overall quality assessment - as such an assessment will always be in relation to some specific purpose. The corpus text in itself is a sample of some actual linguistic behaviour and style, and this behaviour and style can and should be described to ensure that the corpus is employed for the best possible purposes.

European Language Resources Association (ELRA) has developed a methodology for validation of written LRs against some criteria [3,4]. These validation criteria include (1) descriptive corpus information (resource name, copyright issues, language etc.), (2) annotations; examples are structural information (sections/subsections/headers etc.) and interpretive information (e.g. part-of-speech). Alignments (combining different language versions of the same text) can also be an obvious validation criterion.

One general finding of the ELRA validation committee is that the unpredictability of resource applications impeded the creation of normative guidelines considerably. ELRA therefore stresses that the result of a validation process should be an accurate description of a corpus, and that it is up to the individual user to determine the extent to which a corpus so described is likely to be fit for a given purpose. We have followed ELRA's recommendations and have prioritized to evaluate and ensure high quality of corpus descriptive information.

For terminology resources, the degree of authoritativeness is an important indicator for quality. The main indicator is the originator involved in the preparation of the resource [5]. For a large number of domains (e.g. legal, administrative), national and international authorities determined by legislation or jurisdiction, followed by officially authorized harmonization bodies are the data originators with the highest degree of authoritativeness. This authoritativeness principle was followed in the selection for our catalogue.

2.3 Existing Resources

LRs originally created with a specific purpose are not always generally reusable. An LR may lack information, e.g. on domain or copyright issues, because this information seemed of little importance in the creation phase, but this subsequently impedes reuse by other users. Therefore, the project also valorized the LRs by optimizing the existing metadata and adding new metadata where needed.

Based on early user contacts we initially operated with a very limited number of metadata. In a later phase of the project potential users evaluated a preliminary version of the repository with this short metadata list, and gave feedback. The feedback mainly focused on metadata types such as copyright issues (for commercial use), the importance of in-domain monolingual as well as parallel data, quality issues and reasonable prices. Consequently, new metadata fields were added to the metadata list.

The resulting list of metadata corresponds to some extent to the Dublin Core (DC) metadata set for resources with a few adjustments. A few metadata categories were added, e.g. size which the users stressed as an important factor in MT creation, the keyword-like value tag since it is very useful in a search context, and availability that includes information on the possible price of the resource.

The project experience was that identification of relevant information for the various metadata fields is not necessarily easy; but information can often be derived from various descriptions of the resource or from the framework in which they were created.

2.4 Tools for Resources

One of the findings in connection with collecting parallel data cf. above was the identified gap between user needs on the one hand and available LRs on the other hand. In order to bridge this gap, it is obvious and relevant to exploit the possibilities of extracting domain specific and parallel data from the Web.

Acquiring high quality parallel data from the Web involves usage of a wide package of language tools that can be executed canonically in a tool chain.

The most significant elements of such a pipeline are identification of domain relevant websites containing bilingual documents, assessment of the quality of the documents found, removal of duplicates, exclusion of boilerplate elements, and then finally generation of sentence aligned versions of the parallel, in domain-specific data.

Access to user-friendly tool chains easy to use would be beneficial and ideal seen from a user's point of view. Observations made in the LT_Observatory project, however, indicate that in the real world such software packages are rarely found. Even though many useful open source software programmes can be identified, they are often developed as stand-alone research prototypes, leaving it up to the users themselves to implement scripts that link the applications into one workflow.

Although a similar gap was identified in connection with collecting terminology resources, the users additionally reported a strong need for preparing their own terminology resources. There are mainly two reasons for this: Firstly, it may be required due to specific in-house or corporate terminology for a specific project, in which the corporate terminology should not be polluted with terminology from resources in public domain. Secondly, when translating from and to morphologically rich languages, implementing a terminology resource from an authoritative source does not show quality improvements for SMT systems [6] due to deviations from the canonical forms. For these purposes, the terminology firstly needs to be automatically extracted from parallel or comparable data provided by the client, supported by terminology extraction tools. These tools are currently mainly available either as stand-alone tools and research prototypes, or integrated into computer-assisted translation tools (CAT tools). The extracted candidates often require a certain amount of manual post-processing and validation. The creation of project-based terminology resources and their integration into workflows for MT should ideally be integrated into the tool chain, but with some exceptions, users are left to link the tools into one workflow.

2.5   Results – Gap Discussion

The LT_Observatory project has revealed a number of gaps. Below we draw some conclusions in terms of coverage of languages and domains. Gaps can be considered along four dimensions:

Quality gap: Very few LRs that are presently in repositories correspond to minimum quality requirements on metadata. Further, the project revealed that the notion of quality issues is often closely related to misapplication of resources. The reason is that the various domains have an insufficient amount of resources and consequently resources are used for unsuitable purposes; people simply use what they can lay their hands on. I.e. what is initially perceived as quality issues are really often quantity issues.

Quantity gap: As just mentioned the LR quantities available for commercial use today are largely insufficient to have a positive impact on the quality of (S)MT in a commercial context. One of the reasons is that most resources made available by repositories are only for academic use, i.e. their licenses do not allow commercial use. Europe urgently needs a new legislation that will allow fair use of data for this type of purposes.

A large combined effort should be launched to produce new LRs that correspond to a set of agreed usability criteria.

Awareness gap: User feedback showed that potential users are not generally aware of the existence of LR repositories. This can probably be explained by the scarcity of LRs – if the user always finds that there are no usable LRs, then he/she stops looking for them.

Coverage gap: For corpora English has the best coverage in terms of combinations with other languages, but still the amount of LRs identified is pretty low. We see gaps for most of the languages, and for nearly all domains. For terminology resources, English, French and German have a good coverage of the domains.

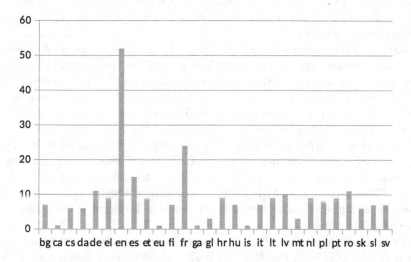

Fig. 1. Number of parallel corpora identified per language (EU and regional languages)

Figure 1 shows the total number of parallel corpora identified for EU and regional languages in all domains. Languages from other parts of the world, e.g. Arabic, Chinese, and Russian, appear in some of the corpora but are not included in these figures.

2.6 Future Steps – a Strategy Is Needed

Only English has some coverage in relation to volume as well as in relation to domains. LR creation, identification and operational management must be organized by means of a clear strategy of identifying, usability-checking and promoting all those LRs that can contribute to better MT productivity in the years ahead. This provision of LRs can be very well supported through the use of the fast developing automatic methods of creating parallel corpora e.g. from crawling the web, as mentioned above.

LT_Observatory has taken the first step in making LRs more easily accessible: simplifying access to usable translation data from repositories in the EU via a one-stop access point, the LT_Observatory Catalogue[2], functioning at present, and to be further developed over time.

3   Language Strategies and National/Regional Funding

3.1   Introduction

An additional dimension of the LT_Observatory project was to investigate European language strategies of the EU Member States and identify funding opportunities for LT projects that are complementary to European Funding programmes. The results are put on-line at: http://www.lt-innovate.org/lt-observe/public-policy-observatory.

Language is intrinsic to the expression of culture. As a means of communicating values, beliefs and custom. Therefore, there is no "categorical imperative" on how the EU or Member States deal with languages. At the same time, languages are of considerable economic relevance but are barriers to building the Digital Single Market. In the course of the LT_Observatory project, national and regional language strategies were investigated and the financial means available from all possible sources identified: national/regional budgets or from ESIF - European Social and Investment Funds e.g. ERDF, Cohesion Fund, European Social Fund to finance necessary/desirable improvements to language corpora and tools. These sources are highly fragmented and as a result, often under-used. A more efficient and effective use of them can help implement the multilingual Digital Single Market.

Since the start of Horizon 2020, strong emphasis was put on synergies among different funding options, like Horizon 2020 and ESIF that found its repercussion at several instances in the H2020 work programmes[3] and in DG REGIO's "Enabling synergies between European Structural and Investment Funds, Horizon 2020 and other research, innovation and competitiveness-related Union programmes"[4] co-authored by one of the authors of this article. However, practice showed that it is not easy to match different funding sources.

---

[2] http://www.lt-innovate.org/lt-observe/language-resources-observatory.

[3] E.g. in the Introduction to the 2014/15 work programmes, p. 10, http://ec.europa.eu/research/participants/data/ref/h2020/wp/2014_2015/main/h2020-wp1415-intro_en.pdf.

[4] http://ec.europa.eu/regional_policy/sources/docgener/guides/synergy/synergies_en.pdf.

3.2   LT_Observatory Findings

Language Strategies. Language Strategies usually must make a decision: one or many? A lingua franca may be ideal for understanding (e.g. in a working environment) but may discriminate against minorities (e.g. in a territory).

A Harvard Business School report[5] found out that many large companies do not have a language strategy which leads to inefficiency or miscommunication. Countries are not far behind: Very few have something that may be called a "language strategy", most feature a language preservation policy or a language learning strategy.

Not all European constitutions are as clear as the French one that, without compromise or tolerance, states that "la langue de la République est le français" (Art. 2 of the French constitution), to the chagrin of many historically spoken languages on French territory. Other countries boost their languages (e.g. Latvia) or collaborate with adjacent countries that speak the same language (e.g. Dutch).

EU Level. The European Commission has supported Human Language Technologies - HLT for some 40 years now. There was a lot of sustained effort throughout 1980s–1990s which resulted in some pioneering Machine Translation and Translation Memory technologies. The EU support for HLT is now being revived due to renewed political commitment following the ambition to create a Digital Single Market.

At European Commission level, DG CONNECT is a main driver, together with DG Translation that is a pioneer in realising the MT@EC tool for their internal services. Based on this, the CEF – Connecting Europe Facility building block on automated translation (CEF.AT[6]) will help European and national public administrations information exchange across language barriers. The main purpose of CEF.AT is to make all Digital Service Infrastructures (DSIs) multilingual.

Since 1 July 2016, a new Unit G3 at DG CONNECT takes care of LT under the heading of "Learning, multilingualism and accessibility". Its description says: "The mission of the unit is to make the Digital Single Market more accessible, secure and inclusive. To this end, the unit supports policy, research, innovation and deployment of learning technologies and key enabling digital language technologies and services to allow all European consumers and businesses to fully benefit from the Digital Single Market." Marco Marsella, Head of Unit, emphasises the human element that connects all three chapters of his unit. At a recent (December 2016) brain-storming Round Table in Luxembourg[7], priorities for LT were discussed. While the "wish list" was divers depending on stakeholders' interests, repeated discussions pivoted around a European Language Infrastructure as some sort of multilingual one-stop-shop for all Europeans.

EU Member States' Level. The citizens of the 28 Members States of the European Union speak 24 official languages and altogether 60+ languages. This

---

[5] https://hbr.org/2014/09/whats-your-language-strategy.

[6] https://ec.europa.eu/cefdigital/wiki/display/CEFDIGITAL/eTranslation.

[7] https://ec.europa.eu/digital-single-market/en/news/language-technologies-round-table.

represents a rich cultural heritage but at the same time, is a tremendous barrier for effective and efficient communication across borders (or even across regions). Language technologies help maintaining the linguistic diversity and at the same time, fostering cross-lingual communication, be it for e-commerce, e-government, culture or education.

Currently best practice example for an all-encompassing language technology strategy is Spain that published its "Plan de Impulso" (Plan for the advancement of language technologies)[8] on 20 October 2015. It dedicates 90+MEUR to language technologies for Spain's national and regional languages. As such, it is currently the highest doted national initiative in the area of language technologies. Another example is Ireland with its "20 years strategy for the Irish language"[9] 2010 to 2030 that explicitly includes language technologies.

Funding Opportunities. Horizon 2020 is worldwide the highest doted funding programme for research and innovation. It puts emphasis on pre-competitive collaboration at European level, strongly advocating the European dimension. It is an important tool to foster research and market-near innovations in Europe, the more so as Europe does not have the culture of pan-European seed money or Venture Capital. However, even this highly doted programme has financial limits, and many good project ideas must be turned down by lack of budget. Therefore, the LT_Observatory project looked into "complementary" funding sources.

ESIF[10]: European Structural and Investment Funds have a fundamentally different aim than Horizon 2020: to contribute to the cohesion of the EU and to develop less advanced regions/countries. Therefore, funding taken from ESIF funds need to comply with certain conditions[11]. Added to it comes the "Smart Specialisation Strategy – S3" for research: Regions/countries must pre-define their priorities in order to receive funds. These topics are the regional strengths to be developed.

As LT does not figure as a priority in its own right, any funding can only be related to a specific topic. To give one example: innovative machine translation tools in the area of eHealth or culture, in regions where eHealth or culture are priority topics. To summarise, one can say that Spain, Ireland, Austria, Latvia and Lithuania offer some opportunities, as well as Finland, Germany, Hungary and Greece.

---

[8] http://www.agendadigital.gob.es/tecnologias-lenguaje/Paginas/plan-impulso-tecnologias-lenguaje.aspx.

[9] http://www.ahg.gov.ie/app/uploads/2015/07/20-Year-Strategy-English-version.pdf.

[10] Information was gathered through direct contacts with Managing Authorities and agencies in the Member States.

[11] For more details, see: How does ESIF work? http://www.lt-innovate.org/lt-observe/how-does-esif-work.

National/regional including EUREKA/Eurostars[12]: Each EU Member State has its own funding agencies and programmes. These are as divergent as the countries themselves. As with ESIF, one major difference to Horizon 2020 is their subjection to state aid rules. This results in considerably lower funding rates for industry. The percentage of funding depends also on the size, with SMEs usually enjoying a higher funding rate than large enterprises.

Advantages of national/regional funding compared to Horizon 2020:

- A single entity can obtain funding – this is in Horizon 2020 only exceptionally the case, e.g. in the SME instrument.
- Most often easier/quicker procedure to submit a proposal and to receive an evaluation.
- Often direct contact with Funding Agency possible, sometimes even appreciated.
- Sometimes the pre-evaluation of a project idea is possible.

Disadvantages of national/regional funding compared to Horizon 2020:

- Lower funding percentage: a rule of the thumb is: "industrial research" yields a higher funding percentage than "experimental development" as the latter is commonly closer to the market. This is mainly for industrial partners. For SMEs this can be between 35% and 80%, for large enterprises it is usually max. 20–40%. There are Member States that do not support Large Enterprises at all.
- Sometimes no grants, but only loans.
- Some countries do not always have a budget available, which leads to a de facto discrimination of entities located in a specific territory.

The European landscape of funding opportunities is divers and is permanently changing. Therefore, it is good to contact the agencies and programme administrators to obtain accurate, updated information. Countries with a special interest in languages (e.g. Spain, Baltic countries, Ireland) or with a track record in funding innovative projects, also in LT (e.g. Austria, Germany, Belgium) provide funding in an easier way. Some other countries like Finland (TEKES) offer a pre-proposal check with an answer promised within 1 week.

The EUREKA/Eurostars programmes allow for a cooperation between two and more entities with a minimum of two EUREKA member countries (which are comprising 41 members: 40 countries and the EU). EUREKA provides national monies to the partner of the respective country. Two partners from two countries are the minimum. Only if they receive a EUREKA label (from a central unit) and a positive feed-back from both EUREKA countries (national evaluation),

---

[12] Information was gathered in a first round through desk research, and in a second through direct contact with the respective agencies. EUREKA and Eurostars information was collected from the EUREKA (http://www.eurekanetwork.org/eureka-countries) and Eurostars (https://www.eurostars-eureka.eu/eurostars-countries/europe) contacts pages.

can they start the project. The Eurostars programme evaluates centrally, and the funds are national topped up by EU monies.

Similar rules as for national/regional funding apply. This is also valid for the diversity in funding instruments: mostly grants, but occasionally only loans (The Netherlands) or other benefits in addition to grants, like tax credits (e.g. Malta). Total upper levels apply as well. The following countries provide no EUREKA funding: Cyprus, Estonia, Slovakia, UK. Estonia, Italy and Greece do not provide Eurostars funding. It should be noted that, despite of the fact that some countries indicate available funds, they are de facto difficult to obtain.

3.3   Access to Results

The design of LT-Observatory project was such that any on-line presence would be integrated into the already existing LT-Innovate platform to guarantee a continuation of information after the project phase. Main website for funding opportunities is the landing page: http://www.lt-innovate. org/lt-observe/public-policy-observatory/national-funding-opportunities It is a "one-stop-shop" for funding information with a clickable map of Europe that leads to the country in questions, where links to websites and interactive pdfs provide further information. Each country page contains:

- Short summaries of available funds (for ESIF, EURKEA and Eurostars), as well as links to funding agencies and programmes
- For national/regional funding opportunities, information is displayed in interactive pdf tables.

While contact persons or programme names may change, the main web addresses and agencies usually remain the same. Thus, interested people can contact them for the newest updates.

All funding information is compiled in a practical guide called "Path through the Funding Maze" that can be downloaded at: http://www.lt-innovate.org/ sites/default/files/National_regional_funding_opportunities_online_nov16.pdf.

It contains a practical 8-Steps Vademecum that will help potential funding applicants to be successful. These steps are:

1. Be clear about **WHAT** you want to do
2. Establish **WHERE** the seat of your legal entity is located
3. Make up your mind about **WHO** shall perform the project
4. Get **INFORMATION** on funding programmes
5. Establish good **COMMUNICATION** with local/regional/national funding agencies
6. **IDENTIFICATION** of the best suited funding programme
7. **ACTION** time: Write the proposal
8. **MARKETING** your success - in terms of receiving funding and promoting results!

Although geared at language technologies, the practical Vademecum is valid for all types of projects and may benefit a broader range of potential applicants.

4   Navigating the MT Ecosystem in Europe: MT EcoGuide

With MT slowly reaching a critical mass of awareness and performance, more and more stakeholders are getting involved in deployment of machine translation (MT) at various levels. Navigating the rich and varied European MT ecosystem is not straightforward, and participants often act in information silo. One of the aims of the LT-Observatory project was to adapt the findings of the project for various stakeholder groups. MT EcoGuide could be understood as a pathfinder through the European MT ecosystem for the following stakeholders:

- MT developers and providers (vendors).
- Providers of language resources (LR) and LR-related services.
- Policy and decision makers and
- End-users.

R&D as well as training in academic or other settings were understood to be integral parts of all stakeholder groups. MT EcoGuide provides practical information for operational usability of LRs and tools for MT use, funding opportunities, and recommendations geared at European, national and regional policy and decision makers. It is available as a downloadable version[13], and is integrated into the existing LT-Innovate platform as an online tool, linking all the other services developed in the scope of the LT-Observatory project: LR catalogue, information on public policies and funding, directory of LR stakeholders and LR policy makers.

4.1   Components of the European MT Ecosystem

This section gives a brief overview over two key stakeholder groups in European MT ecosystem. In addition, it outlines two drivers of language technology at large that are of importance for all stakeholders: research and development and training, and standardization. For policies and strategies – also crucial drivers –see Sect. 3.

MT Developers and Providers of MT-Related Services. Developers of MT systems develop MT systems and adapt existing MT systems for individual customers. The directory of LT-Innovate provides a solid overview over European vendors of language technologies[14] and includes MT developers and vendors of MT-related solutions and services.

Language Service Providers (LSPs), often also known as translation agencies, provide translations to end-clients. European LSPs have been early adopters of language technologies and are still the worldwide leaders in the production of post-edited MT [7]. Open-source systems, such as Moses[15], and hosted MT

---

[13] http://www.lt-innovate.org/lt-observe/mt-ecoguide.
[14] http://www.lt-innovate.org/directory/lt-vendors.
[15] http://statmt.org/moses/.

solutions have made MT accessible also to smaller LSPs, for which post-edited MT has been the solution for their growing translation volumes. Adaptive MT may result in an even bigger reception of MT at all levels of the translation service industry. LSPs get the data to prime their MT engines from various sources and often combine data from several provenances. A survey by LT-Innovate[16] showed that 70% would attempt to find third party sources. Few would be prepared to buy such data, a large majority would acquire the data by crawling the web, and 83% of them expect more free resources to become available. Although a high percentage of LSPs acquire data from third party sources or expect free resources to become available, consultations in the scope of the LT_Observatory project showed that the level of awareness for language resource repositories and catalogues is not prevalent among those users who would need them most.

MT EcoGuide gives practical information on finding and reusing data for MT. Since few LRs are available for commercial use, it also gives practical hints how to build LR for MT from scratch and how to deal with intellectual property rights (IPR).

Users. MT is no longer just a solution for multilingual needs for large enterprises. Recent developments have made MT more accessible to the full array of companies and public services. The main demand is for translating high volumes content (e.g. product documentation, online help, FAQs, knowledge bases, websites), but the need for translation of user-generated content is increasing, although it remains challenging. Business and public sector users alike profit from the implementation of MT to speed up time-to-market or to publication by reducing the length of the translation cycle. In global enterprises and multilingual public services, it increases internal knowledge sharing, and enhances staff effectiveness by making real time and on-demand translation a 'regular' part of their process.

In terms of MT for public services at the European level, MT@EC is the operational service built around the open source MT system Moses. MT@EC is part of the Automated Translation platform (CEF.AT)[17], one of the key building blocks of the CEF Digital Service Infrastructures (DSIs)[18] that will provide services to support the development of the European Digital Single Market (DSM). The European Commission has contracted the European Language Resource Coordination consortium (ELRC)[19] to work jointly with the Member States, Iceland and Norway to collect LRs for all official EU languages (and two affiliated languages) for the purpose of the CEF.AT platform.

R&D and Training. Several European R&D and similar initiatives have driven innovation in the field of language technology and language resources:

---

[16] http://ltinnovate.blogspot.co.at/.

[17] https://ec.europa.eu/digital-single-market/en/automated-translation.

[18] https://ec.europa.eu/digital-single-market/en/news/connecting-europe-facility-cef-digital-service-infrastructures.

[19] http://lr-coordination.eu/.

LT-Innovate[20] – the language technology industry association; CLARIN – European Research Infrastructure for Language Resources and Technology[21]; META – the Network of Excellence forging the Multilingual Europe Technology Alliance[22]; ELRA/ELDA – European Language Resources Association/Evaluations and Language Resources Distribution Agency[23]; FLaReNet – Fostering Language Resources Network[24], TAUS[25], and initiative Cracking the Language Barrier[26].

The European Commission has been instrumental in setting incentives for many R&D initiatives to flourish supporting research and industry communities in carrying out R&D projects such as EuroMatrix[27], Euromatrix Plus[28], Lets MT[29], QT LaunchPad[30] and others.

Education and training in language technologies in general and in machine translation in particular has been another key driver in progress of language technology industry. Numerous academic programmes include topics in translation technologies, LRs and related topics. The European Master of Translation[31] is a quality label initiated by the Directorate General for Translation of the European Commission in cooperation with universities all over Europe. Language technology is in the core of this programme as it is imperative that translators are trained in using MT systems and other language technology as they are not only users of LRs, but also important producers of such resources, and could contribute to larger availability of LRs.

Standardization. The development of technical standards is the main purpose of standardization and this type of standardization activity has been prevalent so far in the language industry, but increasingly process-oriented standards processes are getting ground, for example for example ISO 17100:2015 Translation services – Requirements for translation services[32].

At least in official, standardizing organizations, standardizing activities are open to experts from various backgrounds and should therefore be explored as an important venue for horizontal collaboration of stakeholders in MT. The integration of language technology solutions into the European Digital Single

---

[20] http://www.lt-innovate.org.
[21] https://www.clarin.eu/.
[22] http://www.meta-net.eu/.
[23] http://www.elra.info/.
[24] http://www.flarenet.eu/.
[25] http://www.taus.net/.
[26] http://www.cracking-the-language-barrier.eu.
[27] http://www.euromatrix.net.
[28] http://www.euromatrixplus.net/.
[29] https://www.letsmt.eu.
[30] http://www.qt21.eu/launchpad/.
[31] https://ec.europa.eu/info/resources-partners/european-masters-translation-emt_en.
[32] http://www.iso.org/iso/catalogue_detail.htm?csnumber=59149.

Market relies also on EU Rolling Plan for ICT Standardisation[33], linking EU policies to standardisation activities.

4.2 Current Situation and Recommendations to Policy Makers

Strategies for Digital Multilingualism at European Level. For the last 15 years, there has been a need at the level of the European Union to formulate strategies for dealing with technologies enabling, facilitating and automating multilingualism and multilingual communication in all spheres of society. This form of "digital multilingualism" [8] should be distinguished from other manifestations of multilingualism, such as in language policies with socio-linguistic and socio-cultural perspectives, or language learning policies where a broader concept has developed called "translanguaging" [9] focusing on multilingual education in migration contexts.

Digital multilingualism covers a broad range of language technologies that are considered as key enabling technologies for a "Future Multilingual European Information Society", as conceptualized in the strategic initiative META [10,11]. In recent years, the development of language technology strategies has focused on the DSM and CEF (also see Users), which led to the initiation and co-funding of strategic-action projects such as LT_Observatory and CRACKER[34] with the joint task of formulating a Strategic Research and Innovation Agenda[35].

The common aim of all the stakeholders in the European MT landscape should be a ubiquitous deployment of MT across Europe as part of an overall strategy for language technology and digital multilingualism. The following analysis, carried out in scope of the LT_Observatory project, is based on discussions and consultations with all stakeholder groups. It therefore gives a broad picture that was confirmed by most stakeholders in the language technology community.

Status Quo in Europe. The strengths of the European language technology landscape could be summarised as follows: Europe is still a leader in translation technology and has a strong position in speech technology and analytics. The reason for this may be found in the ingrained nature of European multilingualism, policy choices in the past, and a thriving community in terms of research groups, as well as numerous organisations and initiatives in the field of language technology and language resources. On the downside, this plurality leads to a fragmented market that is getting even more dispersed due to a lack of strong and coordinated strategies for language technologies in European countries, despite the effort carried out by the EC for supporting language technology development. These circumstances are already showing real threads

---

[33] https://ec.europa.eu/digital-single-market/en/rolling-plan-ict-standardisation.

[34] http://cracker-project.eu/.

[35] The LT_Observatory project contributed to the Strategic Research and Innovation Agenda for the Multilingual Digital Single Market, see http://www.cracking-the-language-barrier.eu/wp-content/uploads/SRIA-V0.9-final-online.pdf.

in the form of quick-acting competition outside of Europe, and acquisition of European companies that have evolved from publicly funded R&D projects by large foreign companies. The situation is further exacerbated by lack of awareness for language technology at policy levels. On the one hand, this is showcased by European public institutions and companies relying on language technologies developed outside Europe, often on free solutions that harvest data in return. On the other hand, the support for language technology is inconsistent, uncoordinated and dispersed between regional, national, and European levels (see also Sect. 3).

Recommendations. Given the strategic importance of language technology in a digitally connected world, ignoring the challenges would fundamentally set back the economic and political development of Europe. A borderless infrastructure is needed to guarantee access to all (official) languages and tools for all European citizens, businesses, researchers, and public administrations. From the industry side, the need for languages of trade partners (Chinese, Arabic, Russian) is getting more insistent. Singular solutions and modules are currently available, but not yet connected into an interoperable language technology ecosystem. CEF.AT for public services could become an infrastructure for the European Language Infrastructure (with already existing basic layers e.g. LRs) and a driver for the European language technology industry.

The accessibility of LRs to feed MT could be accelerated by creating an IPR regime that supports language technology, for example by modelling it on the existing provision from the "reverse engineering/decompilation" exception inscribed in the EC Software Directive - art. 6). A similar clause like the "fair use clause" in the US that would allow web crawling for LR collection for MT training. In terms of standardizing licensing models, coordination is needed among the existing (federated) LR repositories.

Above all, a closer cooperation and coordination is needed between all stakeholders at regional, national, and European level, in terms of awareness raising, opening up LRs of the public sector for all purposes, improving the existing LRs, and increasing the number of available LRs in terms of languages, domains and genres.

5 Conclusions

Europe has a long-standing excellence in Language Technologies. This is due to its multilingual culture and the support R&D(&I) received over more than 40 years to improve these technologies. Language Resources are crucial for a next-to-perfect machine translation, no matter if statistical, rule-base, hybrid or neural. And MT is crucial to truly create the Digital Single Market, without language barriers. There are many resources spread over different repositories, but very few are adopted for commercial use and not all MT practitioners are familiar with the major repositories. Furthermore, there are about 150 identified LRs (corpora, terminology, lexica) that fulfil the required selection criteria (see above, 2.1) but huge gaps still exist in terms of languages and domains: widely spoken languages (FR, DE, ES) appear more often in multilingual corpora (e.g. the EU Acquis Communautaire) than in bilingual ones; the situation is worse for less used languages which hardly appear in bilingual corpora[36]. Moreover, the 19 domains identified in the corpora have considerable variation in coverage (amount/languages). Additionally, most domains are public sector LRs meaning that they are written in "administrative language" that is not always very useful. Lastly, the creation and sharing of new LRs is made more challenging due to European copyright, privacy and data protection rules.

To improve the situation in terms of a LT Strategy, the LT_Observatory partners recommend that all EU stakeholders including decision-makers should participate in and support the following shared actions: firstly, it is important to strengthen EU initiatives (including funding) to better coordinate national/regional initiatives and create a European Language Infrastructure. Improved coordination should take place also among existing (federated) LR repositories, particularly in terms of standardizing licensing models. Secondly, an awareness raising campaign illustrating the benefits of LT at all levels, including benefits of CEF.AT for the public sector, should be conceived and followed by an opening up of public sector LRs for all purposes, including commercial uses. This should go hand in hand with an open mind of funding agencies to provide monies for innovative projects e.g. for safeguarding the presence of lesser used languages in the digital ecosystem. Thirdly, there is a need to increase the number of LRs in terms of languages and domains and to improve LRs in terms of: Metadata, Accessibility and Usability. Finally, the creation and easy sharing of LRs in a legal manner should be considered and discussed with the corresponding authorities in order to facilitate a European regulatory framework (IPR).

References

1. Mastropavlos, N., Papavassiliou, V.: Domain adaptation of statistical machine translation using web-crawled resources: a case study. In: Proceedings from the 10th International Conference of Greek Linguistics (2011)
2. Maegaard, B., Henriksen, L., Joscelyne, A., Lusicky, V., Mazura, M., Olsen, S., Povlsen, C., Wacker, P.: Providing a catalogue of language resources for commercial users. In: Calzolari, N., Choukri, K., Declerck, T., Goggi, S., Grobelnik, M., Maegaard, B., Mariani, J., Mazo, H., Moreno, A., Odijk, J., Piperidis, S. (eds.) Proceedings of the Tenth International Conference on Language Resources and Evaluation (LREC 2016), Portoroz, pp. 449–456 (2016)
3. Lou, B., McEnery, T., Baker, P., Wilson, A.: Validation of Linguistic Corpora (1998)
4. Fersøe, H., Monachini, M.: ELRA validation methodology and standard promotion for linguistic resources. In: Proceedings of the Fourth International Conference on Language Resources and Evaluation (LREC 2004), ELRA, Lisboa (2004)

---

[36] Bilingual corpora are "true translation corpora", whereas two language versions of a multilingual corpus are not necessarily translations of each other.

5. Rirdance, S., Vasiljevs, A.: Towards Consolidation of European Terminology Resources. Tilde, Riga (2006)
6. Pinnis, M., Skadins, R.: MT adaptation for under-resourced domains - what works and what not. In: Tavast, A. et al. (eds.) Human Language Technologies - The Baltic Perspective (2012). http://ebooks.iospress.nl/publication/7500
7. Lommel, A.R., DePalma, D.A.: How Europe Is Driving the Shift to MT. Common Sense Advisory (2016)
8. Budin, G.: Digital humanities, language industry, and multilingualism: global networking and innovation in collaborative methods. In: Forstner, M., Lee-Jahnke, H., Lang, P. (eds.) Proceedings of CIUTI-Forum 2014: Pooling Academic Excellence with Entrepreneurship for New Partnerships, pp. 423–448 (2015)
9. García, O., Wei, L.: Translanguaging. Language, Bilingualism and Education. Palgrave Macmillan, Basingstoke (2014)
10. Burchardt, A., Rehm, G., Sasaki, F. (eds.): The Future European Multilingual Information Society. Vision Paper for a Strategic Research Agenda (2011). http://www.meta-net.eu/
11. Rehm, G., et al.: The strategic impact of META-NET on the regional, national and international level. Lang. Resour. Eval. 50(2), 351–374 (2016)

The Rise of the Conversational Interface: A New Kid on the Block?

Michael F. McTear[✉]

Ulster University, Newtownabbey, Northern Ireland, UK
mf.mctear@ulster.ac.uk

Abstract. The conversational interface has become a hot topic in the past year or so, providing the primary means of interaction with chatbots, messaging apps, and virtual personal assistants. Major tech companies have been making huge investments in the supporting technologies of artificial intelligence, such as deep learning and natural language processing, with the aim of creating systems that will enable users of smartphones and other devices to obtain information and access services in a natural, conversational way. Yet the vision of the conversational interface is not new, and indeed there is a history of research in dialogue systems, voice user interfaces, embodied conversational agents, and chatbots that goes back more than fifty years. This chapter explores what has changed to make the conversational interface particularly relevant today, examines some key issues from earlier work that could inform the next generation of conversational systems, and highlights some challenges for future work.

Keywords: Conversational interface · Chatbot · Spoken dialogue system · Voice user interface · Embodied conversational agent · Design guidelines

1 The Rise of the Conversational Interface

The year 2016 marked a tipping point for chatbots and conversational interfaces. Major tech companies started to invest heavily in the technologies required to develop sophisticated systems capable of interacting with users in a natural, conversational style, such as artificial intelligence (AI), particularly deep learning and natural language processing (NLP). They have also been hiring many of the best researchers from university research labs and buying up smaller companies that had specialized in these technologies. Microsofts CEO Satya Natella declared that "conversational interfaces will be born on the devices you use today" and that "chatbots will fundamentally revolutionize how computing is experienced by everybody",[1] while David Marcus, VP of Facebook Messaging

---

[1] http://uk.businessinsider.com/microsoft-ceo-satya-nadella-chatbots-wpc-2016-7?r=US&IR=T.

© Springer International Publishing AG 2017
J.F. Quesada et al. (Eds.): FETLT 2016, LNAI 10341, pp. 38–49, 2017.
https://doi.org/10.1007/978-3-319-69365-1_3

stated that "threads (of conversation) are the new app",[2] and Chris Messina of Uber announced that "2016 will be the year of conversational commerce".[3]

There are many reasons why chatbots, also known as messaging apps, have suddenly come to the fore. One reason is to do with usage. BI Intelligence reported that the usage of messaging apps on smartphones has surpassed the usage of social networks.[4] Another factor is that interaction with a messaging app is easier than with a traditional smartphone app that has to be downloaded and installed. In contrast messaging apps run on a standard platform such as Facebook Messenger or Skype that users are already familiar with. Although users often have a large number of apps on their device, it has been shown that many of these are only used once or twice and then abandoned. In fact, only a small number of all the apps on a user's device are used regularly. A further advantage is that chatbots do not have to be built separately for different operating systems, such as Android, iOS, or Windows – they can work across apps such as Skype, Facebook Messenger, Line, or any other messaging service. This makes life easier for users as well as developers.

There are also various technological drivers that have facilitated the development and deployment of chatbots and conversational interfaces:

- Advances in AI, particularly in deep learning (deep neural networks).
- Greater computing processing power to support the massive parallel computations required to run deep neural networks.
- The availability of vast amounts of data (known as *big data*) that enable AI systems to learn and become increasingly more intelligent.
- Increased connectivity, allowing users to connect their smart devices to vast cloud-based resources.
- Advances in Speech Recognition and Natural Language Processing technologies, mainly as a result of the application of deep neural networks.
- The interest of the major technology companies in chatbots and conversational interfaces, enabling them to more accurately profile their users and thus gain a competitive advantage in the promotion of their e-commerce services.

2   Defining Chatbots and Conversational Interfaces

Various terms are used to refer to systems that provide conversational interaction for users, including *bot*, *chatbot*, *virtual personal assistant*, *digital assistant*, *conversational agent*, *conversational bot*, and *messaging app*.

---

[2] https://www.facebook.com/notes/david-marcus/heres-to-2016-with-messenger/10154485804004148/.

[3] https://medium.com/chris-messina/2016-will-be-the-year-of-conversational-commerce-1586e85e3991#.7e2ctqfo2 .

[4] http://uk.businessinsider.com/messaging-apps-have-completely-overtaken-social-networks-to-become-the-dominant-platforms-on-phones-2015-4?r=US&IR=T.

2.1 Bots and Chatbots

It is useful to distinguish between bots and chatbots. Bots can be defined as software applications that perform automated tasks. Bots are used to automatically post messages to social media, to crawl search results, and for various other routine and mundane tasks that would otherwise be costly and time-consuming for humans to do. For example, bots are used by Wikipedia to scan its millions of articles to fix errors, add links to other pages, and perform various other housekeeping tasks. In some cases bots are used for less desirable purposes, such as spreading spam emails, and there is a growing use of political bots that can send large numbers of automated messages on social media to sway opinions at elections and to spread propaganda [25].

A chatbot is also a software application that performs automated tasks, but it differs from a bot in that it also engages in a conversation (or chat) with the user. We can distinguish between task-oriented chatbots that use conversation to automate a task, such as scheduling a meeting[5] or ordering a pizza,[6] and those chatbots that engage in conversation mainly for entertainment or to take part in competitions to find the most humanlike chatbot.[7]

2.2 Conversational Interface

A conversational interface, also known as *conversational user interface (CUI)*, provides the front-end to a chatbot or virtual personal assistant, allowing the user to interact with the app using speech, text, touch, and various other input and output modes.

What does it mean to be conversational? The term *conversational* covers two different dimensions of a conversational interface.

Firstly, in terms of language, a conversational interface can mean a system in which the language being used is *natural*, as in naturally occurring conversation, as opposed to language restricted to a fixed set of commands and phrases. Conversational language also implies flexibility, so that messages can be expressed in a variety of different ways as opposed to a single fixed expression. For chatbots the language may also take the form of *textese* or *chatspeak*, terms that refer to the special forms of language, including abbreviations and syntactic variations, that are used commonly in messaging apps.

A second meaning of *conversational* can refer to the interactional style supported in the interface. At a basic level this can refer simply to the interaction style used in messaging apps where the user and system interact on a turn-by-turn basis, as opposed to clicking and selecting from drop-down menus on a graphical user interface. A more advanced usage refers to a style of interaction that is more flexible, as in human-human conversation, where both system and user can make contributions to the conversation (known as *mixed-initiative*

---

[5] https://x.ai/.

[6] http://uk.businessinsider.com/you-can-now-order-dominos-pizza-through-a-chatbot-on-facebook-messenger-2016-9?r=US&IR=T.

[7] http://www.mitsuku.com/.

interaction). A more advanced conversational system should also keep track of the context of the conversation in order to allow follow-up questions and topic tracking. Most current chatbots support one-shot queries that are stateless, i.e. the user asks a question and the system answers, but any subsequent question is treated as completely independent of previously asked questions.

In sum, the interaction afforded by a conversational app can range in complexity from a tightly constrained form in which the user is restricted to simple inputs or selecting from a small set of options (also known as *quick replies*), to a form that is similar to a conversation between humans.

3 Origins of the Conversational Interface

Although conversational interfaces and chatbots became hot topics in 2016, the idea of creating a conversational computer has been around for a long time, going back in fact to the 1960s. It is worth considering the main achievements and findings of this work, both in order to inform current efforts and also to avoid the problem of unnecessarily re-inventing the wheel.

There are four different communities that have worked on conversational interfaces, largely independently of one another (for more detail, see [14]):

- Spoken dialogue systems (SDSs)
- Voice user interfaces (VUIs)
- Embodied conversational agents (ECAs)
- Chatbots

3.1 Spoken Dialogue Systems

Spoken dialogue systems allow humans to interact with a computer on a turn-by-turn basis using spoken natural language for input and output. The earliest dialogue systems, developed in the 1960s and 1970s, were text-based and mainly motivated by efforts to apply techniques from linguistics to dialogue. In the 1980s researchers focused more on the nature of conversational competence, looking at issues such as how to recover from conversational breakdowns arising from the user's misconceptions and false assumptions. This work also built on areas of artificial intelligence such as user modeling and planning. For a detailed account of early text-based dialogue systems, see [13].

Around the late 1980s and early 1990s, with the emergence of more powerful and more accurate speech recognition engines, spoken dialogue systems began to appear. Early examples were the ATIS (Air Travel Information Service) in the USA, [6], while in Europe SUNDIAL was a major project funded by the European community [12]. Later systems include MIT's Mercury [19], the DARPA Communicator systems [24], Ravenclaw[8], and TRIPS [2].

Some of the achievements from research and development in spoken dialogue systems are still relevant today, including:

---

[8] http://www.cs.cmu.edu/dbohus/ravenclaw-olympus/links.html.

- The application of techniques from logic-based AI, such as plan-based dialogue [1], Information State Update Theory [22], and dialogue as rational
  interaction [9].
- The application of techniques from data-driven and statistical AI, such as
  reinforcement learning [18], corpus-based dialogue systems [8], and deep
  neural networks for sequence to sequence learning [21].
- The production of toolkits to support developers of spoken dialogue systems,
  including the CSLU Toolkit,[9] TRINDIKIT,[10] and OpenDial[11].

3.2   Voice User Interfaces

While spoken dialogue systems were developed in academic and industrial
research laboratories, at the same time similar systems were being developed
by various companies and enterprises for commercial deployment. These were
called *Voice User Interfaces*. AT&T's *How May I help You? (HMIHY)* system is an early example [7]. HMIHY supported call routing and by the end of
2001 was handling more than 2 million calls per month and showing significant
improvements in customer satisfaction over alternative solutions. Many similar systems have been developed subsequently to support automated customer
self-service tasks such as directory assistance, information enquiries, and simple
transactions.

Some of the achievements of the voice user interface community are:

- The production of design and evaluation guidelines [4,11,16].
- The development of standards, such as VoiceXML, a W3C standard for scripting spoken dialogues. For a recent book on W3C standards for voice user
  interfaces, see [5].
- Toolkits, especially for developing VoiceXML-based applications, for example,
  Voxeo Evolution.[12]
- Speech Analytics – the process of mining recorded conversations between a
  company's service agents and customers to obtain information about the quality of the interaction, agent performance, customer engagement, and other
  factors that determine customer satisfaction and loyalty.[13]
- Usability testing – the application of effective metrics and methods for the
  evaluation of the usability of voice user interfaces.[14]

3.3   Embodied Conversational Agents

Embodied conversational agents (ECAs) are computer-generated animated characters that combine facial expression, body stance, hand gestures, and speech to
provide a more human-like and more engaging interaction. Examples are:

---

[9] http://www.cslu.ogi.edu/toolkit/.
[10] http://www.ling.gu.se/projekt/trindi/trindikit/.
[11] http://www.opendial-toolkit.net/.
[12] https://evolution.voxeo.com/.
[13] http://www.nexidia.com/.
[14] http://speechusability.com/.

- Smartakus, an animated character used in the SmartKom project to present information [23].
- REA, a real-time, multimodal, life-sized ECA that plays the role of a real estate agent [3].
- GRETA, a real-time three dimensional embodied ECA that talks and displays facial expressions, gestures, gaze, and head movements.[15]
- The Aldebaran robots: Pepper, NAO, and Romeo.[16]
- Jibo, a social robot with a single eye and a moving head and body that are used to give him a personality and promote social engagement.[17]
- Furhat, a robotic head based on a projection system that renders facial expressions, with motors to move the neck and head.[18]
- Hello Barbie, a commercially available conversational toy that responds to children's inputs and retrieves answers from data sources on the Web.[19]

The achievements of the ECA community include the following:

- Advances in technology, such as how to handle multimodal input and output, the development of avatars and talking heads, and the production and interpretation of gestures and emotions.
- The development of standards, such as SAIBA (Situation, Agent, Intention, Behaviour, Animation), BML (Behavior Markup Language), FML (Functional Markup Language), MURML (Multimodal Utterance Representation Language), and EML (Emotion Markup Language). See [5] for descriptions of many of these standards.
- Toolkits, for example, the Virtual Human Toolkit[20] and ACE (Articulated Communicator Engine).[21]

For more detailed descriptions of ECAs, see [14], especially Chaps. 13–16.

3.4 Chatbots

Chatbots, also known as chatterbots, produce simulated conversations in which the human user inputs some text and the chatbot makes a response. One of the motivations for developers of chatbots is to try to fool the user into thinking that they are conversing with another human. Competitions such as the Loebner prize, launched in 1991 by the late Dr Hugh Loebner, have the aim of finding the most human-like chatbot.

To date most conversations with chatbots have been text-based, although some more recent chatbots make use of spoken input and output and in some cases also include avatars or talking heads to endow the chatbot with a more

---

[15] http://perso.telecom-paristech.fr/~pelachau/Greta/.
[16] https://www.aldebaran.com/en/humanoid-robot/nao-robot.
[17] https://www.jibo.com/.
[18] http://www.furhatrobotics.com/.
[19] http://hellobarbiefaq.mattel.com/.
[20] https://vhtoolkit.ict.usc.edu/.
[21] http://www.techfak.uni-bielefeld.de/*skopp/max.html.

human-like personality. Generally, the interaction with chatbots takes the form of small talk as opposed to the task-oriented dialogues of SDSs and VUIs.

The achievements of the chatbot community include the following:

- The development of scripting languages such as AIML (Artificial Intelligence Markup Language)[22] and ChatScript.[23]
- Toolkits, for example, Pandorabots[24] and PullString.[25]
- Advances in technology, such as the use of knowledge repositories to provide some degree of world knowledge and discourse mechanisms to provide limited support for anaphora resolution and topic tracking.
- The incorporation of mobile functions to enable the deployment of chatbots on smartphones and other smart devices.
- Machine learning of conversational patterns from a corpus of conversational data [20].

4   What Is Different Now?

Given the extensive work on conversational interfaces described in the previous section, we might ask what is different now with present-day chatbots and conversational interfaces. While there is much to be learned from the achievements and also some of the failures of the past, many of the systems described above suffered from one or more of the following limitations:

- Some early systems were extremely brittle and would fall over or crash if there was the slightest deviation from the expected input.
- The systems worked well for the purposes for which they were designed but did not scale up or transfer easily to other domains.
- They were often developed using proprietary toolkits and languages.
- They were deployed on specialized platforms and could not be easily ported and deployed on other platforms.

In contrast, present-day chatbots and conversational interfaces benefit from the following advantages:

- As mentioned earlier, they can be developed and deployed on messaging apps that users are already familiar with and thus they work seamlessly across multiple devices and platforms. Moreover, the user does not need to download and install separate apps for each application.
- Chatbots have access to contextual information about users, such as their location, health, and other data that may have been acquired through sensors. This allows them to provide a more personalised experience for each user.
- Chatbots can learn from experience in contrast with earlier systems that were static and did not alter or improve their behaviour over time.

---

[22] http://www.alicebot.org/aiml.html.

[23] http://chatscript.sourceforge.net/.

[24] http://www.pandorabots.com/.

[25] https://www.pullstring.com/.

– A number of toolkits have become available that incorporate the latest developments in AI, machine learning, and NLP, and provide an intuitive and easy-to-learn facility for developers. Examples include:
  • Microsoft Bot Framework.[26] and Microsoft LUIS.[27]
  • IBM Watson.[28]
  • Amazon Alexa.[29]
  • Google Actions.[30]
  • Facebook Messenger Developer.[31]
  • Api.ai (now part of Google).[32]
  • Wit.ai (now part of Facebook).[33]
  • and many others.[34]

5   Some Issues for Future Work

Chatbots and conversational interfaces provide a new and easy interface for users as well as an opportunity for businesses to promote goods and services more effectively. However, as mentioned earlier, there is a danger with all the hype that lessons learned in the past are being ignored. Two areas are of particular interest here:

– How to design and evaluate a conversational interface.
– How to provide a satisfying conversational experience.

5.1   Guidelines for Design and Evaluation

Many articles are being published on an almost daily basis setting out how to design chatbots, providing tips and highlighting common design mistakes, with titles such as "Eleven rules to follow when designing a chatbot"[35] and "Top 6 conversational skills to teach your chatbots",[36] While articles such as these often provide useful hints for novice developers, in some cases the advice given is very high-level and not easy to actually operationalise, for example:

---

[26] https://dev.botframework.com/.
[27] https://www.luis.ai/.
[28] https://www.ibm.com/watson/.
[29] https://developer.amazon.com/alexa.
[30] https://developers.google.com/actions/.
[31] https://developers.facebook.com/products/messenger/.
[32] https://api.ai/.
[33] https://wit.ai/.
[34] https://botpublication.com/10-bot-building-platforms-and-why-you-need-to-build-a-bot-for-your-business-b86fd26ba9f9#.ivdnsmxq4.
[35] http://venturebeat.com/2016/08/02/11-rules-to-follow-when-building-a-chatbot/.
[36] https://medium.com/topbot/top-6-conversational-skills-to-teach-your-chatbotsec4 eb019a23d.dg37ymo27.

- Make life easier.
- Make interactions simpler.
- Don't be a broken record.
- Don't sound like a robot.

Instead of a proliferation of hints and suggestions, what is needed is a coherent set of design and evaluation guidelines. As one commentator has written:

> With the hype around bots, everyone is running around like headless chickens to build bots that will solve every existing problem in the world.[37]

Chatbot developers are in danger of re-inventing the wheel when there has already been considerable work done in areas such as voice user interfaces, backed by years of experience in commercial deployment. See, for example, [5, 11, 16].

Little has been written on how a chatbot should be evaluated, although companies are beginning to emerge that specialise in the analysis of conversational data with bots).[38]

A common distinction has been made in the evaluation of spoken dialogue systems and voice user interfaces between objective and subjective measures:

- Objective metrics are computed from logs of the interactions of users with the system, such as the duration of the dialogue, the number of system corrections, word error rate, and the containment rate i.e. the number of interactions handled by the automated system.
- Subjective metrics elicit the opinions of users about some aspect of quality, such as the intelligibility of the synthesized speech, the overall user experience, and the expected future usage of the system.

An initial step in developing evaluation guidelines for chatbots and conversational interfaces should be to consider and possibly further develop and amend metrics that have been used successfully over several decades for spoken dialogue systems and voice user interfaces. For more detail on the evaluation of conversational interfaces, see [14], Chap. 17.

There are two interesting new initiatives within the speech and W3C communities that are currently addressing issues of design guidelines and standards:

- **Guidelines for conversational interfaces** – this initiative has been launched by the Association for Voice Interaction Design (AVIxD),[39] aiming to investigate issues such as:
  - How to evaluate conversational interfaces.
  - Contexts of use.
  - Interactions between different modalities (visual, spoken, touch).
  - Should conversations always be user-initiated or sometimes system-initiated and under what circumstances?

---

[37] http://venturebeat.com/2016/09/19/why-we-are-still-a-long-way-from-a-killer chatbot/.

[38] https://botanalytics.co/.

[39] http://avixd.org/.

- **Standards for virtual assistants** – this is a W3C community group, led by Deborah Dahl,[40] investigating issues such as:
  - Collection of new use cases for voice interaction.
  - Languages for defining intelligent, conversational dialogues.
  - Standard semantic representations for common concepts, e.g. time, location, etc.
  - Communication standards between different virtual assistants.

5.2 Providing a Satisfying Conversational Experience

As yet there has been little written on how to provide a satisfying conversational experience for users. One aspect concerns the management of the conversation flow in a chatbot application. Some toolkits allow the designer to design the conversation flow using a graphical tool.[41] However, while this approach is useful for simple conversations with few choices, it has been shown in spoken dialogue research that when a dialogue increases in complexity with several branches at each dialogue state, trying to represent the complete dialogue flow as a graph becomes difficult, if not impossible [15,17]. Other methods for dealing with conversation flow need to be considered (see, for example, discussion in [14], Chap. 10).

There are many other issues that have been addressed in research on dialogue management for spoken dialogue systems and voice user interfaces that are also potentially relevant for chatbots, including:

- How to manage multi-turn conversations as opposed to one-shot queries, where the conversation either involves slot-filling or simply an extended interaction. See [14], Chap. 10 for discussion of dialogue management issues.
- Within a multi-turn conversation how to handle requests for clarification and follow-up questions.
- How to manage context, including the conversational context, the user's physical context, and other relevant contextual factors such as user preferences and attributes.
- How to handle more advanced pragmatic features of conversation, such as the interpretation of indirect speech acts, conversational implicature, and presupposition (see [10] for a comprehensive treatment of these issues).
- How to deal with elements of conversational behaviour, such as social engagement, personality, and emotion (see [14], Chap. 14 for a detailed discussion of these issues).

6 Concluding Remarks

Chatbots with conversational interfaces provide a new and exciting medium for users interacting with smart devices. There are great opportunities but also many

---

[40] http://www.speechtechmag.com/Articles/Editorial/FYI/New-Standards-for-Virtual-Assistants-Sought-112671.aspx.
[41] http://www.converse.ai/features.

challenges ahead. It is important that developers should not ignore the rich body of scientific work on conversational interfaces that has produced guidelines and standards as well as highlighting some of the pitfalls to be avoided.

References

1. Allen, J.F.: Natural Language Understanding, 2nd edn. Benjamin Cummings Publishing Company Inc., Redwood (1995)
2. Allen, J.F., Byron, D.K., Dzikovska, M., Ferguson, G., Galescu, L., Stent, A.: Towards conversational human-computer interaction. AI Mag. **22**(4), 27–38 (2001)
3. Bickmore, T., Cassell, J.: Social dialongue with embodied conversational agents. In: van Kuppevelt, J.C.J., Dybkjær, L., Bernsen, N.O. (eds.) Advances in Natural Multimodal Dialogue Systems. Text, Speech and Language Technology, vol. 30. Springer, Dordrecht (2005). doi:10.1007/1-4020-3933-6_2
4. Cohen, M.H., Giangola, J.P., Balogh, J.: Voice User Interface Design. Addison Wesley, New York (2004)
5. Dahl, D.A. (ed.): Multimodal Interaction with W3C Standards: Toward Natural User Interfaces to Everything. Springer, Cham (2017). doi:10.1007/978-3-319-42816-1
6. Hempill, C.T., Godfrey, J.J., Doddington, G.R.: The ATIS spoken language systems pilot corpus. In: Proceedings of the DARPA Speech and Natural Language Workshop, Hidden Valley, pp. 96–101 (1990). doi:10.3115/116580.116613
7. Gorin, A.L., Riccardi, G., Wright, J.H.: How may i help you? Speech Commun. **23**, 113–127 (1997). doi:10.1016/s0167-6393(97)00040-x
8. Griol, D., Callejas, Z., Lopez-Cozar, R., Riccardi, G.: A domain-independent statistical methodology for dialog management in spoken dialog systems. Comput. Speech Lang. **28**(3), 743–768 (2014). doi:10.1016/j.csl.2013.09.002
9. Jokinen, K.: Constructive Dialogue Modelling: Speech Interaction and Rational Agents. Wiley, Chichester (2009). doi:10.1002/9780470511275
10. Levinson, S.C.: Pragmatics. Cambridge University Press, Cambridge (1983)
11. Lewis, J.R.: Practical Speech User Interface Design. CRC Press, Boca Raton (2011). doi:10.1201/b10461
12. McGlashan, S., Fraser, N., Gilbert, N., Bilange, E., Heisterkamp, P., Youd, N.: Dialogue management for telephone information systems. In: Proceedings of the Third Conference on Applied Language Processing. Association for Computational Linguistics, Stroudsburg, pp. 245–246 (1992) doi:10.3115/974499.974549
13. McTear, M.: The Articulate Computer. Blackwell, Oxford (1987)
14. McTear, M., Callejas, Z., Griol, D.: The Conversational Interface: Talking to Smart Devices. Springer, Cham (2016). doi:10.1007/978-3-319-32967-3
15. Paek, T., Pieraccini, R.: Automating spoken dialogue management design using machine learning: an industry perspective. Speech Commun. **50**, 716–729 (2008). doi:10.1016/j.specom.2008.03.010
16. Pearl, C.: Designing Voice User Interfaces: Principles of Conversational Experiences. O'Reilly Media Inc., Sebastapol (2017)
17. Pieraccini, R., Huerta, J.M.: Where do we go from here? In: Dybkjær, L., Minker, W. (eds.) Recent Trends in Discourse and Dialogue. Text, Speech and Language Technology, vol. 39. Springer, Dordrecht (2008). doi:10.1007/978-1-4020-6821-8_1
18. Rieser, V., Lemon, O.: Reinforcement Learning for Adaptive Dialogue Systems: A Data-Driven Methodology for Dialogue Management and Natural Language Generation. Springer, New York (2011). doi:10.1007/978-3-642-24942-6

19. Seneff, S., Polifroni, J.: Dialog management in the mercury flight reservation system. In: Proceedings of ANLP-NAACL 2000, Stroudsburg, 11–16 May 2000. doi:10.3115/1117562.1117565

20. Shawar, B.A., Atwell, E.S.: Using corpora in machine-learning chatbot systems. Int. J. Corpus Linguist. **10**(4), 489–516 (2005). doi:10.1075/ijcl.10.4.06sha

21. Sutskever, I., Vinyals, O., Le, K.V.: Sequence to sequence learning with neural networks. In: Advances in Neural Information Processing Systems (NIPS 2014), vol. 27, pp. 3104–3112 (2014). http://papers.nips.cc/paper/5346-sequence-to-sequence-learning-with-neural-networks.pdf

22. Traum, D.R., Larsson, S.: The information state approach to dialog management. In: Smith, R., Kuppevelt, J. (eds.) Current and New Directions in Discourse and Dialog, pp. 325–353. Kluwer Academic Publishers, Dordrecht (2003). doi:10.1007/978-94-010-0019-2_15

23. Wahlster, W., Reithinger, N., Blocher, A.: Smartkom: multimodal communication with a life-like character. In: Proceedings of the 7th European Conference on Speech Communication and Technology (Eurospeech 2001), Aalborg, pp. 1547–1550, 3–7 September 2001. http://www.isca-speech.org/archive/eurospeech_2001/e01_1547.html

24. Walker, M.A., Aberdeen, J., Boland, J., Bratt, E., Garofolo, J., Hirschman, L., Le, A., Lee, S., Narayanan, K., Papineni, B., Pellom, B., Polifroni, J., Potamianos, A., Prabhu, P., Rudnicky, A., Sanders, G., Seneff, S., Stallard, D., Whittaker, S.: DARPA communicator dialog travel planning systems: the June 2000 data collection. In: Proceedings of the 7th European Conference on Speech Communication and Technology (INTERSPEECH 2001), Aalborg, 3–7 September 2001, pp. 1371–1374 (2001). http://www.isca-speech.org/archive/eurospeech_2001/e01_1371.html

25. Woolley, S.C., Howard, P.N.: Political communication, computational propaganda, and autonomous agents. Int. J. Commun. **10**(2016), 4882–4890 (2016). doi:10.1016/0022-2836(81)90087-5

Spanish Language Technologies Plan

David Pérez Fernandez[✉][iD], Doaa Samy[iD],
and Juan de Dios Llorens Gonzalez[iD]

State Secretariat for Information Society and Digital Agenda, Madrid, Spain
PlanTecnologiasLenguaje@minetad.es

Abstract. The paper aims at introducing the Language Technologies Plan launched by the Spanish State Secretariat for Information Society and Digital Agenda. Since its launch in October 2015, several steps have been taken to integrate Human Language Technologies (HLT) in a number of initiatives targeting different sectors in Public Administration, considered as a driving force to promote HLT industry. The paper outlines the rationale behind the Plan, its objectives and its structure. The paper is divided into three sections: An introduction explaining the rationale behind the adoption of the Plan and its scope of action. The second section outlines the HLT ecosystem in Spain through a SWOT analysis. The third section gives a detailed explanation of the objectives and the adopted structure for the implementation of the Plan. Finally, conclusions are included in the fourth section.

Keywords: Human Language Technologies · HLT · Natural Language Processing · NLP · Machine Translation · MT · Open data · Language resources · Data analysis

1 Introduction

The ongoing development of the Internet and Information Communication Technologies in general provides access to enormous—and growing—volumes of textual information. These volumes of textual information are varied and in different languages. However, IT systems, which are able to easily process data, cannot directly process human language. The emergence of new technologies, based on increased computation power and access to huge amounts of data in this post digitalization era are converting Human Language Technologies (HLT) into a real solution to overcome language barriers. In this sense, HLT is a critical enabling technology to exploit the available amounts of digital resources [1].

HLT applies scientific methods and information technology to the understanding of human language. Tools such as search engines, intelligent personal assistants, text classifiers and machine translation have become essential to our day-to-day work. However, there are many other situations in which the application of natural language processing and machine translation might be a key for offering citizens new advanced services and for optimizing processes in both

© Springer International Publishing AG 2017
J.F. Quesada et al. (Eds.): FETLT 2016, LNAI 10341, pp. 50–60, 2017.
https://doi.org/10.1007/978-3-319-69365-1_4

business and in public administrations. Any step towards improved understanding, synthesis, classification or machine translation of unstructured information generates value for society and could apply to all business sectors.

To have a better understanding, it is important to highlight the reasons behind adopting a Plan for Language Technologies at the national level. Language technologies market is growing rapidly. Recent reports estimate substantial growth in the global market over the coming years, among the Top 10 Strategic Technology Trends, natural language processing appears as essential technology under the first trend "Artificial Intelligence and Advanced Machine Learning". This technology is directly linked with massive data and extensive parallel processing power characterizing this era aiming at the development of systems which "can learn and change future behavior, leading to the creation of more intelligent devices and programs". Moreover, conversational systems appear as the seventh trend [2]. In addition to this technological progress, other key factors support the adoption of a plan for the advancement of language technologies in Spain. These factors could be explained within different contexts: the national, the European and the international contexts.

At the Spanish national level, both the Digital Agenda for Spain and the Spanish Strategy for Science, Technology and Innovation establish the development of "Digital Economy and Society" as one of the general challenges that require the greatest efforts in Scientific and Technological Research, Development and Innovation (R&D&I) [3]; they also highlight the potential of Information and Communication Technologies (ICT) sector as one of Spain's strengths for leading scientific, technological and business development. This industry is identified as a Strategic Innovative Area [3]. Furthermore, the Autonomous Regions of Spain also highlight the potential for ICT to be a driving force for the economy in their Research and Innovation Strategies for Smart Specialization (RIS3) [4].

The State Secretariat for Information Society and the Digital Agenda (hereinafter SESIAD, its Spanish acronym) is the responsible body for the implementation and coordination of the Digital Agenda as part of the Strategic Action Plan for the Digital Economy and Society of Spain. In this respect, SESIAD has opted for the adoption of the Plan of Language Technologies as integrating natural language processing and machine translation could optimize services and processes in terms of quality and quantity.

At the European Union level, there are 24 official languages and more than 60 national and regional minority languages [5]. Spanish language is one of the 24 official languages, while co-official languages of Spain: Catalan, Galician and Euskera (Basque) are among the 60 national and regional minority languages. Language diversity is one of the greatest cultural assets, however this asset is also considered a barrier that needs to be overcome, especially when new initiatives are taken at the European level, such as the establishment of a Digital Single Market (DSM). HLT industry could play a crucial role since language technologies components are embedded in many digital products [6,9].

However, development of applications for a specific language and, in many cases, for a particular area of knowledge, is dependent on the availability of technology and resources for the language in a designated field of expertise.

In the case of Spain, the availability of such resources for the Spanish language—but to a lesser extent and with some considerable gaps—is similar to that for German or French, despite the number of Spanish speakers being much higher. For the co-official languages of Spain, the level is lower. The cost of these resources is substantial and cannot be borne by small- and medium-sized enterprises (SMEs).

To ensure that applications are available in Spanish and the co-official languages of Spain, a comprehensive plan for fostering HLT should take into consideration some measures such as:

- Improving the quantity, quality, variety and availability of the supporting language resources and tools. In this respect, language resources could be built from the vast amount of information generated by the Public sector within the framework of RPSI Policy, i.e. Policy of Re-use of Public Sector Information [7].
- Expanding training in these technologies to ICT professionals in the private and public sectors.
- Introducing Natural Language Processing (NLP) and Machine Translation (MT) technologies into the content managed by Public Administration. The impact of introducing these technologies in sectors such as Health or Justice could significantly improve public services quantitatively and qualitatively.

At the International level, Spanish is the world's second most widely spoken language after Mandarin Chinese, based on the number of native speakers, and third in terms of total number of speakers, after English [8]. Thus, the Spanish language's capacity for internationalization is huge, as nine of every ten speakers are located outside Spain [8]. In addition, Spanish is estimated to be the second most widely used language in business transactions globally, due to growth in the Latin American market. Sharing a common language represents an opportunity to strengthen ties with the Ibero-American community and reach out for a wider market in the field of HLT industry.

The Spanish Language Technologies Plan is launched by State Secretariat for Information Society and Digital Agenda (SESIAD) is a five-year plan, framed within the Digital Agenda for Spain. Its geographical and institutional scope cover the various Autonomous Regions and the three co-official languages of Spain: Catalan, Galician and Euskera (Basque) languages.

Given the multidisciplinary nature of language technology, the Plan is inter-institutional and it is based on promoting language technologies by coordinating all the actions of Spain's Central Administration, in conjunction with the authorities of Spain's Autonomous Regions.

The Plan is structured in five pillars with different measures under each pillar.

2   HTL in Spain

Based on the steps taken at the ministerial levels, the Committee of Experts was asked to prepare a report in which an analysis of the HLT situation in Spain is presented together with needs assessment within the Spanish context. The report pointed out the strengths, weaknesses, opportunities and threats as shown in Table 1.

Table 1. SOWT Analysis of HLT in Spain.

Strengths	Weaknesses
– A high standard of research in natural language processing, coordinated by the Spanish Society for Natural Language Processing – Good governance of the Spanish language (Royal Spanish Academy and the Association of Spanish Language Academies in Ibero-America) – Extensive experience in multilingualism, due to the presence of co-official languages in Spain	– The sector comprises small- and medium-sized enterprises that do not have the industrial capacity to compete on international markets or complete the value chain within Spain – The difficulty of transferring knowledge from the research sector to the business sector, primarily due to the cross-sector and multidisciplinary nature of natural language processing
Opportunities	Threats
– The Spanish language's high potential for internationalisation and cooperation with Ibero-America – New public services for citizens and companies in strategic sectors (e.g. healthcare, tourism and education) – A fast-expanding market tied to innovation and development – The potential of RPSI as a source of extremely valuable language resources for business and research	– The loss of economic and industrial competitiveness of Spain and of Ibero-America – The digital underdevelopment of the Spanish language – The digital extinction of co-official languages of Spain Brain drain of researchers and professionals

From the above analysis, the following conclusions could be driven:

– The language technology sector is a cross-cutting emerging sector, linked to innovation, with the capacity to drive growth, competitiveness and high quality employment.
– Development in HLT is unstoppable and Spain should seize upon this opportunity.

Spain has the means, but the country's Central Administration must promote and coordinate initiatives in conjunction with the authorities of Spain's Autonomous Regions and with the countries of Ibero-America, to make the most of this opportunity.

3   Objectives and Implementation

The general objective of the Spanish Language Technology is to promote HLT in Spanish and Spain's co-official languages. Three specific objectives are identified:

1. Development of Linguistic Infrastructure
2. Promoting HLT Industry
3. Counting on Public Administration as a Promoter of HLT Industry

The break down into activities is structured within an implementation plan that guarantees coordination of efforts to find possible synergies and to avoid overlapping. The Implementation Plan is structured in five pillars with a set of measures identified under each pillar. The five pillars are the following:

1. A governance pillar to ensure the management and follow up of the activities.
2. Three core technical pillars corresponding to the three specific objectives.
3. A fifth pillar for the implementation of a set of flagship projects.

3.1   Governance Pillar

This pillar is operating horizontally through the lifetime of the Plan to ensure coordination, complementarity, collaboration and mutual assistance among the involved parties at the different levels of Spanish Administration: national, regional and local. Compatibility and complementarity with European strategies and initiatives is also an important dimension in the governance pillar [1]. It contemplates the operational planning and the periodic evaluation of the Plan.

Two established committees are responsible of the governance of the plan: The Steering Committee and the Experts' Committee. The first is a decision making body focusing on managerial aspects, while the second acts as a liaison between the Steering Committee and the stakeholders providing technical advice to the decision makers. Both implement the governance through three measures:

- Operational Planning
- Evaluation and Follow up
- Coordination with Public Administrations

3.2   Development of Linguistic Infrastructure

This the first of the three pillars which directly map to the following specific objectives of the Plan. This pillar focuses on building a robust infrastructure for Language Technologies including both language resources and processing tools for Spanish and co-official languages. It is important to adopt an integrative approach which avoids overlapping and seeks coordination of efforts and synergies between stakeholders. The following four measures are planned to develop the Linguistic Infrastructure:

1. Design a plan for the development of linguistic infrastructure after creating an inventory of the currently available linguistic infrastructures classified and assessed according to their quantity, quality and availability.
2. The designed plan should consider as an aim reducing the gap between linguistic infrastructure for NLP and MT in Spanish and co-official languages of Spain and those in English. In addition, campaigns should be organized for the assessment and evaluation of language resources.
3. Select technical interoperability standards, appropriate licence policies and mechanisms for protecting personal data in the generation of language resources.
4. Purchase or develop common tools for generating and evaluating linguistic infrastructures.
5. Facilitate accessibility to available high-quality linguistic infrastructure in Spanish and the co-official languages of Spain, free of charge or at a low cost (at least for innovative SMEs, the research sector and the public administrations).

3.3   Promoting HLT Industry

The report conducted by the Committee of Experts in NLP and MT in Spain shed light on the need to boost the HLT industry as Public Administrations and many sectors in the industry are not aware of its potential and its useful role, if applied, in a broad range of products and services. To face this challenge, it is necessary to increase the visibility of HLT industry both locally and internationally.

HLT Visibility. At the local level, support should be given to HLT industry in order to reach a high profile that enables it to attract talented specialists to Spain and to compete internationally.

This support should consider setting the mechanisms to encourage the transfer of knowledge from academia to industry. Furthermore, it should contemplate training of researchers and developers in the field as a necessary step to a create critical mass of specialists in the HLT field in Spain.

For the implementation, the following measures are planned

1. Design a plan to raise the industry's profile and improve transfer from research to industry.
2. Train professionals and specialists in the HLT field through coordinated actions aiming at improving the profile of HLT providers. Among these actions, the following are planned:
   - including specific courses on language technology in university programmes
   - creating online training (MOOCs)
   - organizing competitions such as hackathons
   - supporting industrial doctorate and master's programmes
   - offering specialised grants.

3. Enhance visibility through the following actions:
   - organizing training seminars for SMEs and professionals;
   - organizing conferences, seminars and forums
   - participation in national and international trade fairs
   - promoting cloud computing (SaaS)

Internationalization of HLT Sector. At the international level, support should be provided to Spanish companies in the HLT sector to enable them to reach out to the international markets, especially the Ibero-American and North American markets among other emerging markets. For corporations that are already well-established in the Ibero-American market, different support should be given to consolidate their competitiveness and their position in this market.

On the other hand, it is indispensable to strengthen cooperation with Ibero-American counterparts to seek their support and active involvement in order to join efforts to lead the HLT industry for the Spanish language.

A set of measures are identified for implementing the HLT internationalization:

1. Conducting a study on the state of the art of the internationalisation of Spanish companies in the HLT industry, especially in countries with biggest markets for internationalisation.
2. Design an internationalisation plan.
3. Cooperation with Ibero-America through participation in key events such as the Ibero-American Summit and through collaboration with the Secretariat-General for Ibero-America (SEGIB) in addition to other Ibero-American institutions.
4. Coordination with Spanish Agency for International Cooperation and Development (AECID), Network of Science Counsellors Abroad and other existing associations of Spanish scientists abroad.
5. Integration of HLT into the areas that are currently being funded within the international dimension of the Strategic Action Plan for the Economy and Digital Society.
6. Including HLT industry among the investment opportunities in Spain under the ICT sector of the "Invest in Spain Programme" which targets attracting foreign investment to Spain.
7. Including HLT in the agreements and memoranda of understanding (MoU) signed with Ibero-American countries (or from other regions) in the future.
8. Promoting the development of linguistic infrastructure and availability of open public information on variants of Spanish.
9. Identifying trade fairs, conferences or other events for marketing the products and projects being carried out by Spanish companies in HLT industry. These activities could be carried out in collaboration with entities such as ICEX1, the Spanish public entity responsible of promoting exportation, investment and internationalization for the Spanish industry.
10. Studying the possibility of providing grants to incubators or accelerators, or of presenting twinning projects between small and large companies with an international dimension.

3.4 Public Administration as Promoter of HLT Industry

This pillar could be seen from two perspectives: The Public Administration as a user of NLP and MT on one hand, and the Public Administration as provider of resources for NLP and MT, on the other hand.

Creating Shared Platforms Within Public Administrations for HLT. Considering the Public Administration as a user, HLT components could be integrated in its processes and systems. This integration would apply the recommendations of the Commission for the Reform of the Public Administrations (CORA) [10] as public services could be improved significantly in terms of quality, capacity, efficiency and cost.

A shared platform for resources implies saving costs and avoiding duplication of efforts. Thus, making procedures more efficient. Moreover, HLT could provide Public Administration with useful insights through data analysis. The suggested platform will be based on re-usable and interoperable components, preferably with unrestrictive, open source licences.

A set of measures are identified to implement this line:

1. Design a development plan for natural language processing and machine translation platforms in the public administrations.
2. Establish a clear organisational and financial structure to ensure the sustainability of the platform beyond the lifetime of the Plan.
3. Development of a common natural language processing and machine translation platform for the public administrations, with the following essential requirements:
   - Facilitate the launching of advanced services based on natural language processing and machine translation in the national and regional administrations.
   - Develop a scalable infrastructure based on components for the parallel processing of large corpora of documents.
   - Guarantee confidentiality of public services.
   - Add different components and language resources to the flow of language processing with different licensing models and processing methods.
   - Introducing tools for anonymization, editing, post-editing of machine translations, etc.
   - Facilitate access to general-purpose language resources pillar and field-specific resources (mainly those specialized resources necessary for the development of the flagship projects proposed in the fifth pillar.
   - Ensure exploitation and standardization of the language resources generated under the RPSI policy.
   - Enable different models of implementation and distribution (embedded, local cluster, remote, and implementation at supercomputing centres).

Linguistic Resources Generated from Public Administrations Within the Policy for Re-use of Public Sector Information. This line contemplates the Public Administration as provider of resources for HLT. This objective is based on the basic assumption that the huge amounts of data and information generated by Public Administration could be used as valuable linguistic resources.

Nevertheless, converting these resources into freely available linguistic resources (or available at a low cost) requires a set of measures for the development of tools and the adoption of technical interoperability standards, appropriate licence policy and mechanisms for protecting personal data. These measures are detailed as follows:

1. Apply the recommendations of the "Re-use of Public Sector Information" (RPSI) [7] policy through:
   - Introducing the concept of linguistic linked open data in RPSI.
   - Promoting this concept within the public administrations.
   - Introducing the concept of linguistic linked open data at international forums and events such as the International Open Data Conference (IODC), in collaboration with Ibero-America, to raise the profile of the linguistic linked open data policy.
2. Identify corpora of public-sector information that could be converted into language resources.
3. Select technical interoperability standards, open-licence policies and personal data protection mechanisms.
4. Facilitate access to the common tools necessary for generating and exploiting these language resources (e.g. anonymisers, text alignment, processing flows) on the natural language processing platform of the public administrations foreseen in this Plan.
5. Develop a catalogue of these open language resources within the open data portal, with an advanced user experience.

3.5 Flagship HLT Projects in Public Administration

This pillar focuses on developing a set of flagship HLT projects within strategic sectors in the Public Administration. These projects should address well identified problems in which the integration of HLT would highly impact the services or the products offered by the public administration on a wide scale. Thus, they require a vertical and horizontal scalability to process large amounts of information and to serve many users at the same time. Succeeding in implementing these projects would create a high social impact and, hence, would convert them into a reference model for other public administrations. It would also prove the latent potential of HLT if integrated in public services (Fig. 1).

The Plan contemplates strategic sectors of high impact such as Health, Justice, Education and Tourism. However, more sectors might be considered during the lifetime of the Plan based on the following criteria:

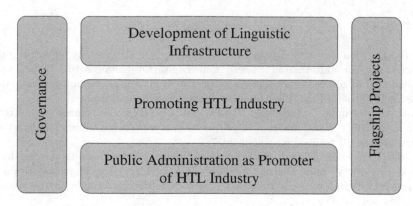

Fig. 1. Structure of the Plan

- Commitment of the competent bodies to ensure leadership by those who understand the problem well and are competent to solve it.
- Clear and demonstrated benefits of HLT.
- High economic and social impact.
- Development of the entire value chain.
- Generation of re-usable resources to avoid dependency on certain exclusive solutions and technologies which prevent resource portability.
- Synergies with the other measures in the Plan for the Advancement of Language Technology and, in particular, with the generation of language resources and with the public administrations' natural language processing and machine translation platform.
- Transferability to future projects.

4 Concluding Remarks

Since its official launch in October 2015, implementation is in progress according to the activities of the different pillars. Steps have been taken to join efforts and bring together different actors in HLT from public administration, academia and industry. Activities and initiatives taken are available on the official webpage of the Plan: http://www.agendadigital.gob.es/tecnologias-lenguaje/Paginas/plan-impulso-tecnologias-lenguaje.aspx.

Acknowledgments. The English version of the Spanish Language Technologies Plan has been translated thanks to the team of the Language Interpretation Office (Oficina de Interpretación de Lenguas OIL), Spanish Ministry of Foreign Affairs.

References

1. SESIAD: Plan for the Advancement of Language Technology. Spanish State Secretariat for Information Society and Digital Agenda (2015). http://www. agendadigital.gob.es/tecnologias-lenguaje/Bibliotecaimpulsotecnologiaslenguaje/ Detalle%20del%20Plan/Plan-Impulso-Tecnologias-Lenguaje.pdf
2. Gartner Group: Gartner's Top. 10 Strategic Technology Trends for 2017 (2016). http://www.gartner.com/smarterwithgartner/ gartners-top-10-technology-trends-2017/
3. SESIAD: Agenda Digital para España. Spanish State Secretariat for Information Society and Digital Agenda (2013). http://www.agendadigital.gob. es/agenda-digital/recursos/Recursos/1.Versi'ondefinitiva/Agenda_Digital_para_ Espana.pdf
4. European Commission: Estrategias nacionales y regionales para la especialización inteligente (RIS3) (2014). http://ec.europa.eu/regional_policy/sources/docgener/ informat/2014/smart_specialisation_es.pdf
5. Special Eurobarmeter: Europeans and their Languages 386 (2012). http://ec. europa.eu/public_opinion/archives/ebs/ebs_386_en.pdf
6. European Commission: Language Technologies and Big Data— Digital Single Market (2015). https://ec.europa.eu/digital-single-market/en/ language-technologies-and-big-data
7. Boletín Oficial de Estado BOE: Norma Técnica de Interoperabilidad de reutilización de recursos de la información (2013). https://www.boe.es/boe/dias/2013/ 03/04/pdfs/BOE-A-2013-2380.pdf
8. Ethnoloue: Languages of the World (2013)
9. LT-Innovate: Status and Potential of the European Language Technology Markets (2013). https://ec.europa.eu/digital-single-market/en/news/ lt2013-status-and-potential-european-language-technology-markets
10. State Secretariat for Public Functions, Spanish Ministry of Finance, Public Administration: Reform of the Public Administrations (2013). http://www.sefp.minhafp. gob.es/en/web/areas/reforma_aapp

Improving Collaboration Between the European Language Technology Industry and Research: A New Framework for Supply and Demand

Philippe Wacker$^{(\boxtimes)}$ and Andrew Joscelyne

LT-Innovate, Brussels, Belgium
info@lt-innovate.org

Abstract. It is vital to develop more intensive and intelligent collaboration between industry and research to create true win-win situations for all stakeholders in language technology. LT-Innovate, as the key language technology industry organisation, proposes a tentative strategy and methodology to federate actions that improve industry/research collaboration throughout Europe.

Keywords: (human) Language technology · Natural language processing · Multilingual and cross-lingual processing · Interactive communication · Intelligent content · R&D&I · Relationship between research and industry · Innovation support · Speeding up research-to-market · Language technology strategy · Digital single market

1 Supporting Language Technology: The Role of LT-Innovate

LT-Innovate is the Language Technology Industry Association. It was founded in 2012 with the main objectives of:

- strengthening the Language Technology Industry for increased competitiveness in global markets;
- promoting language technologies as drivers of economic success, societal well-being and cultural integrity;
- encouraging collaboration within the Industry and with other stakeholders of the Language Technology value-chains;
- articulating the Industry's collective interests vis-à-vis buyers, researchers, investors and policy makers.

LT-Innovate is a global association with 400 members, composed of LT vendors, buyers, integrators, researchers, as well as language service providers, associations and policy makers.

In order to promote and inform about the language technology sector, LT-Innovate runs a website (www.lt-innovate.org) that provides a Language Technology Directory with profiled technology vendors, users and applied researchers

© Springer International Publishing AG 2017
J.F. Quesada et al. (Eds.): FETLT 2016, LNAI 10341, pp. 61–69, 2017.
https://doi.org/10.1007/978-3-319-69365-1_5

allowing easy one-stop searches for information about players in the field. Each year, LT-Innovate holds an annual Language Technology Industry Summit (for the sixth time on 9–11 October 2017 in Brussels) that brings together the industry, its clients, research partners and policy makers. It also publishes a recognised news channel (Lang Tech News) available on Scoop.it and Twitter to share relevant industry and research news from around the world within the community.

The Language Technology industry is not a "vertical" industry on a par with automotive, pharmaceuticals, publishing or chemicals. It forms part of the intelligent services sector, providing critical software and some hardware solutions and applications horizontally across many distinct verticals. As a fairly recent growth sector in the computing, data and information industry, it covers a wide range of scientific and technological solutions for language-based–and especially multilingual–processes and activities.

Today, human language-based processes play an increasing role in a wide range of knowledge-management tasks carried out in both vertical industries and inside individual companies and organisations of many different kinds. These tasks are being increasingly digitised and assimilated into the more general field of artificial intelligence (AI), but 'LT' (or 'Natural Language Processing - NLP' as it is referred to in the USA) retains a powerful identity as a language-centric sector, focused on the following three core fields, all related to fundamental linguistic issues, yet often separated in terms of business applications:

- Multilingual processing, in which the understanding, translation and localisation of information and content is the core activity,
- Interactive communication, in which automated speech/voice communication, understanding and conversational exchanges are the central concerns,
- Intelligent content, in which text and speech analytics, understanding, summarisation, and sentiment evaluation play a key role in automating knowledge creation, processing and extraction processes.

We estimate that growth in the LT sector in the EU will reach an impressive 10% a year for the coming decade. Other predictions in the specific sector of cognitive computing systems cite 33.9% global growth to 2020. Content analytics (to which LT offers decisive technology support) could grow globally by 22.1% to 2021 and speech analytics (mostly covering contact centre and media analysis processes) may even grow by 22% to 2020. LT itself is largely a software business, whereas the afore-mentioned markets often include hardware and related services in the figures. But a 10% growth rate means that both private and public investors should understand that the LT market is productive and has the potential to create new jobs.

2 Working with LT Users and Buyers

There are very few surveys of the language technology markets as such, and no one has a clear, comprehensive view of end-user needs. The translation business can depend on fairly reliable figures, but translation mixes technology with human productivity and management processes.

In March 2013, LT-Innovate published a major report[1] on the state of LT in Europe, one of the first that analysed in depth the opportunities as well as the brakes and challenges on developments in this field[2]. It found that the LT arena in Europe was extremely fragmented and dysfunctional, with many small companies in different countries often reinventing the wheel.

At that time, large-scale technology transitions such as mobile telephony, cloud computing, and the initial collection of extensive language data were beginning to radically accelerate the potential role of computational linguistics in IT application development (speech recognition for phones, data-driven statistical translation systems, the arrival of textual analysis for big data, etc.). Simultaneously,the European Commission formulated its ambitious Digital Single Market project. It is now time to consolidate the field, leverage the power of the new platforms, and transform years of funding for LT research (notably through the R&D Framework Programmes at European level) into a viable marketplace for multilingual applications and services that IT platforms could benefit from in e-commerce, business intelligence, the Internet of Things and the soaring market for personalised devices.

LT-Innovate is committed to making a greater effort in monitoring the specific technology and application fields for Language Technology, in particular by continuously analysing the relationship between LT buyers and vendors.

To this end, LT-Innovate has embarked on a campaign to engage with companies operating in different vertical sectors with a view to better understanding their emerging needs in the LT area. Over the last three years, in-depth discussions[3] have been held with organisations such as Segittur in the tourist industry, Bayer in the chemicals and pharmaceuticals industry, Oracle in the computing industry, Daimler in the automotive industry and StepStone, a large human resources company.

This experience provided useful knowledge about the kinds of processes and applications in which LT could play a key role. It also illustrated the growing importance of automatable language/knowledge-based processes which are impacting companies today. But it equally demonstrated that the European LT industry needed to consolidate and improve its own capacity to develop and market its products more effectively.

To summarise, LT-Innovate attempts to facilitate the interaction of LT end users who require new services, LT buyers (big industries that use LT in their business processes or embed it in their products), LT vendors who need to expand

---

[1] LT2013: Status and Potential of the European Language Technology Markets - http://www.lt-innovate.org/sites/default/files/2216-LT2013_Report_Medium Quality.pdf#overlay-context=lt-observe/document/lt-innovate-innovation-agenda-manifesto .

[2] The LT2013 Report is quoted at several instances in Spain's "Plan for the Advancement of LT" - http://www.agendadigital.gob.es/tecnologias-lenguaje/Bib liotecaimpulsotecnologiaslenguaje/Detalle%20del%20Plan/Plan-Advancement-Language-Technology.pdf .

[3] See details about LT-Innovate's Innovation Acceleration Programme at http://www. lt-innovate.org/programmes/innovation-acceleration.

their market reach, and also LT researchers, who will increasingly be called upon to provide proof of concept solutions that address the speed of innovation required by society as a whole.

3 Research and Innovation: The Hoover and Hairdryer Effects

The European Commission aims at stimulating research and technological development (R&D) by funding projects bringing together research and industry with the aim of delivering a proof of concept (technology) and then exploring the opportunities to industrialise/productise the technology within verticals.

Under the Horizon 2020 Programme, the focus shifted from research and development (R&D) to research and innovation (R&I) with the aim of bringing research closer to the market. It is the opinion of LT-Innovate - and many others - that research is not in itself a form of innovation. Funding the two activities in one programme is rather like trying to use a hairdryer in lieu of a vacuum cleaner or vice versa. In reality, research can attempt to blow out (disseminate) ideas like a hairdryer; but innovation needs to deliver the right solution for a specific innovation challenge like a vacuum cleaner. We believe that mixing the two processes in one and the same programme is counter-productive. There should be a research programme on the one hand, driven by researchers and an innovation programme on the other hand, driven by industry. Meanwhile, there should also be an increased effort to build bridges between research and innovation by making publicly funded research results more systematically and proactively available to industry.

4 Towards a European Language Technology Strategy

Since 2013, a number of papers attempting to outline the needs of LT in terms of European policy support have been circulating stakeholders and amongst policy makers. We shall list only the most recent:

2013: the META-NET Strategic Research Agenda for Multilingual Europe 2020[4] June 2014: LT-Innovate's Innovation Agenda & Manifesto[5] February 2015: the CITIA Roadmap for Conversational Interaction Technologies[6] April 2015: the Declaration of Common Interest at the Riga Summit on the Multilingual Digital Single Market[7] July 2016: Language as a Data Type and Key Challenge for Big Data - Strategic Research and Innovation Agenda (v0.9)[8]

---

[4] http://www.meta-net.eu/sra-en.
[5] http://www.lt-innovate.org/lt-observe/document/lt-innovate-innovation-agenda-manifesto.
[6] http://www.lt-innovate.org/citia/citia-roadmap-conversational-interaction-technologies.
[7] http://www.lt-innovate.org/sites/default/files/Riga-Summit-2015-Declaration.pdf.
[8] http://cracker-project.eu/wp-content/uploads/SRIA-V0.9-final-online.pdf.

LT-Innovate considers that these documents are not really "strategy" papers that set out a clear path for the European Commission to successfully support the LT innovation ecosystem over the coming 5 to 10 years. An innovation strategy cannot simply be a shopping list of research challenges. Research covers everything from "blue sky" research to engineering solutions for specific problems. However, research should not be shackled to the needs of innovation. Its task is to explore, inspire and suggest. Conversely, innovation should focus on declared aims and challenges and show how to commit to them.

In a recent paper[9], entitled Assessment of the State of Language Technologies and EU Policy Recommendations, LT-Innovate suggested what should be, in our view, the three main building blocks of a European language technology strategy.

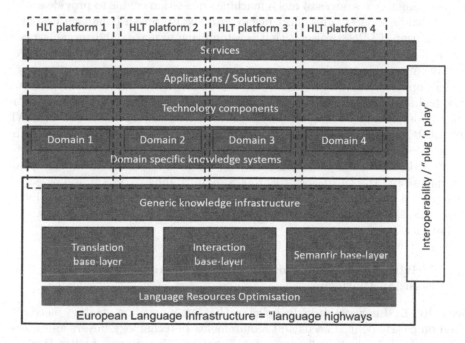

4.1   The European Language Infrastructure (ELI)

Firstly, Europe needs a basic infrastructure for natural language processing (NLP). All language processing applications (search, mining, writing, speech, translation, etc.) depend on such an NLP infrastructure. These different infrastructure components are tedious to develop and maintain, and are thus expensive, since they are required for every single language. The development of such an infrastructure, maintained and accessible as a layer of resources and technologies would enable the emergence of LT-based solutions in multiple languages–e.g. the entire range of languages necessary to bring about the Digital Single Market.

---

[9] http://www.lt-innovate.org/sites/default/files/Assessment of the state of Language Technologies and EU policy recommendations.pdf.

The European Language Infrastructure should therefore provide the basic functionalities required to process unstructured content. Through Application Programming Interfaces (APIs) it should provide basic language technology services such as tokenization, stemming, part of speech tagging, named entity detection, identification of measurements, currencies, formulas, etc. for all languages, in the same basic quality, and under the same favourable terms.

LT-Innovate believes that building this collective infrastructure layer would be the quantum leap empowering every other innovation project in the EU built around complex language technology.

An effort is underway in the European Commission as part of the Connecting Europe Facility (CEF.AT)[10] to identify, collect and, where necessary, create parallel language resources to fuel a machine translation engine to provide multilingual public services. This effort began with the European Language Resource Coordination (ELRC) project[11] that is attempting to make public organisations aware of the potential for identifying and eventually creating parallel resources to drive automatic translation solutions.

LT-Innovate considers that this resource collection process is likely to be too slow to have a real impact on the market for quicker, better translation solutions underpinning the Digital Single Market. At the very least, the CEF.AT and ELRC initiatives should be opened up to private companies as well as public agencies. Furthermore, LT-Innovate calls upon the European Commission to extend this effort so as to generate the full range of resources for all European languages (and the languages of Europe's main trading partners) and assemble them into a publicly-maintained infrastructure available as a translation, interaction and semantic "base layer" for all private and public LT-based applications and services.

4.2   Driving Innovation: Domain-Specific European-Scale LT Solution Platforms

Secondly, LT-Innovate strongly believes that an innovation strategy needs to build on clearly defined needs and requirements of technology buyers and users.

Hence, LT-Innovate calls upon the European Commission to use Horizon 2020 funding to launch 4 to 5 powerful demonstrator projects combining domain-specific knowledge systems and relevant technologies into powerful, user-driven, solution platforms. These platforms could then serve as launch pads (or "market places") for ecosystems of multilingual applications and services tailored for the specific needs of verticals in which Europe has already strong positions (e.g. public administration & services, transport & logistics, defence & security, banking & insurance, travel & tourism, chemicals & pharmaceuticals, trade & commerce, entertainment & publishing, etc.).

---

[10] https://ec.europa.eu/cefdigital/wiki/display/CEFDIGITAL/eTranslation.
[11] http://lr-coordination.eu/.

Once the European Language Infrastructure and a few domain-specific LT platforms are in place, additional innovation projects, aiming at delivering language-neutral products and services of European and global scale, could then boost the entire ecosystem.

4.3 Language Interoperability

Thirdly, LT-Innovate believes that language interoperability, as foreseen in the European Interoperability Framework, is a key prerequisite in achieving the European Language Infrastructure and would considerably speed up and facilitate the launch of domain-specific European-scale LT solution platforms. Language interoperability should operate mandatorily on a par with rail, road, telecoms, information systems, banking systems, and similar interoperable networks that simplify and accelerate traffic and data exchange within the EU and globally. Using public IT standards and shared intelligence, interoperability will mean that both businesses and public agencies will no more need to pay constant attention to the "language knowledge" level of their institutions, systems or daily practices. Language interoperability must become as automatic as packet switching around the internet, resulting in a seamless Digital Single Market.

Language interoperability of this kind will involve the use of common APIs at all levels (within the services/applications/technologies/ infrastructure layers and between them) to ensure that meanings are maintained in data between languages expressed in different containers, simplifying the work of all citizens as they search, shop, travel, play, pay and learn.

To set a powerful example of and also benefit from the leverage of interoperability, EU institutions should act as pioneers in this domain, demonstrating its full multilingual potential for citizens needing to consult services in their own languages, and agents wishing to share and exchange information and knowledge of all kinds. The current MT@EC and CEF.AT initiatives constitute a step in the right direction but are, by far, insufficient to achieve the above. Instead, EU Institutions should ensure that the precise meaning of information is understood in all languages and that it is preserved throughout exchanges. They can achieve this by maintaining, deploying, and improving Multilingual Knowledge Systems such as EuroVoc and TMClass.

Once a reasonable degree of language interoperability has been achieved by exploiting the European Language Infrastructure and associated domain-specific LT solution platforms, steps will need to be taken to review progress, seek improved solutions, and establish language interoperability as a legal requirement for certain processes throughout the EU.

5   Interacting and Collaborating More Effectively

Improving the process that relates fundamental research, applied research, in-company R&D and productisation and innovation is a long-standing issue.

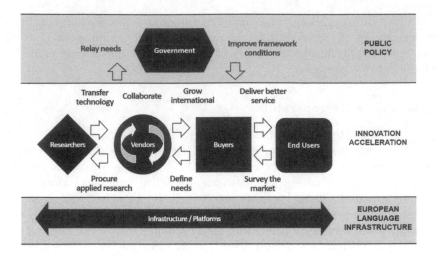

Over the past half-decade in the LT sector, not much has been achieved to clarify the situation, which is initially very much about communication.

Increasingly, the "time to market" for outcomes from certain university research projects is accelerating. Governments want to capitalise on the research institutes they fund and encourage industry to explore competitive opportunities from the work accomplished by the research community. At the same time, part of the research community should be more motivated by the need for solutions targeting all kinds of industries.

Industry buyers need to better communicate about the challenges they are facing and the opportunities that could stimulate the supplier community to propose plausible technology solutions. One way to achieve this would be to build "clusters" around vertical industries that enable all players within vertical value-chains to meet, brainstorm and work on specific LT-based solutions together (see domain-specific LT solution platforms proposed above).

LT-Innovate believes that the best way to promote and improve shared knowledge about research advances and industry needs for given verticals is to build up vibrant communities. What is needed is an efficient clearing house where vertical buyers, suppliers and the research community can meet, find out about needs and attend efficiently-organised webinars, workshops and conferences.

Concretely, LT-Innovate proposes to the research community:

- To collaborate in developing a common vision/strategy for LT in Europe in which research takes the lead on research and industry takes the lead on innovation.
- To join forces to deliver the European Language Infrastructure in less than five years.
- To make research results visible and available to industry, for example through LT-Innovate's Language Technology Directory.
- To present research results to industry at LT-Innovate events and/or through webinars.

– To become involved in industry-led innovation acceleration projects in the context of domain-specific LT solution platforms, with the perspective of applying research results towards delivering solutions corresponding to well-defined user requirements/needs.

LT-Innovate is ready to play its role towards achieving these goals and looks forward to collaborating with the research community in their pursuance.

Contributed Papers

LifeLine Dialogues with Roberta

Asier López[1], Ahmed Ratni[2], Trung Ngo Trong[3], Javier Mikel Olaso[1],
Seth Montenegro[4], Minha Lee[5], Fasih Haider[6], Stephan Schlögl[7],
Gérard Chollet[8], Kristiina Jokinen[3], Dijana Petrovska-Delacrétaz[2],
Hugues Sansen[9], and María Inés Torres[1(✉)]

[1] Universidad del País Vasco (UPV/EHU), Bilbao, Spain
manes.torres@ehu.eus
[2] CNRS SAMOVAR UMR 5157, Télécom SudParis,
Université Paris-Saclay, Paris, France
[3] University of Helsinki, Helsinki, Finland
[4] Hyx, London, UK
[5] Eindhoven University of Technology, Eindhoven, The Netherlands
[6] Trinity College Dublin, University of Dublin, Dublin, Ireland
[7] Management Center Innsbruck, Innsbruck, Austria
[8] Intelligent Voice, London, UK
[9] Shankaa, Paris, France

Abstract. This paper describes work on dialogue data collection and
dialogue system design for personal assistant humanoid robots undertaken at eNTERFACE 2016. The emphasis has been on the system's
speech capabilities and dialogue modeling of what we call LifeLine Dialogues, i.e. dialogues that help people tell stories about their lives. The
main goal behind this type of application is to help elderly people exercise their speech and memory capabilities. The system further aims at
acquiring a good level of knowledge about the person's interests and thus
is expected to feature open-domain conversations, presenting useful and
interesting information to the user. The novel contributions of this work
are: (1) a flexible spoken dialogue system that extends the Ravenclaw-
type agent-based dialogue management model with topic management
and multi-modal capabilities, especially with face recognition technologies, (2) a collection of WOZ-data related to initial encounters and presentation of information to the user, and (3) the establishment of a closer
conversational relationship with the user by utilizing additional data (e.g.
context, dialogue history, emotions, user goals, etc.).

Keywords: Dialogue system · Speech input · Agent-based dialogue
management · Topic trees

1 Introduction

Human-robot interaction provides a new and promising area for the study of
a dialogue partner's engagement in conversational interactions, and for experimenting with various presentation strategies, their cultural differences and the

© Springer International Publishing AG 2017
J.F. Quesada et al. (Eds.): FETLT 2016, LNAI 10341, pp. 73–85, 2017.
https://doi.org/10.1007/978-3-319-69365-1_6

impact on the user's perception, understanding, and evaluation of the interaction. Robots have also opened up novel possibilities in practical applications, e.g. in scenarios which focus on providing tools for the aging population, such as maintaining companionship, detecting health problems, and assisting dependent people. In addition, adaptation to the user can be learned. Roberta Ironside is a personal assistant humanoid robot project that emphasizes speech capabilities for interacting with dependent persons. The project covers: speech processing and dialogue management, affective computing, human behavior analysis, and human robot interaction and assistance. In this paper we focus on the development of Roberta's LifeLine Dialogues, which was one of the topics pursued during the eNTERFACE 2016 workshop series held at the University of Twente, The Netherlands[1]. During four weeks, a team consisting of research students and a number of faculty members worked on different dialogues for Roberta. The results of this undertaking are summarized below. A more extended version of this paper will be available later this year, or early next year, as a report published in the digital CTIT proceedings of the University of Twente.

As a start we worked on dialogue management. The task was to produce clear, natural, engaging, and intuitively easy-to-follow mixed-initiative interactions where both the user and the system are engaged in satisfying and smooth conversational-type situations. While the long-term goal of Roberta Ironside is that both the human as well as the robot can initiate topics and ask questions, for this workshop we focused on the initial encounter and presentation dialogues. In addition to spoken input Roberta was able to obtain information from the environment (incl. an interlocutor's face) and from the system through a dialogue manager that integrates this information within its dialogue tasks and strategies. It was designed to help people tell stories about their lives and consequently help them exercise their speech and memory capabilities. It further aims at acquiring a good level of knowledge about the person and his/her context and thus is expected to feature an open-domain conversational system, presenting useful and interesting information to the user. The novel contributions of this project can thus be summarized in providing a real world application:

- to build a robot-driven spoken dialogue system that integrates and improves face recognition technologies into its dialogue models, and
- to utilize these data (e.g. context, dialogue history, emotions, user goals, etc.) so as to establish a closer conversational relationship with the user, by considering both knowledge of the user as well as the dialogue history.

2   Background

A Spoken Dialogue System (SDS) is a collection of natural language processing components which enables speech-based interaction between a user and a situated agent or knowledge base. Multimodal dialogue systems extend the basic notion of a spoken dialogue system with additional input and output modalities

---

[1] http://hmi.ewi.utwente.nl/enterface16/.

such as visual, tactile, or biosensor information, and thus need extra processing components to take care of sensor fusion and sensor fission.

The basic tasks around dialogue management include: (1) interpretation of the user utterance in a given context (i.e. Natural Language Understanding), (2) decision of what action the system should take (i.e. actual Dialogue Management), and (3) production of an appropriate response (Natural Language Generation).

Moreover, the dialogue manager component keeps track of the dialogue context by integrating the recognized user messages as well as the produced system messages into the dialogue history. Often a separate User Model (UM) is provided to record the user specific characteristics and preference information, and a specific World Model (WM) to store the general knowledge of the world and the environment.

An important part of the dialogue manager is the handling of the grounding process, i.e. overseeing the way how information uttered by the participants is used to form 'common ground', or assumed to be mutually known by the participants [2,20]. This requires that interlocutors actively contribute to the dialogue and let their partner(s) know that they have heard and accepted their contribution. Feedback may be verbal acknowledgments and/or non-verbal communicative acts like head nods, facial expressions and other gestures.

The dialogue manager decides upon the action a system should perform at any given state in the dialogue. Common dialogue techniques are described in [9] where script-based, frame-based, agent-based, and statistical dialogue management models are distinguished.

Script-based dialogue management designs the dialogue as a state diagram where each state and dialogue action are paired. Although easy to design and implement for simple dialogue tasks, they require significant effort to be built and maintained for complex dialogues. A frame-based DM provides more flexible dialogue management by separating knowledge from dialogue actions, so that the actions can be executed in various orders depending on the current information state (e.g. [19,21]). The frame also provides a dialogue context. However, more extended control algorithms and natural language grammar capabilities are necessary.

Many advanced dialogue management architectures use an agent-based approach like the one employed by CMU's Ravenclaw [1]. Originally developed in the Galaxy Communicator project, and further enhanced by [11], Ravenclaw provides an advanced management structure with distributed software agents; i.e. dialogue flow can be modeled by the software agents' reasoning about their own state and the next action. Dialogue structure and reasoning can be flexibly designed, and it is also possible to take multimodal information and dynamic context into account. Similar architectures have been proposed for example in TRIPS [5], EDECAN [12] and JASPIS [22].

Interactive systems are an ongoing field of research, in particular such applications that face the challenges of real world users [4,7,18] and those that deal with adaptive and multi-modal systems. For the initial work on Roberta Ironside we have focused on building a basic dialogue system based on Ravenclaw and from there study more advanced issues in a systematic way.

3   System Architecture

The system we developed consists of an input perception layer, an understanding module, an interaction module that includes the dialogue manager which also manages a user blackboard, a dialogue history blackboard and an open domain conversational agent that gets information from a digital repository and a final output layer. While eventually all these components will be integrated into the body of a humanoid robot, our work group at eNTERFACE 2016 focused solely on the spoken interaction aspects, for which the physical system representation was currently neglected.

3.1   Perception and Understanding

Automatic Speech Recognition – For Automatic Speech Recognition (ASR) our goal was to distribute processing between a local and a remote module. Remote access should be used to allow for richer linguistic data and knowledge processing (note: at eNTERFACE 2016 we used remote servers of Intelligent Voice[2] and Google[3]). Locally, an HMM/DNN decoder running on an NVIDIA GPU platform should serve as a backup. Although a number of different languages were available, at eNTERFACE 2016 we focused on English.

Audio-Visual Signal Processing – As for audio-visual signal processing we used the SudFrog (Telecom SudParis Face Recognition open-source reference software)[4]. It is part of the open-source reference systems initially developed by the BioSecure Network of excellence [13], and has been extensively tested on different large scale and challenging biometric databases, such as the FRGC [14] and the MOBIO [10] databases. Recently it has further been implemented in an audio-visual verification application running on the iPad [23]. It offers 2D face recognition, speaker verification as well as the synchronization of lip movements with the speech signal. At eNTERFACE 2016 we used SudFrog to add an additional input channel, which should help us contextualize interactions. That is, a number of our study participants enrolled into a dialogue with Roberta with their faces. The enrollment phase consisted of the face detection, the normalization, and the creation of a template that represented the subject for further comparisons. In case of a second encounter with the same participant, Roberta would check whether she would 'recognize' this face, and if yes would provide the dialogue manager with the name of the participant.

Natural Language Understanding – With respect to Natural Language Understanding (NLU), we have seen that a semantic parser that uses statistical classifiers outperforms semantic decoders that use manually constructed semantic grammars [8]. However, such a parser needs to be trained by a sufficient number of sentences representing the task. Thus, a main goal of our eNTERFACE 2016

---

[2] http://www.intelligentvoice.com/.

[3] https://cloud.google.com/speech/.

[4] http://share.int-evry.fr/svnview-eph/.

efforts was to collect a respective dataset of sentences, and transform them in corresponding grammar rules and concepts using the Phoenix Semantic Parser [24]. We were able to collect data from interactions with 15 participants, which gave us some initial constructs and vocabulary to work with. Additional interactions increasing the scope of our dialogues are planned for the future.

3.2   Interaction and Dialogue Management

As already mentioned above, our system used Ravenclaw to offer independent agenda-based dialogue management. Ravenclaw is a plan-based and task-independent framework for dialogue management. Domain specific logic is designed through a task specification level using a tree of dialogue agents. A domain-independent dialogue engine then executes the specified dialogue task and thus controls the dialogue [1]. The dialogue specification task is just a plan for interaction described as a hierarchy of sub-dialogues. A small set of fundamental dialogue agents are located at terminal positions of the tree. This set consists of an *Inform*, an *Expect*, a *Request* and an *Execute* agent that produces output, expects information, requests information and performs a domain-specific action. Then dialogue-agencies occupy non-terminal positions in the tree, i.e. representing sub-tasks or sub-dialogues. The execution of agencies is controlled by preconditions, triggers and success and failure criteria. An important feature of Ravenclaw is that the information flow trough the tree is encapsulated in concepts. A more detailed description of this can be found in [1]. Using Ravenclaw allowed us to design a flexible topic dependent dialogue manager, extending the initial capabilities of this framework.

3.3   Output

The goal was to provide facial animation in sync with text-to-speech output. For this we used Unity's game engine. We started by using GRFL's Base Liza 3D model[5]. This saved time since it included animation clips for facial expressions and pre-generated viseme articulations. The phonemes served by the MaryTTS text-to-speech instance were then mapped to their matching visemes for the English language and synchronized with the 3D animations. From there we just had to integrate it with ActiveMQ (the messaging service we used to connect all our components) and push the messages to be read aloud by the Linux build of Roberta's Unity project.

Figure 1 shows the main components of the Roberta dialogue framework developed at eNTERFACE 2016.

4   Audiovisual Dialogues Through Wizard of Oz

In order to design and shape interactions with complex technical solutions such as the ones envisaged by Roberta Ironside, researchers require tools and methods

---

[5] https://www.assetstore.unity3d.com/en/#!/content/52234.

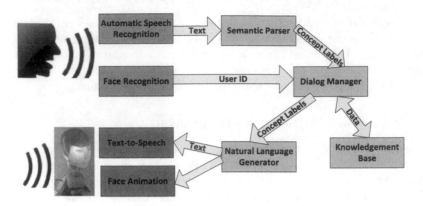

Fig. 1. Main modules of Roberta developed at eNTERFACE 2016

that allow for the early stage prototyping and evaluation of potential development directions. One approach often used for such low-fidelity evaluations is
Wizard of Oz (WOZ) [3]. WOZ constitutes a prototyping method employed
by researchers and designers to obtain initial feedback on features that usually
require significant resources to be implemented. In a so called 'WOZ experiment' a human 'wizard' mimics the functionality of a system, either entirely or
in part, which allows for the evaluation of potential user experiences and interaction strategies without the need for building the actual product. Language based
interaction with systems has been one of the main fields of application for this
type of prototyping, as building high-end prototypes in this domain tends to be
rather costly and time intensive. For example, in order to be able to obtain a basic
understanding of an envisioned spoken interaction, systems may require several
hours of recorded speech, valid transcriptions, and an implemented framework of
rules, as well as a solid error-recovery strategy. Obtaining these types of resources
usually requires several person months of work. Here WOZ experimentation can
help collect data as well as test overall design directions. The two main ingredients required to successfully conduct WOZ experiments are (1) a prototyping
framework/software that allows for the creation of a more or less realistic experimental setting (i.e. the wizard should be hidden from test participants so that
they may feel as if they would be interacting with a real system) and (2) a set
of scenarios which reflect the capabilities and features of the envisioned future
solution. Both was available for our work at eNTERFACE 2016.

4.1 The WOZ Prototyping Tool

We used the WebWOZ prototyping platform[6], a tool specifically geared towards
designing and evaluating natural language based interactions [16]. It is entirely
web-based and allows for the integration of existing language technologies such
as automatic speech recognition and text-to-speech synthesis modules. In order

---

[6] https://github.com/stephanschloegl/WebWOZ.

to collect the above mentioned interaction data (i.e. an initial corpus based on 15 participants) and to obtain a general understanding of potential user strategies we used a pre-configured version of WebWOZ running within a VirtualBox system image [17]. The system used the Google Speech API[7] for speech recognition to provide the input to the wizard and the Open-Mary TTS engine[8] for synthesis. The dialogue management at this stage was entirely wizard-based. That is, we prepared a number of utterances from which the wizard could choose so as to engage a participant into a dialogue. Initially those utterance came from how we expected the envisioned dialogue would progress. Yet, each experiment produced a new set of what one may call 'realistic' utterances, which gradually increased our 'interaction pool' and also produced new insight with respect to potential dialogue strategies (note: utterances could also be produced on the fly so that the wizard was not restricted to the initial set). While our long-term goal for Roberta is to offer the possibility for open domain conversations, this initial design stage was focused on a limited number of interaction scenarios.

4.2   WOZ Driven Roberta Scenarios

Flandorfer advises on having an interdisciplinary team in constructing user scenarios to better understand users' needs instead of just typecasting potential users [6]. We followed this advice and employed a team with diverse expertise including engineers and human-computer interaction researchers. We first wanted to know what kind of personal data we can gather through the intake conversation with Roberta. We used WebWOZ to conduct a study with 15 volunteers on four pre-identified topics i.e. (1) introduction, (2) professional life, (3) hobbies, and (4) conversation closing. These topics constitute the starting points of building a unified storyline about a person, which is the overall aim of the LifeLine module Roberta should eventually be assembled with.

Dahlbäck et al. [3] described the importance of learning from real-life conversations when building natural language dialogue structures because human-machine interactions are full of unexpected conversational turns [3]. Also, sociodemographic information is an important part of whether or not assistive robots will be accepted by their users, yet various researchers, system designers, and engineers do not incorporate sociodemographic information [6]. Our WOZ study showed that it is possible to identify a user's sociodemographic background during an initial conversation with Roberta. Roberta begins by checking if a person's face is registered in her database. If it is not, then first, Roberta asks for permission to record the new user into her database. Second, Roberta asks for his/her name and spelling of the name when it is not easily identified. Third, she asks where the user is from and where the user now lives. Fourth, she asks about the user's age, although we learned that age can be a sensitive question. Thus, if no answer is given, Roberta does not immediately repeat the question but rather saves it for later. Fifth, she asks for an opinion about the

---

[7] https://cloud.google.com/speech/.

[8] http://mary.dfki.de/.

user's hometown and/or his/her place of residence. Roberta was also able to provide some answers about herself (e.g. "I am Roberta"; "I am infinite"; "I'm from Enschede"), which makes information gathering conversational. Below are two sample conversations from our experiments which demonstrate this:

Conversation 1
Roberta: Hi I am Roberta. Do you want to register and talk with me?
User: Yes I would like that.
R: What is your name?
U: John.
R: Where are you from?
U: Israel. And you?
R: I'm from Enschede. Do you know it?
U: Yes I do, but I still prefer Israel.

Conversation 2
R: Hi I am Roberta. Do you want to register and talk with me?
U: Yes, I am here to talk to you. I am glad to know you.
R: Good. What is your name?
U: I'm Sungjin from Korea.
R: Can you spell that for me?
U: S-u-n-g-j-i-n.
R: Great. Where do you actually live?
U: Sorry I don't understand your question.
R: Where do you live?
U: Ah you mean where do I now live. I live in Amsterdam.
R: Do you like it there?
U: It's okay. It's nice, but can be challenging.

4.3   Moving to LifeLine Dialogues

The pre-defined conversational topics we used for our WOZ study were inspired by the idea of providing Roberta with what we call a LifeLine module. The goal of LifeLine is to help a person tell the story of his/her life [15]. Such offers an infinite number of subjects to talk about while requiring a rather simplistic framework of questions and answers. Also, it helps a person to work on his/her memory capabilities. With LifeLine, we hope that elderly persons will find a permanent ear for discussing about the past. At the same time, the Roberta system obtains more knowledge about the person. LifeLine could thus be seen as a social network where people's life lines could cross and be linked for a certain period of their life. By sharing information about an event, people will be able to enrich the event, which again could be a subject for later discussion.

We have seen that even with very little information gathered from an initial conversation with a user, we are able to build a rich picture of this person, including relevant sociodemographic information. This initial intake conversation is useful for two reasons. First, it begins a user's LifeLine that is semi-autobiographic, with Roberta acting as a *ghostwriter* who categorizes and places stories from the user's life in a timeline as she gets to know the user better. Second, Roberta establishes a user's sociodemographic background, which helps tailor conversational approaches to fit each user.

Our study participants at eNTERFACE 2016 may not have been the exact right target group for LifeLine. They all received at least undergraduate education and were more knowledgeable about technology than the average population. Yet, they provided an initial starting point. Going from here, future studies will be conducted with older, less educated users that are potentially less knowledgeable about technology.

5 System Building

Figure 2 shows the topic-based dialogue structure we developed based on the conducted WOZ study and its gathered data. An agency was defined for each topic defined during the WOZ scenarios. Then the acquired dialogues guided us through the design of agencies. Note that the use of concepts as triggers allowed us to control the execution of each agency or sub-tree so that a change of topic could appear as often as required, resulting in a very natural and flexible topic-based dialogue structure. As an example, if a participant names a place this can trigger a Roberta interest in said place. She is then able to access a knowledge repository to retrieve information of this place, or, in case the place is already an attribute value in the user blackboard or in the history of the dialogue blackboard, she can ask the user about the place, using a request agent.

The WOZ data served as the foundation for developing the 'Authentication" and the 'Intro" agencies in Fig. 2. On top of that, Roberta can either ask about a user's professional life or hobbies according to the tree shown in Fig. 2. In case the user first talks about his/her professional life, Roberta asks about the person's current job, tasks related to the job, a typical workday, and his/her educational background. If the user does not currently have a job, Roberta asks about what the user used to do or study.

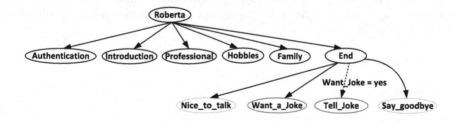

Fig. 2. Topic-based dialogue structure

Conversation 3
R: What's your job?
U: I'm now working on an airport security project.
R: What tasks do you do?
U: That's very specific. Right now I am working on voice activation.
R: Tell me about your typical workday.
U: Well I wake up around eight and come to work.
R: Wonderful. What did you study?
U: I studied electrical engineering in France.

Roberta can then ask about hobbies. If the user does not have any hobbies, Roberta will ask more specifically about music, sports or traveling. All three categories have anticipatory questions and/or statements. For example, Roberta will ask "do you like music?", followed by "who is your favorite musician?" or "what is your favorite genre?" or "do you play any instruments?".

Conversation 4
R: What is your hobby?
U: I don't have a lot of time for hobbies.
R: Do you like music?
U: Yes I like music.
R: What is your favorite genre?
U: I like classical music.
R: Do you play any instruments?
U: I used to play piano when I was very very young, but not anymore.

Conversation 5
R: What is your hobby?
U: I like photography and traveling.
R: Tell me more about the places you've visited.
U: I visited so many countries... Germany, Ireland, England, Mexico, Brazil...

The end of the conversation can also be controlled by some trigger conditions, as shown in Fig. 2. At this point Roberta may tell a joke and/or ask for permission to talk at a later time.

Conversation 6
R: Do you want to listen to a joke?
U: Yes please.
R: Why was 7 afraid of 9?
U: Why?
R: Because 789.
U: Very funny.
R: Do you want to talk more some other time?
U: Yeah maybe some other time.
R: Talk to you later.
U: Bye.

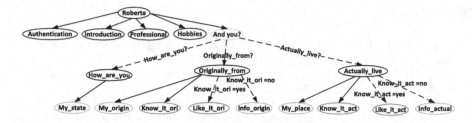

Fig. 3. Allowing for user questions

The WOZ study further showed that some people liked to ask questions back. So we also built an 'and-you' agency. This agency used some expectation agents that added naturalness to the dialogue and some information agents providing Roberta's answers (cf. Fig. 3).

Finally we developed the preliminary design of a feedback agent able to provide Roberta with the capability of giving feedback to the user. It uses inform and execution agents allowing for sufficient dialogue flexibility.

Conversation 7
R: Where are you originally from?
U: I'm originally from Spain. And you Roberta?
R: Nice question, I'm from the Cybernation.

6   Concluding Remarks and Future Work

The paper has described work on dialogue data collection and dialogue system design for personal assistant humanoid robots undertaken at eNTERFACE 2016. The emphasis has been on the system's speech capabilities and dialogue modeling of LifeLine dialogues. Hence, WOZ data based on 15 video recorded conversations is currently available. This collection served as the basis for designing our face recognition, speech understanding, dialogue task and natural language generator modules. The current system includes a flexible spoken dialogue system that extends the initial Ravenclaw dialogue management framework with topic management and multimodal capabilities.

Roberta's LifeLine module is, however, still work-in-progress. Some efforts are currently spent on using the same WOZ study design to compile an audiovisual database in more realistic environments, like in the houses of elderly people, and in several languages with the help of tele-assistance services.

Acknowledgments. The authors want to acknowledge the organizers of eNTER-FACE 2016 and the University of Twente for providing the opportunity to develop this project. We also want to acknowledge the institutions supporting some of the authors e.g. the Spanish Science Minister under grant TIN2014-54288-C4, 'ADAPT 13/RC/2106', and the Academy of Finland project Digital Citizens grant number 270082.

References

1. Bohus, D., Rudnicky, A.I.: The RavenClaw dialog management framework: architecture and systems. Comput. Speech Lang. **23**(3), 332–361 (2009)
2. Clark, H.H., Schaefer, E.F.: Contributing to discourse. Cogn. Sci. **13**(2), 259–294 (1989)
3. Dahlbäck, N., Jönsson, A., Ahrenberg, L.: Wizard of Oz studies: why and how. In: Proceedings of the 1st International Conference on Intelligent User Interfaces, pp. 193–200. ACM (1993)
4. Eskenazi, M., Black, A.W., Raux, A., Langner, B.: Lets Go Lab: a platform for evaluation of spoken dialog systems with real world users. In: InterSpeech (2008)
5. Ferguson, G., Allen, J.F.: TRIPs: an integrated intelligent problem-solving assistant. In: Proceedings of the AAAI/IAAI Conference on Artificial Intelligence/Innovative Applications of Artificial Intelligence, pp. 567–572 (1998)
6. Flandorfer, P.: Population ageing and socially assistive robots for elderly persons: the importance of sociodemographic factors for user acceptance. Int. J. Popul. Res. **2012**, Article ID 829835, 13 (2012). doi:10.1155/2012/829835
7. Ghigi, F., Eskenazi, M., Torres, M.I., Lee, S.: Incremental dialog processing in a task-oriented dialog. In: InterSpeech, pp. 308–312 (2014)
8. Henderson, J., Merlo, P., Titov, I., Musillo, G.: Multilingual joint parsing of syntactic and semantic dependencies with a latent variable model. Comput. Linguist. **39**(4), 949–998 (2013)
9. Jokinen, K., McTear, M.: Spoken Dialogue Systems, vol. 2. Morgan & Claypool Publishers, Princeton (2009)
10. McCool, C., Marcel, S., Hadid, A., Pietikäinen, M., Matejka, P., Cernockỳ, J., Poh, N., Kittler, J., Larcher, A., Levy, C., et al.: Bi-modal person recognition on a mobile phone: using mobile phone data. In: 2012 IEEE International Conference on Multimedia and Expo Workshops (ICMEW), pp. 635–640. IEEE (2012)
11. Olaso, J.M., Milhorat, P., Himmelsbach, J., Boudy, J., Chollet, G., Schlögl, S., Torres, M.I.: A Multi-lingual evaluation of the vAssist spoken dialog system. Comparing Disco and RavenClaw. In: International Workshop on Spoken Dialogue Systems (2016)
12. Olaso, J.M., Torres, M.I.: Dialogue system based on EDECÁN architecture. In: Sojka, P., Horák, A., Kopeček, I., Pala, K. (eds.) TSD 2010. LNCS, vol. 6231, pp. 547–551. Springer, Heidelberg (2010). doi:10.1007/978-3-642-15760-8_69
13. Petrovska-Delacrétaz, D., Chollet, G., Dorizzi, B. (eds.): Guide to Biometric Reference Systems and Performance Evaluation. Springer, London (2009). doi:10.1007/978-1-84800-292-0
14. Phillips, P.J., Flynn, P.J., Scruggs, T., Bowyer, K.W., Chang, J., Hoffman, K., Marques, J., Min, J., Worek, W.: Overview of the face recognition grand challenge. In: 2005 IEEE Computer Society Conference on Computer Vision and Pattern Recognition (CVPR 2005), vol. 1, pp. 947–954. IEEE (2005)
15. Sansen, H., Torres, M.I., Chollet, G., Glackin, C., Petrovska-Delacretaz, D., Boudy, J., Badii, A., Schlögl, S.: The Roberta IRONSIDE project: a dialog capable humanoid personal assistant in a wheelchair for dependent persons. In: 2016 2nd International Conference on Advanced Technologies for Signal and Image Proceedings (ATSIP), pp. 381–386 (2016)
16. Schlögl, S., Doherty, G., Luz, S.: Wizard of Oz experimentation for language technology applications: challenges and tools. Interact. Comput. **27**(6), 592–615 (2015)

17. Schlögl, S., Milhorat, P., Chollet, G., Boudy, J.: Designing language technology applications: a Wizard of Oz driven prototyping framework. In: Proceedings of the EACL Conference of the European Chapter of the Association for Computer Linguistics, pp. 85–88 (2014)
18. Serrras, M., Pére, N., Torres, M.I., Del Pozo, A.: Entropy-driven dialog for topic classification: detecting and tackling uncertainty. In: International Workshop on Spoken Dialogue Systems (2016)
19. ter Maat, M., Heylen, D.: Flipper: an information state component for spoken dialogue systems. In: Vilhjálmsson, H.H., Kopp, S., Marsella, S., Thórisson, K.R. (eds.) IVA 2011. LNCS, vol. 6895, pp. 470–472. Springer, Heidelberg (2011). doi:10. 1007/978-3-642-23974-8_67
20. Traum, D.R.: A computational theory of grounding in natural language conversation. Technical report, University of Rochester, Rochester, NY, USA (1994)
21. Traum, D.R., Larsson, S.: The information state approach to dialogue management. In: van Kuppevelt, J., Smith, R.W. (eds.) Current and New Directions in Discourse and Dialogue. Text, Speech and Language Technology, vol. 22, pp. 325–353. Springer, Dordrecht (2003)
22. Turunen, M., Hakulinen, J.: Jaspis-a framework for multilingual adaptive speech applications. In: InterSpeech, pp. 719–722 (2000)
23. Usoltsev, A., Petrovska-Delacrétaz, D., Houssemeddine, K.: Full video processing for mobile audio-visual identity verification. In: International Conference on Pattern Recognition Applications and Methods ICPRAM 2016 (2016)
24. Ward, W., et al.: The CMU air travel information service: understanding spontaneous speech. In: Proceedings of the DARPA Speech and Natural Language Workshop, vol. 1, pp. 127–129 (1990)

An Affective Utility Model of User Motivation for Counselling Dialogue Systems

Zoraida Callejas[1]([✉]) and David Griol[2]

[1] Department of Languages and Computer Systems,
University of Granada, Granada, Spain
zoraida@ugr.es
[2] Computer Science Department,
Carlos III University of Madrid, Madrid, Spain
dgriol@inf.uc3m.es

Abstract. Counselling dialogue systems are designed to help users to change and monitor their behaviours in order to achieve beneficial goals, such as the acquisition of healthy habits. To be effective, it is important that these systems include a model that accounts for the effort that users are investing to achieve the goals. However, most of the systems available nowadays carry out a naïve calculation based on the attained results, rather than on the reasons behind the successes or failures and their consequences for future user behaviour. In contrast to this, in this paper we propose a model that characterizes user motivation considering various aspects of psychological theories on subjective expected utility and attribution. Moreover, we provide a specification that allows carrying out calculations that replicate the users' decision-making process considering its emotional implications. The model is general-purpose and can be employed in standard architectures to make interpretations that adapt to each user, thus fostering more flexible and personalized interactions.

Keywords: Dialogue systems · User models · User motivation · Counselling · Emotion

1 Introduction

Counselling dialogue systems are usually aimed at engaging users in a persuasive dialogue on positive attitudes towards a beneficial goal. Usually the goal is long-term and requires a significant effort by the user to achieve it, as it usually implies a change in behaviour.

Some of the most studied application domains for these systems are healthcare and pedagogy. In the health domain, counselling systems are employed to change attitudes or behaviours towards more healthy habits, such as adherence to medication [17], smoking cessation [26], sugar and blood pressure control [5], regular exercising [29] and diet promotion [4]. In the pedagogic domain, students must be engaged to learn, thus one goal of tutoring dialogue systems is to maintain their motivation [6].

© Springer International Publishing AG 2017
J.F. Quesada et al. (Eds.): FETLT 2016, LNAI 10341, pp. 86–97, 2017.
https://doi.org/10.1007/978-3-319-69365-1_7

As explained in [14], the effectiveness of counselling dialogue systems has been proven, and their use is likely to increase in the near future. Thus, different architectures and models have been proposed in order to build such systems over a variety of devices, and to make them portable across different domains. For example, [4] proposed a reusable framework based on ontologies and a standard task modelling language that allows to easily port a dialogue system between different health counselling domains. However, these systems must still achieve another level of effective tailoring to users, as it has been demonstrated that users who disengage from their regular use are those who find that the system is not addressing their needs [14, 15].

State-of-the-art user models are regularly based on fixed parameters, such as education level or ethnicity [14], and on the achievement of the settled objectives, for instance frequency of exercise, frequency of control of health parameters, and weight reduction. This way, motivation is considered implicitly through these parameters, and not modelled explicitly, which makes it difficult to fully adapt systems to users and prevent disengagement.

In [20], a study of over 200 papers in the topic revealed that the key to solve this problem might be in more collaboration between disciplines such as Psychology, Computer Science and Cognitive Science. In a similar survey of tutoring systems [15], the authors identify adaptation to affect as one the main challenges to be addressed.

In this paper we propose a novel approach. We consider user motivation with an affective utility model that takes into account the psychological theories on attribution and decision making in order to estimate the internal mechanisms that influence the motivation of the users. The benefit is that dialogue systems can adapt their interaction strategies to maintain or increase user motivation. Our approach can be used to complement existing user models, and may be implemented as a separate module in the systems' architecture.

2   Fundamentals

In this section we describe the decision and attribution theories in which we base our proposal. On the one hand, decision theory explains the reasons why individuals decide to take some action instead of another, which is relevant to study why users choose to make the effort necessary to follow the suggestions made by the dialogue system. On the other hand, attribution theory describes how users might attribute their failure or success to their own continued effort or to uncontrolled external factors, which allows to understand their motivation to reach the established goals and interact with the system.

2.1   Decision Theory

Early works in the field of human decision making formalized decision under uncertainty as a value-maximizing behaviour: people usually choose the action that provides a higher expected value. This way, it is possible to define a consistent preference relation in the finite set A of actions $(\succeq_A)$ as a preference function $EV : A \rightarrow \Re$. That is to say, it is possible to define an *expected value* function that provides a numeric value for all the possible actions, so that an action a_1 is preferable to an action a_2 if the expected value for a_1 is higher than for a_2 $(EV(a_1) > EV(a_2) \rightarrow a_1 \succ a_2)$. The expected value of the action a_i is computed as shown in Eq. 1, as the sum of the expected values of all the possible outcomes of the action multiplied by their probabilities. For example, in a gambling game where you flip a coin and if you get heads you win \$2 and if you get tails you loose \$1, the expected value of flipping the coin would be $2\,x\,0.5 + (-1)\,x\,0.5 = 0.5$.

$$EV(a_i) = \sum_{j=1}^{n} value(o_i)p(s_j) \tag{1}$$

However, different people might choose different actions even when identical expected values apply. For example, most persons would choose \$25 for certain rather than a 25% chance of earning \$100 and a 75% chance of earning \$0, even when the expected value is \$25 in both gambles. This problem was addressed by defining perceived or subjective *expected utility* (SEU) instead of *expected value* [28]. SEU is a function of the perceived attractiveness (utility) of each outcome of the considered actions along with its perceived likelihood. This theory accounts for the individualisms in choice, as different people may have different utility functions and beliefs about the probabilities of outcomes.

Following Eq. 2, the subjective expected utility of action a_i is defined as the sum of the perceived utility of the outcomes of such action $u(o_{ij})$ and the perceived likelihood or subjective probability of the state of the world $(p(s_j))$. This way, decision under uncertainty consists in choosing the action, among all the possibilities in the given scenario, that maximizes expected utility $(SEU(a_1) > SEU(a_2) \rightarrow a_1 \succ a_2)$.

$$SEU(a_i) = \sum_{j=1}^{n} u(o_{ij})p(s_j) \tag{2}$$

Expected utility is a very expressive model for decision making. On the one hand, the perceived likelihood or subjective probability represents beliefs about the probabilities of the outcomes. On the other hand, the utility function explains the different attitudes towards risk.

Only recently, affective decision making has been taken into account in decision models. For example, in [7] the authors describe two psychological processes that determine choice in decision making: a rational process and an emotional process. The former is deliberative and chooses the optimal action that maximizes expected utility, whereas the latter forms risk perception and finds optimal beliefs that maximize mental profile.

In [12], there is a discussion about the importance of anticipatory feelings such as anxiety or suspense when making decisions in scenarios of uncertainty.

Other works also corroborate that the anticipation of rewards is not a purely cognitive procedure, and it is modulated by emotion [21]. Emotions make it possible to explain some of the inconsistencies of the expected utility model. For example, anxiety explains why probability changes from 50 to 51% have less impact on the decision maker than differences between 0 and 1.

In [1], the authors claim that an affective agent must have cognition and emotion, and that both play an important role on motivation. They propose to model motivation as a reward in an internal simulation loop and define ad-hoc six models: attention model, cognition model, emotion model, decision making model, cognitive reward model, and emotional reward model.

For our proposal, we consider the anticipation of emotion as a key aspect that affects the subjective utility of the actions that users may choose. However, instead of considering multiple models, we contribute an integrated framework that can be employed in different systems.

2.2 Attribution Theory

Attribution theory reveals what individuals believe about the reasons for the outcomes of their actions. As argued by Weiner [32], personally relevant and/or unexpected outcomes leverage a positive or negative affective response that initiates a process that forms a causal attribution for the outcome. These attributions have been categorized in three dimensions: stability (stable/unstable), locus of control (internal/external), and control (controllable/uncontrollable).

Based on the type of attribution formed in this process, a more refined emotional response is generated. According to Weiner, negative outcomes that are attributed to external and controllable factors (e.g. attributing failing an exam to teacher injustice) will promote anger. Conversely, the attribution of negative outcomes to internal and controllable factors (e.g. attributing a poor performance to insufficient effort) is thought to cause guilt. Also shame is likely when negative outcomes are associated with internal uncontrollable factors (e.g. attributing poor performance to insufficient intelligence). With regard to positive emotions, internal attributions for positive outcomes are associated with pride, whereas external attribution is associated with gratitude. These attribution-driven emotions, provoke behavioural responses to the outcome.

The perceptions or attributions that individuals have about why they succeed or fail at an activity determine the amount of effort they will engage in similar activities in the future. This is why we have considered attributions into our motivation model. In our proposal, when attributions lead to positive affect and high expectancy of future success, they result in a greater motivation than with attributions that produce negative affect and low expectancy of future success.

3 Proposal

We formulate the motivation to engage in an activity towards a beneficial objective as a process of decision under uncertainty in which the user must choose between two actions: to make the effort of carrying out the proposed changes (e.g. acquire healthy habits, addiction cessation, and health control), or not to make the effort (e.g. having sedentary habits, smoking, and not controlling their health). We consider that the user is motivated when he prefers to do the effort, which occurs when the subjective utility of doing the effort is greater than the utility of not doing it, as show in Eq. 3.

$$SEU(eff) > SEU(\overline{eff}) \rightarrow eff \succ \overline{eff}$$
$$eff \succ \overline{eff} \rightarrow User\ is\ motivated \tag{3}$$

We have defined a *subjective utility* function that provides a numeric value for the two possible actions, as shown in Eq. 4 (the equivalent equation holds for $SEU(\overline{eff})$). For counselling dialogue systems, the model of the decision making process can be simplified by considering only two possibilities: success ($succ$) and failure ($\overline{succ}$), which may have different meaning depending on the application domain. For example, in a smoke cessation scenario, success means that the user was able to quit (or decrease) smoking, whereas in a pedagogical domain success would imply that the student learned the proposed contents.

$$SEU(eff) = u(succ)p(succ|eff) + u(\overline{succ})p(\overline{succ}|eff)$$
$$= u(succ)p(succ|eff) + u(\overline{succ})(1 - p(succ|eff)) \tag{4}$$
$$= p(succ|eff)(u(succ) - u(\overline{succ})) + u(\overline{succ})$$

Counselling dialogue systems maintain a stable relation with users, supporting them while they pursue long-term goals. During this time, users provide feedback about their achievements at specific moments. We will refer to these moments as "feedback interactions". In these interactions, the system must inform users about their progress, discuss about the success or failure of the current objective, and provide advice to achieve the next goal. In this setting, motivation can be computed and used by the system to provide more adequate help to the users.

Figure 1 shows the process carried out at each feedback interaction to update the motivation model following our proposal. The result is an update of the motivation model that includes information about the subjective utility of effort taking into account the attribution scenario, the user emotional responses in the scenario, and the achievement history. Also, it outputs a boolean value for motivation, which is true when the subjective expected utility of making the effort is higher than the one of not making the effort.

During this process, the system obtains several pieces of information from the user. Firstly, in order to assess the causes to which the user attributes his outcomes at each feedback interaction, the dialogue system employs standardized locus of control tests. There exist many standardized tests with hundred of questions [13,16,24,31], so that each time the user is presented with different questions, and predictions do not loose reliability [3]. Also, developers can easily add new tests or questions specially designed for specific application domains (e.g. health promotion [23]) or even create their own.

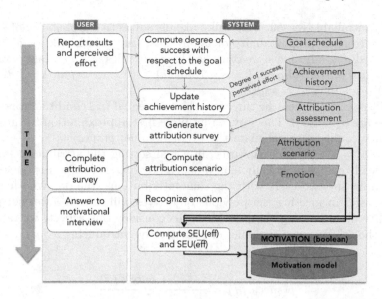

Fig. 1. Procedure followed at each feedback interaction to update the motivation model

Secondly, to assess emotion, the system uses a motivational interviewing approach, in which the goal is to elicit statements of the user's existing beliefs. In [30] the authors use this approach with the aim of helping the user to notice discrepancies between his stated beliefs and values, and his current behaviour. These user descriptions can be employed to carry out emotion recognition. The obtained emotions can be represented in an activation-evaluation bi-dimensional space, indicating their valence (negative or positive) and arousal [11]. We have employed this approach successfully for the recognition of emotions in previous works [8–10].

Thirdly, the achievement history is updated based on the success percentage and the subjective effort. Success percentage measures the extent to which the objective settled for the current feedback interaction has been achieved. Subjective effort represents whether the user considers he has done a considerable effort to achieve the goal.

Finally, with these sources of information, the system computes the values for the subjective utilities (u) and probabilities (p), as explained in the next sections.

3.1 Proposed Model for Subjective Probability

To compute subjective probability (p), we take into account that external, uncontrollable and unstable attributions make success subjectively less probable for the user than when he considers that success depends of his own effort (controllable, stable and internal attribution). For example, if a student thinks that he is not intelligent enough to learn about a topic, he is attributing his failure to an uncontrollable reason. This will make his subjective probability of success be near zero and the probability of failure near one, which will make him be demotivated to study. Thus, we consider three variables that can take a value of 0 or 1, x ($0 = uncontrollable$, $1 = controllable$), y ($0 = external$, $1 = internal$), and z ($0 = unstable$, $1 = stable$).

The best case is when the three variables are equal to 1, and the worst when the three are equal to 0. This way, an intuitive first approximation to subjective probability could be to calculate the average value: $p(succ) = (x + y + z)/3$, and $p(\overline{succ}) = 1 - p(succ)$. However, in a real setting the attribution factor is optimistically or pessimistically biased depending on the user's previous results. For example, for two users with the same attributions, the one who has been less successful in meeting the previous objectives will have a lower subjective probability of succeeding the next time. To consider this aspect, we take into account the achievement dynamics of each user by introducing a $bias$, as shown in Eq. 5.

$$p(succ|eff) = \frac{\frac{x+y+z}{3} + bias(eff)}{1.5} \qquad (5)$$

In the equation, $bias \in [-0.5, 0.5]$. It is negative when during the user's achievement history, a majority of the changes in the success tendencies when making effort were from better to worse results, and positive in the opposite case (the same holds for $\overline{eff}$). It can be computed as shown in Eq. 6.

$$bias(eff) = \frac{growth(F(AH_n(eff)))}{inflexion(F(AH_n(eff)))} - 0.5 \qquad (6)$$

In the equation $AH_n(eff)$ represents the achievement history up to the feedback interaction n, a set of m points (with $m \leq n$) where the user reported to have made an effort to achieve the objective in the feedback interaction t ($t \in [0, n]$). The dimensions of each point are the t and the achievement rate in t. The same holds for $\overline{eff}$.

Additionally, $F(AH_n)$ is a polynomial function that interpolates the points in AH_n. It is based on the fact that it is possible to calculate the number of inflexion points in F ($inflexion(F)$) by computing its derivatives. This number indicates how many times F changes from concave to convex or vice versa. Similarly, $growth(F)$ represents the number of those changes that correspond to a transition from convex to concave, i.e. the number of times the achievement history has changed from a decreasing success rate to an increasing one.

3.2   Proposed Model for Subjective Utility

We propose to model subjective utility as the valence and arousal of the emotion experienced by the user in the case of success or failure. We represent it by using real numbers which are higher with higher intensities and are negative or positive depending on the valence. This way, an intense negative emotion denotes a high negative utility, whereas an intense positive emotion represents a high positive utility. We assume that being successful provokes only positive (or neutral) emotions, but not negative; and that being unsuccessful provokes only negative emotions (or neutral), but not positive.

In order to represent the emotional responses to different attribution scenarios, we propose to use two matrices: S and F, that account for the different emotional responses corresponding to varying attributions of success and failure respectively. The elements of these matrices are the numbers representing emotions, and are indexed by the type of attribution made using the x, y, and z indices discussed above. For example, $S[1, 1, 1]$ represents the expected emotional response for success when the user attributes his achievements to internal, controlled and stable reasons, whereas $F[0, 0, 0]$ represents the expected emotional response for failure when the user attributes it to external, uncontrolled and unstable reasons.

Thus, the computation of subjective utility provided the attribution scenario x, y, z follows Eq. 7.

$$Given\ x, y, z :\ u(succ) = S[x, y, z];\ u(\overline{succ}) = F[x, y, z] \tag{7}$$

To initialize S and F, we have considered previous studies that corroborate that negative emotions in the case of failure are more intense when the attribution is external, and milder when it is internal, as individuals tend to be more merciful to themselves [19]. We have additionally considered that the opposite occurs with positive emotions in the case of success, as an internal and stable attribution would imply that the success is caused by the individual effort and not by chance or by the actions of other people. This considers the fact that the expectancy of failure and success would recall those emotions and affect decision making, and also the tendency for individuals to attribute their own successes to internal factors while putting the blame for failures on external factors [27].

Figure 2 shows a graphic representation of our proposal for the initialization of the elements of S (first circle at each position) and F (second circle at each position). In the figure, the x axis represents the dimension controlled/uncontrolled (C and UC), the y axis represents the dimension internal/external (I and E respectively), and the z axis represents the dimension stable/unstable (S and US respectively). The circles represent emotions where valence is represented by the color (gray represents negative and yellow positive), and the size represents the intensity (the bigger the circle, the more intense).

However, the represented values might change depending on the user. For example, it has been reported that some users suffer from a stronger anxiety when they have to report unaccomplished tasks [14]. In these cases, the intensity of the emotion would be higher. In order to account for individual differences, we propose to dynamically adapt the values of the matrices considering the emotional responses of the users during the feedback interactions as described above (Fig. 1).

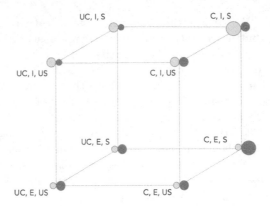

Fig. 2. Relation between emotion and attribution in our model (Color figure online)

4   Discussion

We have expressed motivation as a result of a preference relation between two choices: effort and non-effort $(eff \succ \overline{eff})$, which is computed according to which subjective expected utility is higher (see Eq. 3). As there are only two actions and they are complementary, it is trivial to prove that the proposed preference ordering relation follows all the fundamental properties of such relations: the contraposition principle, the sure-thing principle, the substitutivity condition, the opposite condition, and the maximax condition [18].

With respect to the correctness of the interpretation of motivation, Eq. 8 shows that $SEU(eff) > SEU(\overline{eff}) \rightarrow eff \succ \overline{eff}$ holds, as with this calculation it is interpreted that a user is motivated to do an effort to achieve an objective when the probability of being successful is higher when doing the effort than without doing it.

$$SEU(eff) > SEU(\overline{eff}) \rightarrow$$
$$p(succ|eff)(u(succ) - u(\overline{succ})) + u(\overline{succ}) >$$
$$p(succ|\overline{eff})(u(succ) - u(\overline{succ})) + u(\overline{succ}) \rightarrow$$
$$p(succ|eff) > p(succ|\overline{eff})$$

$$(8)$$

As can be observed, when motivation is computed as a boolean value comparing $SEU(eff)$ to $SEU(\overline{eff})$, as both computations depend on the same variables at each feedback interaction, most terms in the equation become not relevant to the calculation, which ultimately relies on the relative value of the subjective probabilities.

Thus, assessing the appropriateness of the calculation of a boolean value for motivation is a matter of assessing the reliability of the calculation of the subjective probability, i.e., making sure that $p(succ|eff) > p(succ|\overline{eff})$ is true when the user is motivated. As p is calculated following Eq. 5, we have the situation shown in Eq. 9, which means that success is subjectively more probable with effort than without effort when the previous history of achievements indicates so.

$$p(succ|eff) > p(succ|\overline{eff}) \rightarrow$$

$$\frac{growth(F(AH_n(eff)))}{inflexion(F(AH_n(eff)))} > \frac{growth(F(AH_n(\overline{eff})))}{inflexion(F(AH_n(\overline{eff})))} \qquad (9)$$

However, for the dialogue system to be adaptive to its users it is not only important to compute a single boolean motivation value but also to keep track of the complete motivation model. Thus, we compute the complete SEU following Eq. 4, so that the system has information about all the parameters that affect decision, which it can use to adapt to the users' needs.

Equation 4 shows that the expected subjective utility is higher when the probability of success with effort is higher $p(succ|eff)$, and when the difference between the utility of success and the utility of failure $u(succ) - u(\overline{succ})$ is high.

On the one hand, $p(succ|eff)$ is high when x, y, z are high and there is an optimistic *bias* due to the previous history. This makes sense, as according to the studies cited above, the more stable, controllable and internal are the attributions, the higher is the subjective probability of succeeding. With respect to the *bias*, when the user has had an increasing tendency to success, he will make a more optimistic subjective calculation of probability.

On the other hand, if being successful provokes positive or neutral emotions, and being unsuccessful provokes negative or neutral emotions, we have that $\forall\, x, y, z \in \{0, 1\}, S[x, y, z] >= 0$ and $F[x, y, z] <= 0$, thus $\forall\, x, y, z, u(succ) > u(\overline{succ})$.

5 Conclusions and Future Work

Counselling dialogue systems have demonstrated to be very effective in helping users to achieve their goals. However, most systems do not consider motivation explicitly and directly ask users or infer it according to their results in successive controls (e.g. if the user has lost weight, the systems would interpret that he is motivated to loose weight). Such interpretation does not provide enough information to make the systems adaptive to the user's real situation, as it might happen that the user attributes his success to luck or other external or uncontrollable causes.

In this paper we propose a novel model that makes it possible to monitor changes in the user motivation, which the system can consider to adapt its behaviour and try to guide the user towards internal, controlled and stable attributions. Approaches similar to ours have been effective for human managers [22] and tutors [2, 25]. Our proposal builds on the psychological theories of subjective expected utility in decision making and attribution. We have shown that it is expressive enough to account for a wide range of factors that affect motivation.

In future work we will include the proposed user model into a counselling dialogue system for the promotion of healthy habits that we are developing.

Also, we will carry out an evaluation in terms of system performance and user satisfaction with respect to a baseline system that does not include this model.

References

1. Ahn, H., Picard, R.W.: Affective-cognitive learning and decision making: a motivational reward framework for affective agent. In: Proceedings of the 1st International Conference on Affective Computing and Intelligent Interaction (ACII 2005) (2005)
2. Anderman, L.H., Midgley, C.: Motivation and middle school students. In: Irvin, J.L. (ed.) What Current Research Says to the Middle Level Practitioner. National Middle School Association (1997)
3. Beretvas, S.N., Suizzo, M.A., Durham, J.A., Yarnell, L.M.: A reliability generalization study of scores on Rotter's and Nowicki-Strickland's locus of control scales. Educ. Psychol. Meas. **68**(1), 97–119 (2008)
4. Bickmore, T., Schulman, D., Sidner, C.: A reusable framework for health counseling dialogue systems based on a behavioral medicine ontology. J. Biomed. Inform. **44**(2), 183–197 (2011)
5. Black, L.A., McTear, M.F., Black, N.D., Harper, R., Lemon, M.: Evaluating the DI@L-log system on a cohort of elderly, diabetic patients: results from a preliminary study. In: Proceedings of the 9th European Conference on Speech Communication and Technology (Interspeech 2005), pp. 821–824 (2005)
6. du Boulay, B., Avramides, K., Luckin, R., Martínez-Mirón, E., Méndez, G.R., Carr, A.: Towards systems that care: a conceptual framework based on motivation, metacognition and affect. Int. J. Artif. Intell. Educ. **20**(3), 197–229 (2010)
7. Bracha, A., Brown, D.J.: Affective decision making: a behavioral theory of choice. Cowles Foundation Discussion Papers, Cowles Foundation for Research in Economics, Yale University (2009)
8. Callejas, Z., Griol, D., López-Cózar, R.: Predicting user mental states in spoken dialogue systems. EURASIP J. Adv. Signal Process. **2011**, 6 (2011)
9. Callejas, Z., López-Cózar, R.: Influence of contextual information in emotion annotation for spoken dialogue systems. Speech Commun. **50**(5), 416–433 (2008)
10. Callejas, Z., López-Cózar, R.: Improving acceptability assessment for the labelling of affective speech corpora. In: Proceedings of the 10th Annual Conference of the International Speech Communication Association (Interspeech 2009), pp. 2863–2866 (2009)
11. Callejas, Z., López-Cózar, R., Ábalos, N., Griol, D.: Affective conversational agents: the role of personality and emotion in spoken interactions. In: Perez-Marín, D., Pascual-Nieto, I. (ed.) Conversational Agents and Natural Language Interaction. IGI Global (2011)
12. Caplin, A., Leahy, J.: Psychological expected utility theory and anticipatory feelings. Q. J. Econ. **116**(1), 55–79 (2001)
13. Craig, A.R., Franklin, J.A., Andrews, G.: A scale to measure locus of control of behaviour. Br. J. Med. Psychol. **57**(2), 173–180 (1984)
14. Farzanfar, R., Frishkopf, S., Migneault, J., Friedman, R.: Telephone-linked care for physical activity: a qualitative evaluation of the use patterns of an information technology program for patients. J. Biomed. Inform. **38**, 220–228 (2005)

15. Forbes-Riley, K., Litman, D., Friedberg, H.: Annotating disengagement for spoken dialogue computer tutoring. In: Calvo, R.A., D'Mello, S.K. (eds.) New Perspectives on Affect and Learning Technologies, Explorations in the Learning Sciences, Instructional Systems and Performance Technologies, vol. 3, pp. 169–181. Springer, New York (2011). doi:10.1007/978-1-4419-9625-1_13

16. Fournier, G., Jeanrie, C.: Validation of a five-level locus of control scale. J. Career Assess. **7**(1), 63–89 (1999)

17. Friedman, R.H., Kazis, L.E., Jette, A., Smith, M.B., Stollerman, J., Torgerson, J., Carey, K.: A telecommunications system for monitoring and counseling patients with hypertension: impact on medication adherence and blood pressure control. Am. J. Hypertens. **9**(4), 285–292 (1996)

18. Hammond, P.J.: Subjective expected utility. In: Hammond, P.J., Barbera, S., Seidl, C. (eds.) Handbook of Utility Theory. Vol. 1: Principles. Springer, New York (1998)

19. Harvey, P., Martinko, M.J., Borkowski, N.: A re-examination of the attribution-emotion-behavior framework in the context of unethical behavior. In: Zerbe, W.J., Hartel, C.E., Askanasy, N.M. (eds.) Emotions, Ethics and Decision-Making, vol. 4, pp. 259–283. Emeral Group Publishing Limited (2008)

20. Kennedy, C.M., Powell, J., Payne, T.H., Ainsworth, J., Boyd, A., Buchan, I.: Active assistance technology for health-related behavior change: an interdisciplinary review. J. Med. Internet Res. **14**(3) (2012)

21. Knutson, B., Peterson, R.: Neurally reconstructing expected utility. Games Econ. Behav. **52**, 305–315 (2005)

22. Kormanik, M.B., Rocco, T.S.: Internal versus external control of reinforcement: a review of the locus of control construct. Hum. Resour. Dev. Rev. **8**(4), 463–483 (2009)

23. Luszczynska, A., Schwarzer, R.: Multidimensional health locus of control: comments on the construct and its measurement. J. Health Psychol. **10**(5), 633–642 (2005)

24. Marsh, H.W., Richards, G.E.: Generalized expectancies for internal versus external control of reinforcements. Multivar. Behav. Res. **80**, 39–69 (1966)

25. Okolo, C.M.: The effects of computer-based attribution retraining on the attributions, persistence, and mathematics computation of students with learning disabilities. J. Learn. Disabil. **25**(5), 327–334 (1992)

26. Ramelson, H., Friedman, R., Ockene, J.: An automated telephone-based smoking cessation education and counseling system. Patient Educ. Couns. **36**(2), 131–144 (1999)

27. Robbins, S.P., Judge, T.A.: Essentials of Organizational Behavior. Prentice Hall, Englewood Cliffs (2005)

28. Savage, L.: The Foundations of Statistics. Wiley, New York (1954)

29. Schulman, D., Bickmore, T.: Persuading users through counseling dialogue with a conversational agent. In: Proceedings of the 4th International Conference on Persuasive Technology (PERSUASIVE 2009), pp. 251–258 (2009)

30. Schulman, D., Bickmore, T., Sidner, C.L.: An intelligent conversational agent for promoting long-term health behavior change using motivational interviewing. In: Proceedings of the 21th AAAI Conference on Artificial Intelligence, pp. 61–64 (2011)

31. Spector, P.E.: Development of the work locus of control scale. J. Occup. Psychol. **61**(4), 335–340 (1988)

32. Weiner, B.: An attribution theory of achievement motivation and emotion. Psychol. Rev. **7**(92), 548–573 (1985)

Exploring Flexibility in Natural Language Generation Through Discursive Analysis of New Textual Genres

Marta Vicente[(✉)] and Elena Lloret

University of Alicante, Alicante, Spain
{mvicente,elloret}@dlsi.ua.es

Abstract. Since automatic language generation is a task able to enrich applications rooted in most of the language-related areas, from machine translation to interactive dialogue, it seems worthwhile to undertake a strategy focused on enhancing generation system's adaptability and flexibility. It is our first objective to understand the relation between the factors that contribute to discourse articulation in order to devise the techniques that will generate it. From that point, we want to determine the appropriate methods to automatically learn those factors. The role of genre on this approach remains essential as provider of the stable forms that are required in the discourse to meet certain communicative goals. The arising of new web-based genres and the accessibility of the data due to its digital nature, has prompted us to use reviews in our first attempt to learn the characteristics of their singular non-rigid structure. The process and the preliminary results are explained in the present paper.

1 Motivation

Working to develop language generation tools represents, nowadays, a challenging task that could substantially benefit a large number of applications. Natural language generation (NLG) is more than a stand-alone task, its progress impacts on and enriches multiple language-related areas (machine translation, question answering or summarization, for example). Furthermore, its outcomes can be applied in generation of image and video description (involving computer vision, artificial intelligence) along with construction of dialogues, recommendation systems or even instructions for interactive games. Multiple applications whose progress can be boosted by the explosive growth of visual and textual resources and the techniques developed to process them.

Nevertheless, for the time being, the developments on NLG are strongly determined by domain and application, they do not present enough awareness of their context. To introduce pragmatic concerns in order to obtain adaptable systems, it is imperative to understand how that elements affect the compounding of the outcome, how its structure or its contents are concerned. There are multiple factors that can modify how a text is articulated, from the targeted

© Springer International Publishing AG 2017
J.F. Quesada et al. (Eds.): FETLT 2016, LNAI 10341, pp. 98–109, 2017.
https://doi.org/10.1007/978-3-319-69365-1_8

audience to the intention or the communicative aim that is pursued. From a linguistic perspective, is in the figure of the genre that those features take shape.

We believe that we must pay special attention to this matter and looking into that relation poses the main goal of our current work. Additionally, the presence of Internet as a communication channel has fostered the emergence of new genres, as digital reviews or blogs, and the access to that data has become relatively straightforward. Under those circumstances, we have undertaken an approach whose initial steps are reported in the present paper.

The remainder of this document is organised as follows. Section 2 provides further insights on the task of text generation and, specifically, on the stage of Macroplanning. In Sect. 3, we explain some remarks on discourse and genre. Next, on Sect. 4, a deeper analysis of the relation between genre and structure is reported. Relevant research on common areas is summarised on Sect. 5. In order to detect patterns, a clustering methodology has been selected, and is presented in Sect. 6. The first experiments devised are described in Sect. 7 and finally, Sect. 8, outlines some general conclusions and future work.

2   Text Generation and Macroplanning

From a computational perspective, the generation of language is a highly complex process that must be tackled on the premise that the system's outcome will meet certain linguistic and communicative requirements (syntactic, semantic, pragmatic concerns, context related). Much of the work developed until now is focused on expressing some information, which can be given in the form of related concepts, raw data or even texts, through utterances whose elaboration can range from a single sentence to a much more complex structure (sets of paragraphs compounding discourses - reports, articles, stories, for instance). To achieve this, an NLG system must handle two main questions: "*what should be said?*" and "*how to realise it on the desired output?*". Concerning the initial stage, this is known in literature as Macroplanning, and it refers both to the selection and planning of the content, processes that result in a structure called Document Plan [23]. Therefore, the Document Plan could be understood as the guideline for the rest of the process as well as the source of its meaning. Being able to encapsulate in such guidance the relevant content regarding the context implies the incorporation of a pragmatic facet of the linguistic realm which is the main objective of the present research on the long term. To understand and learn how this pragmatic issue affects the content and the structure of the discourse in order to reproduce it, have become our leading goal at the present time. We relate our investigation to the Discourse Theory, the relevance of the genre in the construction of the text and the relationship between genre and the intentionality that lies beneath the use of natural language as an act of communication.

3 Generating the Discourse

When NLG is concerned with the production of text, not as character sequences or single utterances but as sequence of paragraphs, it is fundamental to consider the relation between sentences in order to assure the cohesion and coherence of the text obtained[1]. Discourse theory establishes that to be called discourse, a text must be connected and structured. On the one hand, connection would be provided by linguistic cohesion or by implicatures. On the other hand, the structure would proceed from the contents represented, the intentional and the interactional structure that arise from the goals and conventions of the activity to which the discourse is related: its specific genre [11].

Some theories of the discourse [2,12] have highlighted the fact that genres can be understood as social constructions, as providers of the connection between the discourse and the situation in which it is produced. They condition both the structure and the content of the text generated. According to Swavels [27]:

"A genre comprises a class of communicative events, the members of which share some set of communicative purposes. These purposes are recognised by the expert members of the parent discourse community, and thereby constitute the rationale for the genre. This rationale shapes the schematic structure of the discourse and influences and constraints choice of content and style."

There is yet another definition of genre proposed by Bhatia [5] that also contributes to the fundamentals of our approach:

"Genre essentially refers to language use in a conventionalised communicative setting in order to give expression to a specific set of communicative goals of a disciplinary or social institution, which give rise to *stable structural forms* by imposing constraints on the use of lexico-grammatical as well as discoursal resources."

It is the detection of such patterns or stable forms the first step we are embracing in order to design the mechanisms able to produce natural language involving such discursive features.

Taking this into account, it can be observed that different genres accept different degrees of structural rigidity. In the case of news and research articles, patents, or Wikipedia articles, for instance, some structure can be detected even from a shallow analysis. However, there are other types of texts for which such structure is not as easily perceptible. It is usual in some of the genres intrinsically related to Internet and the new forms of communication arising with it. Reviews, blogs, tweets are examples of texts that can be included in the latter case.

4 Genre and Structure

In order to clarify the novelty of our research, it is necessary to introduce some assumptions regarding the notion of structure that is being pursued. In some

---

[1] Actually, coherence has been accepted as a quality indicator [29].

sense, text structure may be interpreted as the order of the ideas that should be expressed. However, it is not only the order what we have to determine, but the full characterisation of the parts of the discourse: their nature, their relevance for the outcome and, directly linked to our main primary goal, the way their constituents contribute to their purpose or communicative goal, and in turn, to the general aim of the text.

In this regard, the Systemic Functional Theory [12] should be brought up. It provides a notion of discourse and genre that connects situation types with semantic/lexico-grammatic patterns from a conception of language highly related to its socio-semiotic origin. Moreover, coming from this approach, their classification of communicative goals or *"fields of activity"* (*expounding, reporting, recreating, sharing, doing, enabling, recommending, exploring*) along with the related work developed on this line will serve as a cornerstone for our research [21].

Consequently, genres become valuable to our approach since they are meant to bear some communicative purpose: news function would be to inform; reviews, to persuade or fairy tales, to entertain. Nevertheless, it is possible a further analysis, detecting those functions in the sections of the discourse. This would be the case of the parts of any scientific paper or the classical narrative structure: exposition-climax-resolution, that we could relate to the fields of activity previously mentioned. In both cases, the order of such parts must remain the same, in the sense that it would be incoherent to present the conclusions of a research before the results, for example. And this stability provides a benefit when computing is involved.

However, for some genres, the structure is not perceived in a straightforward manner. We worked with reviews, since this genre illustrates such phenomenon. Besides, reviews represent a multi-purpose type of texts depending on several parameters as the object (e.g. books, hotels) or the intention of the writer (e.g. recommend, criticise). In respect to sections and their functions, they contain at the same time parts that expound the personal experience of the user, but also those that convey why a user went to that hotel or chose that book, the description of the room or the plot, or recommendations for anyone reading.

In Table 1, manual analysis over hotel reviews shows both differences and similarities between two documents. In this case, there are three types of sections, relating respectively personal experience, description of the hotel (amenities, building, restaurants, ...) and evaluation. Each review presents different number and order of the parts, but the language on each of them displays some visible regularities. For instance, the sentences in the descriptions share the use of the verb "to be" in a similar way (e.g. *the hotel is, the grounds were, The room was*); first person and past tense for sentences in personal experience fragments (e.g. *we visited this, we travelled in, I had stayed*) and so on.

The flexibility of such kind of structure leads to problems when automatic processes tackle the generation of this type of texts. Therefore, several questions arise: *how a text to be generated should be organised or planned in order to be coherent? in the case of reviews, are they written in a similar fashion, even not showing that rigid structure?* These questions would be worth investigating

Table 1. Hotel review ordering from a functional approach. Even at first sight some different features can be distinguished among parts (Personal Experience, Description, Evaluation): verb tenses, syntactic constructions, lexicon ...

Review 1
Description (1 sentence):
A beautiful hotel, in a perfect location, with large rooms, and an architectural...
Personal Experience (8 sentences):
We visited this resort for our 25th wedding anniversary.
We traveled in March, which tends to be the high rain season...
It rained every day, as we were in the midst of a minor storm...
Description (19 sentences):
The hotel is a very open concept design that sits on 50 acres of the Poipu Beach...
The grounds were beautiful, and the interior of the hotel was open to the outside...
In the lobby were a beautiful collection of live, native birds, of magnificent...
Evaluation (2 sentences):
This hotel is a real winner, complete with it's own 18 hole golf course.
Although I would be cautious about the time of year I visited, I would say...
Review 2
Personal Experience (3 sentences):
In New York for New Years 2003, I had chosen to stay at the Essex House because...
However, I became soon disappointed once I entered my standard room...
It appears to me that the renovation money did not go into the standard rooms...
Description (6 sentences):
My room was very small as it was difficult to maneuver within the room's limited...
The room was dull with worn Old English furnishing.
There where handles missing off cabinet doors and the room lacked isolation...
Personal Experience (1 sentence):
I had stayed at Westin hotels before, and was never disappointed until now.
Description (7 sentences):
The standard rooms lack modern amenities.
They appear to be outdated of at least 10 to 20 years.
The corridors are decorated with non tasteful wallpaper, and the paint...
Evaluation (1 sentence):
Overall, I am very disappointed with the hotel, however I had a good time for...

to address the Macroplanning stage, being that related to genres and their communicative objectives.

Regarding current NLG systems, it is normally assumed a pre-defined structure for a text in their developments [10,14,16]. Nonetheless, most of the cases are focused on very specific domains, such as weather reports [17,18] or specific genres, as Wikipedia articles [26]. It should be noted, however, that some steps have been taken in order to increase flexibility in several areas. This is the case, for example, with storytelling, where the style of narration depends on the communicative goal it is pursued (to entertain, to motivate, to report facts) or on the character's perspective. The work in [19] reflects those pragmatic concerns.

Given this context, our present aim is to explore how to articulate document plans for texts that do not exhibit a structure at a first sight. To achieve this objective, a preliminary study within a set of hotel reviews is conducted, by which using clustering techniques applied to various lexical features, we would be able to determine whether heterogeneous reviews written by a wide range of users from different backgrounds, ages, and nationalities share similarities in their structure or not. Our analysis could be adapted to other genres, since we want to devise a methodology to analyse and determine the structure of a text in an automatic manner.

5   Existing Approaches Addressing Macroplanning and Text Structure

As indicated, Macroplanning consists of selecting and structuring the content that a generation system has to deliver as text. Back in 2003, Dubue and McKeown [8] attempted an approach by which content selection rules could be learnt pairing biographical texts with some semantic information, that would be the selected content. Trying to extend this approach, Barzilay and Lapata [4], included the relations coming from a database, which allowed them to reflect dependency between the involved items, and thus incorporate some structural information, but still very limited. More aware of the structural component, some approaches attempted to determine the distribution of the topics within the document to provide coherence to the result [3], or to extract content templates from an specific domain collection of documents that would incorporate that structure [17, 18, 26]. However, this became its main weakness, the domain restricting the performance of the systems.

Regarding the new digital genres previously mentioned, like the reviews, the research effort has been directed mainly to the area of sentiment analysis or polarity classification [7, 24], but few have been focused on their structure related to text genre. An approach that strongly relies on Systemic Functional Theory can be found in [28], outlining the relation between the genre itself and the structure of the document. An analysis over a corpus of movie reviews is carried out, where the results showed the presence of some parts concerning its purpose that were finally reduced to two main sections: evaluation and description.

There is interesting work on detecting the structure of text using patterns of lexical co-occurrence to identify paragraphs related to the same topic [13]. Taking into account term repetition, subtopics in explanatory texts were recognised, but results were not so good for other genres. Moreover, other features of the discourse were not considered (e.g. syntactic constructions, verb tenses, discourse markers) neither an approach on the functions of the parts of the text.

Bachand's research [1], from another perspective, is focused on the relations between text-type, discourse structures and rhetorical relations. Only considering this time rhetorical relations and markers, the good results obtained indicate that similar but enriched developments can lead to a better generation of accurate document plans.

Our research is novel in the sense that to the best of our knowledge, there is no previous work that attempts to determine and extract the document plan from a *flexible-structure* text genre, such as reviews. Our analysis will set the basis for generating a wide range of texts types, regardless the domain or text genre they belong to.

6   Preliminary Analysis: Clustering to Reach Document Plans

Since the aim of our research is to come up with possible document plans after analysing not strictly organised texts, clustering techniques seem appropriate to detect some patterns across reviews. To accomplish our analysis, the Expectation Maximisation Algorithm (*EM*) implementation provided by Weka has been selected, due to the fact that it allows unsupervised learning over unlabelled data, which is our case. More information on *EM* can be found in [30].

Feature Extraction and Analysis. For now, and regarding the features, our approach is preliminary because there is no set of them already consolidated. We will refine the selection and feed the experiments with several collections to determine the most appropriate for Macroplanning. About the labelling, part-of-speech tags are considered at different levels (a word can contribute as a verb, as a verb in past tense, etc.). Named entities are also labelled. From a semantic perspective, verbs are classified as belonging to one of six categories: mental, material, relational, verbal, existential or modulation [9].

7   Experiments and Preliminary Results

This section describes with some detail the experiments devised to tease out some insights on the structure of reviews. First, the corpus and resources that were used to labelled it and, afterwards, the explanation of the different criteria applied and the analysis of results.

7.1   Corpus

The corpus used in our experiments is a collection of reviews gathered from Tripadvisor, regarding ten different hotels. It consists of roughly 1,400 reviews written in Spanish. The reviews were segmented in sentences (12,467 sentences). Around 200,000 words have been automatically labelled (Table 2).

Table 2. Corpus statistics.

Number of reviews	1400
Sentences	12,467
Words labelled	Approx. 200,000

7.2 Resources

The sentences were analysed and labelled with Freeling [22] using its lemmatiser, its PoS-Tagger and its named entity recogniser. Verb lemmas were confronted with the list of verb meanings from the *ADESSE* project [9] in order to establish their categories (Table 3).

Table 3. Features annotated over the corpus of reviews.

ADESSE verb senses
Mental, material, relational, verbal, existential and modulation
FREELING features
PoS tagging: noun, adjective, pronoun, verb (tense, aspect, ...), etc.

7.3 Review Segmentation and Data Preparation

Firstly, a decision was made about gathering the information that could be computed from the labelled sentences. In this manner, clustering was applied to the corpus four times, each of them over the reviews divided from one to four sections. Our objective was to identify certain relations within those sections and between them. The length of each segment was the result of a equitable division of the number of sentences involved. This would allow us to discover whether reviews tend to condense specific information within a particular area, despite being different in their nature and content. In other words, although two reviews can be written differently, they may contain a section (a set of sentences) expressing similar ideas or written to meet same purposes (e.g. informing about the advantages of the hotel). Even if the area is in different location, some patterns could be extracted.

It is when the division of the text has been set that the process starts computing the features of the sentence constituents and the aggregation of the results according to the number of sections. In order to properly compare the different reviews, we settle the following criterion: taking into account one review divided in sections and a feature f, we calculate for each section the percentage of f regarding the total occurrence of this feature in the review. As a result, two values were obtain: (i) the maximum percentage calculated, and (ii) the section in which this feature is prevalent.

Once this is computed, the Weka implementation of the *EM* algorithm is conducted considering the independence of the features and performing cross-validation.

7.4   Results and Discussion

At the moment, the results obtained are analysed with respect to the following issues: (i) considering only the area in which the maximum percentage of the feature appears (*Area*), (ii) considering only the maximum percentage (*%*); and (iii) considering simultaneously both records (*Area+%*).

For each execution Weka calculates a number of clusters (Table 4) providing the number of instances included in them.

Table 4. Number of clusters obtained for each experiment, being: (i) considering only the area in which the maximum percentage of the feature appears (*Area*), (ii) considering only the maximum percentage (*%*); and (iii) considering simultaneously both records (*Area+%*)

Divisions	Area	%	Area+%
1	1	1	1
2	13	2	4
3	8	2	5
4	10	10	4

Regarding the amount of reviews enclosed on some clusters, some facts seem interesting. For example, in the case of clustering reviews divided in two parts and experiment *(iii)*, the percentage of reviews for each cluster is 39% (0), 2% (1), 44% (2) and 15% (3). It is remarkable to find out how this distribution arises and what are its peculiarities. It is not an isolated case. On the other hand, the distribution of features when the number of clusters is high could be as interesting of this last to discard some relations or study some regularities.

A further examination may revel how could be possible from each cluster to expose correlation or co-occurrence between the features considered, and in a future step, to bound such relations with some communicative goals.

8   Conclusion and Future Work

Questions suggested earlier in this paper can now be addressed from a more informed perspective. How a NLG system would perform the production of a review and if so, could an inner structure be revealed by some automatic analysis? As a result of our experimentation and its analysis, we expect to find the definition of the review genre attending the characteristics of its structure and constituents. Such description would provide appropriate document plans to select and organise the information according to the inner traits of the text genre, and similar methodology could be applied to develop other text types.

Some of the future experiments involve changing the number of features, in order to obtain a comprehensive description, including the sentiment traits, specific semantic characteristics regarding the elements and its discursive relation, and pragmatic information related to the context of the production. Alternatively, the corpus will be increased at different stages to include firstly several types of reviews and afterwards, several types of genres.

Finally, we will take into account some of the resources rooted in Web Semantic technologies. Some research regarding genre have been done in this field. There is the *MARL Ontology Specification*[2] that could be appropriate for reviews, opinion and sentiment annotation. This data schema has been used in the *EuroSentiment Project* [6] and, from a Sentiment Analysis perspective, on reviews [25]. On News, it is relevant the effort invested by the *BBC*, in order to obtain more significant annotation of the documents. They provide a set of ontologies related to their contents and area. *DBPedia* has been already proved useful for Wikipedia articles researchers. *Drammar* [20] and *OntoMedia* [15] are ontology-based models for annotating features of media and cultural narratives. All of them resources that could make a difference in our clustering task and analysis.

Acknowledgments. This work has been supported by the grant ACIF/2016/501 from the Generalitat Valenciana. Funds have been also received from the University of Alicante, Spanish Government and the European Commission through the projects "Explotación y tratamiento de la información disponible en Internet para la anotación y generación de textos adaptados al usuario" (GRE13-15) and "DIIM2.0: Desarrollo de técnicas Inteligentes e Interactivas de Minería y generación de información sobre la web 2.0" (PROMETEOII/2014/001), TIN2015-65100-R, TIN2015-65136-C2-2-R, and 3AM (FP7-611312), respectively.

References

1. Bachand, F.-H., Davoodi, E., Kosseim, L.: An investigation on the influence of genres and textual organisation on the use of discourse relations. In: Gelbukh, A. (ed.) CICLing 2014. LNCS, vol. 8403, pp. 454–468. Springer, Heidelberg (2014). doi:10.1007/978-3-642-54906-9_37
2. Bakhtin, M.M.: Speech Genres and Other Late Essays. University of Texas Press, Austin (2010)
3. Barzilay, R.: Probabilistic approaches for modeling text structure and their application to text-to-text generation. In: Krahmer, E., Theune, M. (eds.) EACL/ENLG -2009. LNCS, vol. 5790, pp. 1–12. Springer, Heidelberg (2010). doi:10.1007/978-3-642-15573-4_1
4. Barzilay, R., Lapata, M.: Collective content selection for concept-to-text generation. In: Proceedings of the Conference on Human Language Technology and Empirical Methods in Natural Language Processing, pp. 331–338. Association for Computational Linguistics (2005)

---

[2] http://www.gsi.dit.upm.es/ontologies/marl.

5. Bhatia, V.: Worlds of Written Discourse: A Genre-Based View. A&C Black, London (2004)
6. Buitelaar, P., Arcan, M., Iglesias Fernandez, C.A., Sánchez Rada, J.F., Strapparava, C.: Linguistic linked data for sentiment analysis (2013)
7. Cambria, E., Schuller, B., Xia, Y., Havasi, C.: New avenues in opinion mining and sentiment analysis. IEEE Intell. Syst. **28**(2), 15–21 (2013)
8. Duboue, P.A., McKeown, K.R.: Statistical acquisition of content selection rules for natural language generation. In: Proceedings of the 2003 Conference on Empirical Methods in Natural Language Processing, pp. 121–128. Association for Computational Linguistics (2003)
9. García-Miguel, J.M., Vaamonde, G., Domínguez, F.G.: Adesse, a database with syntactic and semantic annotation of a corpus of Spanish. In: LREC (2010). http://dblp.uni-trier.de/db/conf/lrec/lrec2010.html#Garcia-MiguelVD10
10. Ge, T., Pei, W., Ji, H., Li, S., Chang, B., Sui, Z.: Bring you to the past: automatic generation of topically relevant event chronicles. In: Proceedings of the 53rd Annual Meeting of the Association for Computational Linguistics and the 7th International Joint Conference on Natural Language Processing (vol. 1: Long Papers), pp. 575–585. Association for Computational Linguistics, Beijing (2015). http://www.aclweb.org/anthology/pp.15-1056
11. Gruber, H., Redeker, G.: The Pragmatics of Discourse Coherence: Theories and Applications, vol. 254. John Benjamins Publishing Company, Amsterdam (2014)
12. Halliday, M., Matthiessen, C.M., Matthiessen, C.: An Introduction to Functional Grammar. Routledge, London (2014)
13. Hearst, M.A.: Texttiling: segmenting text into multi-paragraph subtopic passages. Comput. Linguist. **23**(1), 33–64 (1997)
14. Hu, Y., Wan, X.: Automatic generation of related work sections in scientific papers: an optimization approach. In: Proceedings of the 2014 Conference on Empirical Methods in Natural Language Processing (EMNLP), pp. 1624–1633. Association for Computational Linguistics, Doha (2014). http://www.aclweb.org/anthology/D14-1170
15. Jewell, M.O., Lawrence, K.F., Tuffield, M.M., Prugel-Bennett, A., Millard, D.E., Nixon, M.S., Shadbolt, N.R., et al.: Ontomedia: an ontology for the representation of heterogeneous media. In: Proceeding of SIGIR Workshop on Mutlimedia Information Retrieval. ACM SIGIR (2005)
16. Jha, R., Finegan-Dollak, C., King, B., Coke, R., Radev, D.: Content models for survey generation: a factoid-based evaluation. In: Proceedings of the 53rd Annual Meeting of the Association for Computational Linguistics and the 7th International Joint Conference on Natural Language Processing (vol. 1: Long Papers), pp. 441–450. Association for Computational Linguistics, Beijing (2015). http://www.aclweb.org/anthology/pp.15-1043
17. Kondadadi, R., Howald, B., Schilder, F.: A statistical NLG framework for aggregated planning and realization. In: Proceedings of the 51st Annual Meeting of the Association for Computational Linguistics (vol. 1: Long Papers), pp. 1406–1415. Association for Computational Linguistics, Sofia (2013). http://www.aclweb.org/anthology/pp.13-1138
18. Konstas, I., Lapata, M.: A global model for concept-to-text generation. J. Artif. Intell. Res. **48**, 305–346 (2013)
19. Li, B., Thakkar, M., Wang, Y., Riedl, M.O.: Storytelling with adjustable narrator styles and sentiments. In: Mitchell, A., Fernández-Vara, C., Thue, D. (eds.) ICIDS 2014. LNCS, vol. 8832, pp. 1–12. Springer, Cham (2014). doi:10.1007/978-3-319-12337-0_1

20. Lombardo, V., Damiano, R.: Semantic annotation of narrative media objects. Multimed. Tools Appl. **59**(2), 407–439 (2012)
21. Matthiessen, C.M.: Registerial cartography: context-based mapping of text types and their rhetorical-relational organization (2014)
22. Padró, L., Stanilovsky, E.: FreeLing 3.0: towards wider multilinguality. In: Proceedings of the Eight International Conference on Language Resources and Evaluation (LREC 2012). European Language Resources Association (ELRA) (2012)
23. Reiter, E., Dale, R., Feng, Z.: Building Natural Language Generation Systems, vol. 33. MIT Press, Cambridge (2000)
24. dos Santos, C.N., Gatti, M.: Deep convolutional neural networks for sentiment analysis of short texts. In: COLING, pp. 69–78 (2014)
25. Santosh, D.T., Vardhan, B.V.: Feature and sentiment based linked instance RDF data towards ontology based review categorization. In: Proceedings of the World Congress on Engineering, vol. 1 (2015)
26. Sauper, C., Barzilay, R.: Automatically generating wikipedia articles: a structure-aware approach. In: Proceedings of the Joint Conference of the 47th Annual Meeting of the ACL and the 4th International Joint Conference on Natural Language Processing of the AFNLP, vol. 1, pp. 208–216. Association for Computational Linguistics (2009)
27. Swavels, J.: Genre Analysis: English in Academic and Research Settings. Cambridge University Press, Cambridge (1990)
28. Taboada, M.: Stages in an online review genre: text & talk. Interdisc. J. Lang. Discourse Commun. Stud. **31**(2), 247–269 (2011)
29. Webber, B., Joshi, A.: Discourse structure and computation: past, present and future. In: Proceedings of the ACL-2012 Special Workshop on Rediscovering 50 Years of Discoveries, pp. 42–54. Association for Computational Linguistics (2012)
30. Witten, I.H., Frank, E., Hall, M.A.: Data Mining: Practical Machine Learning Tools and Techniques, 3rd edn. Morgan Kaufmann Publishers Inc., San Francisco (2011)

Bootstrapping Technique + Embeddings = Emotional Corpus Annotated Automatically

Lea Canales[1]([envelope]), Carlo Strapparava[2], Ester Boldrini[1],
and Patricio Matínez-Barco[1]

[1] University of Alicante, Alicante, Spain
{lcanales,eboldrini,patricio}@dlsi.ua.es
[2] Fondazione Bruno Kessler, Trento, Italy
strappa@fbk.eu

Abstract. Detecting depression or personality traits, tutoring and student behaviour systems, or identifying cases of cyber-bulling are a few of the wide range of the applications, in which the automatic detection of emotion is crucial. This task can contribute to the benefit of business, society, politics or education. The main objective of our research is focused on the improvement of the supervised emotion detection systems developed so far, through the definition and implementation of a technique to annotate large scale English emotional corpora automatically and with high standards of reliability. Our proposal is based on a bootstrapping process made up two main steps: the creation of the seed using NRC Emotion Lexicon and its extension employing the distributional semantic similarity through *words embeddings*. The results obtained are promising and allow us to confirm the soundness of the bootstrapping technique combined with the *word embedding* to label emotional corpora automatically.

Keywords: Sentiment analysis · Emotion detection · Emotional corpus · Bootstrapping · Word embedding

1 Introduction

Emotion detection has been widely explored in neuroscience, psychology and behavior science, being an important element of human nature. In computer science, this task has also attracted the attention of many researchers, despite the challenges of dealing computationally with emotions such as the complexity of working exclusively with text as input, due to the lack of para-linguistic information like tone, emphasis and facial expressions.

Automatic detection of affective states in text has wide range of applications for business, society, politics or education. Detecting emotions is becoming more and more important due to the fact that it can bring substantial benefits for different sectors (detecting depression [5], identifying cases of cyber-bullying [10], tracking well-being [26], or contributing to improve the student motivation and

© Springer International Publishing AG 2017
J.F. Quesada et al. (Eds.): FETLT 2016, LNAI 10341, pp. 110–121, 2017.
https://doi.org/10.1007/978-3-319-69365-1_9

performance [21]) that are demanding effective automatic detection systems for multiple purposes.

Many of the machine learning techniques for automatic detection of emotions are supervised, that is, systems first infer a function from a set of examples labeled with the correct emotion (this set of examples is called the training data or labelled corpus). Then the model is able to predict the emotion of new examples. Hence, the training data employed in supervised machine learning algorithms are crucial to build accurate emotion detection systems.

The creation of a labelled corpus is not trivial, since detecting emotion in text can be difficult even for humans. Much of works carried out so far have shown that the amount of agreement between annotations when associating emotion to instances is significantly lower compared to other tasks such as identifying part of speech or detecting named entities. This is due to the fact that manual annotations can be significantly influenced by clarity of instructions, difficulty of task, training of the annotators, and even by the annotation scheme [19]. For this reason, in this paper an innovative automatic technique is proposed to resolve the most important challenge in emotion detection task in text: the problems of the annotation of emotional data.

To do this, our proposal is to exploit a bootstrapping approach for automatic annotations with two main steps: (1) the creation of the seed where NRC Emotion Lexicon [20] is employed to annotate the sentences by its emotional words; and (2) the extension of the seed based on the distributional similarity calculated through *low-dimensional continuous representations* of instances and words (word vectors or *embeddings*). This technique will allow us the annotation of large amount of emotional data in any genre with efficiently and high standards of reliability.

The rest of the paper is organised as follows. Section 2 deals with the related works and a comparative analysis of our approach. In Sect. 3, the proposed method is described in detail. Section 4 is aimed at showing the approaches proposed, the evaluation methodology, the results obtained and a discussion about these results. Finally, Sect. 5 details our conclusions and future works.

2   Related Work

This section summarises the most relevant emotional corpora developed for emotion detection purposes, their features and how they have been developed. In addition, some of works where bootstrapping technique was applied for annotation and the weaknesses that motivate and justify the direction of our research are also analyzed.

Since there are hundreds of emotions that humans can perceive and express, much of the work in the community has been restricted to a reduced of emotions and valence categories.

According to research in psychology, there is a number of theories about how to represent emotions. Among these theories, some of them are focused on defining the set of the basic emotions [11,25]. Although, there is not an universal consensus about which set of emotions are the most basic. Nevertheless, most of works in automatic detection of emotions in text has focused on the limited set of proposed basic emotions, since this allows reducing the cost in terms of time and money. Even though there also are approaches based on non-basic emotions.

Most of the emotional resources developed so far have been annotated manually, since, in this way, machine learning systems learn from human annotations. Among these resources, there are corpora labelled with the six basic emotions categories proposed by Ekman such as: [1] annotated a sentence-level corpus of approximately 185 children stories with emotion categories; [2] annotated blog posts collected directly from Web with emotion categories and intensity; or [27] annotated news headlines with emotion categories and valence.

As mentioned previously, there are corpora labelled with other small set of emotions by manually annotation like: [22] corpus extracted 1,000 sentences from various stories; Emotiblog-corpus that consists of a collection of blog posts manually extracted from the Web and annotated with three annotation levels: document, sentence and element [4]; or EmoTweet-28 corpus that consists of a collection of tweets annotated with 28 emotion categories [15].

The common feature of these emotional corpora is that have been annotated manually, being a hard and time-consuming task where the obtaining an agreement between annotations is a challenge, due to the subjectivity of the task and the need to invest in many resources to annotate large scale emotional corpora.

Consequently, several emotional resources have recently been developed employing emotion word hashtags to create automatic emotional corpus on Twitter. [18] describe how they created a corpus from Twitter post (Twitter Emotional Corpus - TEC) using this technique. In literature, several works can be found with the use emotion word hashtags to create emotional corpora from Twitter [6,28].

Thus, in research community, the interest of developing amounts of emotional corpora has increased because that would allow us to obtain better supervised machine learning systems. The use of emotion word hashtags as technique to label data is really simple and efficient in terms of time and money, but it can be applied on Twitter exclusively. For this reason, our objective is to develop a technique for large-scale annotation of emotional corpora automatically in any domain and with high standards of reliability.

Our proposal consists of a bootstrapping technique because it is a semi-supervised technique whose effectiveness has been demonstrated in a wide range of computational linguistic problems [9,29] and more concretely for annotations task [7,14]. Thus, our hypothesis is that the use of this technique for automatic annotation of emotions will provide us improvements on the emotion labelled task.

3   Bootstrapping Process

This section describes the bootstrapping process developed for automatic annotation.

The process receives as input data a collection of unlabelled sentences/phrases and a set of emotions, concretely the Ekman's six basic emotions [11]. The objective of this task is to annotate unlabelled sentences with the emotions expressed in each sentence.

The overall bootstrapping process is described in Fig. 1.

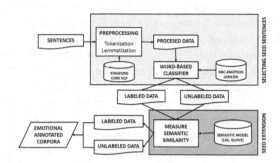

Fig. 1. Overall bootstrapping process.

3.1   Dataset

The dataset employed to test our approaches is Aman corpus that contains sentence-level annotation of 4,000 sentences from blogs posts collected directly from Web. This resource was annotated manually with the six emotion categories proposed by Ekman and the emotion intensity (high, medium, or low).

The reasons to choose this corpus for testing the approach are: (i) it is manually annotated allowing us to compare automatic annotation to manual annotation; (ii) this corpus is relevant to emotion detection task, since it has been employed in many works to detect emotions; and (iii) it is possible to check the usability and effectiveness of our approach in Social Web domain, because this corpus contains sentences from blogs posts.

3.2   Selecting Seed Sentences

In this section, the process of creating the initial seed by exploring NRC Word-Emotion Association Lexicon (Emolex) [20] is presented.

Emolex is a lexicon of general domain consisting of 14,000 English unigrams (words) associated with the Plutchik's eight basic emotions [25], compiled by manual annotation. Our approach only employs the Ekman's basic emotions and for this reason the lexicon is reduced to 3,462 English unigrams.

In this approach, Emolex is applied to annotate each sentence of the Aman corpus which contains emotional words. Each sentence has an emotional vector associated with a value to each emotion ([anger, disgust, fear, joy, sadness, surprise]) initialised to zero (Fig. 2). In Emolex, each word has also an emotional vector associated.

The process starts tokenising and lemmatising each sentence using Stanford Core NLP [16]. Then, each word of the sentence is looked up in Emolex. If a word of the sentence is in Emolex, its emotional values are added to the emotional vector of the sentence. Finally, the emotional vector of the sentence shows the emotions related to the sentence. The sentences are annotated with the emotion whose has the highest value (Fig. 2 - Sentence 1). In this process, a sentence could have an emotional vector associated with several emotions in the same proportion. In this case, the process does not label any emotion because there is not a predominant emotion (Fig. 2 - Sentence 2).

Figure 2 shows two examples of the creation of the seed. Sentence 1: *"We played fun baby games and caught up on some old time"*, whose emotional vector is initialised to zero, contains three emotional word: fun, baby and catch. The values of these three words are added and the sentence has finally associated this vector: [0, 0, 0, 2, 0, 1], this sentence has JOY emotion associated because this emotion has the highest value associated. Sentence 2: *"My manager also went to throw a fake punch."*, whose emotional vector is initialised to zero, contains one emotional word: punch. The sentence has finally associated this vector: [1, 0, 1, 0, 1, 1], hence this sentence has not associated any emotion.

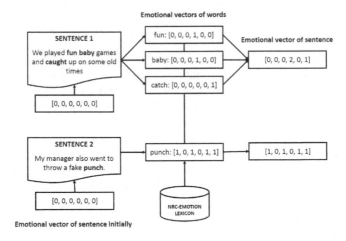

Fig. 2. Examples of the process of selecting seed sentences when a sentence is annotated.

Once the process is completed, there are non-annotated sentences because the sentences do not contain emotional words or do not contain a predominant emotion, and annotated sentences (seed sentences) with one of the emotions.

3.3 Seed Extension

In this step, the purpose is to extend the seed sentences that have been obtained from the process explained in the previous subsection, with the help of a bootstrapping approach.

To achieve that, two Distributional Semantic Models (DSM) are adopted in this step. These models are based on the assumption that the meaning of a word can be inferred from its usage. Therefore, these models dynamically build semantic representations (high-dimensional semantic vector spaces) through a statistical analysis of the contexts in which words occur[1]. Finally, each word is represented with a real-valued vector called word vector or *word embedding*.

There are two main global families for learning word vectors: (1) global matrix factorization methods, and (2) local context windows methods. The methods based on local context windows poorly utilize the statistics of the corpus since they train on separate local context windows instead of on global co-occurrence counts and thus they are not as convenient as global matrix methods on word similarity task.

The extension of the seed of our proposal is based on estimating the similarity among non-annotated sentences and annotated sentences. For this reason, in this paper we test two models based on global matrix factorization methods: LSA and GloVe [23].

Both models are run on the lemmas of the British National Corpus (BNC)[2] that can be considered as a balanced resource since it includes texts from different genres and domains. Concretely, the LSA model employed is the one applied in [12] and GloVe model has been built by us.

The process of extension of the seed consists of measuring the similarity among non-annotated sentences and annotated sentences using the models listed and measuring the standard cosine similarity. When the similarity between a non-annotated sentence and an annotated sentence is higher than 80%, the non-annotated sentence is annotated with the emotions of the annotated one.

In this process, non-annotated sentences could be matched to two or more annotated sentences. The process selects the annotated sentence whose similarity with non-annotated one is higher and annotates it.

3.4 Training a Supervised Classifier

In the second step of the bootstrapping technique, the annotated and the non-annotated sentences from the previous step are exploited to train a supervised classifier. Concretely, a multi-classifier Support Vector Machines (SVM) with Sequential Minimal Optimization [24] is applied, representing the sentences as a vector of words weighted by their counts using Weka [13].

4   Evaluation

The objective of this research is to assess the viability of the use of bootstrapping technique to built emotional corpora. To achieve that, in this paper two evaluation, explained in Sect. 4.3, are carried out.

---

[1] http://wordspace.collocations.de/doku.php/course:acl2010:start.

[2] http://www.natcorp.ox.ac.uk/.

Furthermore, as mentioned previously, Emolex contains 3,462 words when it works with Ekman's emotions compared to the 14,000 words when it works with Plutchik's emotions. Therefore, the improvement of Emolex with synonyms can be considered interesting to test if the creation of the seed improves. For this reason, three approaches have been evaluated employing different versions of Emolex (original, WN synonyms and Oxford synonyms). The extension process of Emolex is completely automatic and is explained in detail in the next sections.

4.1 Enriched Approach by WordNet Synonyms

One of the enriched approach employed consists of the extension of Emolex employing the synonyms of WordNet [17].

In this process, each word contained in Emolex was looked up in WordNet, the synonyms of its more frequent sense were obtained and were annotated with the emotions of the Emolex word. Figure 3 shows an example of the process. The word 'alarm' is contained in Emolex and has the emotions FEAR and SURPRISE associated. The process looks up 'alarm' in WordNet and obtains the synonyms of its more frequent sense: 'dismay' and 'consternation'. These synonyms are added to Emolex and annotated with the same emotions of 'alarm'.

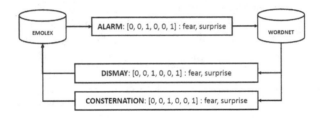

Fig. 3. Process of the extension of Emolex by WordNet synonyms.

After the process, Emolex has been extended with 4,029 words more, resulting a lexicon with 7,491 words.

The enriched approach by WordNet synonyms runs the same process than the original approach, but employing the new version of Emolex.

4.2 Enriched Approach by Oxford Synonyms

The enriched approach by Oxford synonyms was carried out with the aim of analysing the relevance of selecting a set of synonyms or other.

First, each word contained in Emolex was looked up in the Oxford American Writer Thesaurus [3] and all of the synonyms for all of its senses were collected. Then, each synonym of a word was associated with the emotions of the Emolex word and was added in Emolex. If a synonym was already in Emolex, their emotions associated will be the result of matching the emotional vector stored in Emolex and the new emotional vector.

Figure 4 shows an example of the process for the word 'sickness'. The first step is get their Oxford synonyms and for each synonym (in this example the synonym 'vomiting'): (1) associate the emotions of 'sickness', this is, DISGUST, FEAR and SADNESS; and (2) check if 'vomitin' is already in Emolex. If it is not, their emotions associated will be the same that 'sickness'. In another case, their emotional vector will contain the emotion in common between the vector saved in Emolex (old) and the new emotional vector (new). In this case, 'vomiting' will be associated with DISGUST emotion.

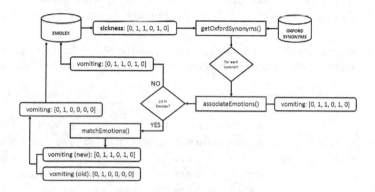

Fig. 4. Process of the extension of Emolex by Oxford synonyms.

After the process, Emolex has been extended with 6,789 words more, resulting a lexicon with 10,251 words.

Once extended, the process of the enriched approach by Oxford synonyms is the same than the original approach, but employing the new version of Emolex.

4.3   Evaluation Methodology

As we mentioned, the evaluation methodology is divided into two steps. On the one hand, an emotional model is built from the corpus annotated automatically to evaluate the usability of this corpus. On the other hand, the quality of automatic annotations is assessed through the measure of agreement between the corpus developed with our approach (automatic annotation) and the gold standard of Aman corpus (manual annotation).

To evaluate the automatic emotion classification, the multi-classifier employed is performed with a 10-fold cross-validation on the corpus annotated automatically. Specifically, precision, recall and F1-score are calculated in each model.

Concerning our evaluation of agreement on Aman corpus, we employ the Cohen's kappa [8] to measure the inter-tagger agreement between automatic and manual annotations like the original work.

4.4 Results

The results obtained by each classifier in all of our approaches are shown in the tables below; Tables 1 and 2 detail results obtained with LSA and GloVe similarity models respectively. Moreover, Table 1 also shows the results obtained by the original Aman corpus, employing SMO classifier with the same features. Precision (P), recall (R) and F1-values (F1) valued are shown for each emotion employing the original approach and the enriched approaches.

Regarding the comparison between automatic and manual annotations, Cohen's kappa values obtained by each one of our approaches when they are compared to the gold standard of Aman corpus are shown in Table 3.

Table 1. Precision, Recall and F1-values obtained by the SMO Multi-Classifier on the Corpus Developed Applying LSA as Semantic Metric in the Extension of the seed.

| | LSA model (Aman corpus) | | | | | | | | | Aman corpus Original | | |
| | Original approach | | | WN approach | | | Oxford approach | | | | | |
	P	R	F1	P	R	F1	P	R	F1	P	R	F1
Anger	0.198	0.137	0.162	0.444	0.348	**0.391**	0.338	0.330	0.334	0.538	0.274	0.363
Disgust	0.250	0.068	0.107	0.308	0.178	**0.225**	0.353	0.120	0.179	0.714	0.320	0.442
Fear	0.401	0.236	0.297	0.392	0.303	**0.342**	0.412	0.251	0.312	0.672	0.357	0.466
Joy	0.574	0.571	0.572	0.677	0.702	**0.689**	0.565	0.604	0.584	0.720	0.513	0.599
Sadness	0.247	0.107	0.149	0.467	0.269	0.341	0.591	0.462	**0.519**	0.577	0.260	0.359
Surprise	0.459	0.224	**0.301**	0.366	0.152	0.214	0.359	0.192	0.250	0.553	0.226	0.321
Neutral	0.706	0.846	**0.770**	0.559	0.676	0.612	0.551	0.668	0.604	0.798	0.955	0.869
Macro Avg.	0.595	0.633	**0.605**	0.571	0.586	0.573	0.525	0.533	0.523	0.753	0.774	0.745

Table 2. Precision, Recall and F1-values obtained by the SMO Multi-Classifier on the Corpus Developed Applying GloVe as Semantic Metric in the Extension of the seed.

| | GloVe model (Aman corpus) | | | | | | | | |
| | Original approach | | | WN approach | | | Oxford approach | | |
	P	R	F1	P	R	F1	P	R	F1
Anger	0.103	0.037	0.054	0.500	0.357	**0.417**	0.353	0.320	0.336
Disgust	0.000	0.000	0.000	0.194	0.085	**0.118**	0.273	0.075	**0.118**
Fear	0.527	0.298	0.381	0.475	0.320	**0.382**	0.341	0.162	0.220
Joy	0.822	0.565	0.670	0.708	0.678	**0.693**	0.594	0.541	0.566
Sadness	0.500	0.109	0.178	0.485	0.263	0.341	0.642	0.480	**0.549**
Surprise	0.787	0.349	**0.484**	0.438	0.097	0.159	0.478	0.180	0.262
Neutral	0.828	0.959	**0.889**	0.650	0.777	0.708	0.631	0.765	0.692
Macro Avg.	0.781	0.812	**0.782**	0.631	0.647	0.631	0.585	0.599	0.583

Table 3. Cohen's kappa values obtained by LSA and GloVe models (the Original Approach and the Enriched Approaches) in the Comparison of their Annotations to the Gold of Aman Corpus.

| | Cohen's kappa values | | | | | |
| | LSA | | | GloVe | | |
	Original Appr.	WN Appr.	Oxford Appr.	Original Appr.	WN Appr.	Oxford Appr.
Anger	**0.9368**	0.9051	0.8882	**0.9470**	0.9133	0.9034
Disgust	0.9495	0.9417	**0.9537**	0.9534	0.9460	**0.9547**
Fear	0.9226	0.8919	**0.9323**	**0.9492**	0.9238	0.9417
Joy	**0.7719**	0.6041	0.7241	**0.8630**	0.6810	0.7814
Sadness	**0.9285**	0.9193	0.8033	**0.9425**	0.9223	0.8508
Surprise	0.9186	**0.9512**	0.9345	0.9504	**0.9574**	0.9470

4.5 Discussion

As seen in the results section in the average F1-values of each approach, the results obtained are promising considering the state-of-art results (around 75% F1-value) and the fact that the features employed in the classifier are the sentences as a vector of words weighted by their counts. Thus, these results could be improved with selecting other features.

Regarding F1-values obtained by original and enriched approaches, the results show the improvements achieved by ANGER, DISGUST, FEAR, JOY and SADNESS emotions when the set of WN and Oxford synonyms are employed. These advances in the results are obtained by both DSMs: LSA and GloVe. Hence, the results confirm the benefit of extending Emolex with synonyms.

In terms of comparison between DSMs, the results demonstrate improvements when GloVe is employed, since this model obtains higher values for nearly all emotions and the global results with respect to LSA model. Hence, GloVe is validated as an effective and proper model to extend the seed in the bootstrapping process.

Concerning agreement values, most of the best values (in bold) are higher than 80% showing the quality of the automatic annotation obtained with our approach. About the comparison of the two DSMs, the best results in LSA approach are improved by GloVe model. Thus, the benefits of GloVe are also endorsed by the agreement values.

5 Conclusion

The basis of our research is the need to develop a technique that allow us to tackle the annotation task of emotions and thus improving supervised learning techniques. Therefore, this paper is focused on exploiting an innovative bootstrapping approach to automatically annotate emotional corpora.

Afterwards the evaluation performed, we can confirm that our approach is appropriate and reliable. Thus, our main conclusions are that: (1) the results confirm the soundness of the proposed approach for automatic annotation of emotions; (2) the relevance of the extension of Emolex with a set of synonyms to improve the result; and (3) the effectiveness of GloVe model to extend the seed.

Our future research will deal with exploring this bootstrapping process in other corpora to verify the results in any genre; analysis of the process to create a more accurate seed; employing other corpora (e.g. social media corpus) to built the GloVe model as well as Word2Vec (W2V) models; and exhaustive manual review to detect potential improvement.

Acknowledgment. This research has been supported by the FPI grant (BES-2013-065950) and the research stay grant (EEBB-I-15-10108) from the Spanish Ministry of Science and Innovation. It has also funded by the Spanish Government (DIG-ITY ref. TIN2015-65136-C02-2-R) and the Valencian Government (grant no. PROM-ETEOII/2014/001).

References

1. Alm, C.O., Roth, D., Sproat, R.: Emotions from text: machine learning for text-based emotion prediction. In: Proceedings of the Conference on HLT-EMNLP, pp. 579–586 (2005)
2. Aman, S., Szpakowicz, S.: Identifying expressions of emotion in text. In: Matoušek, V., Mautner, P. (eds.) TSD 2007. LNCS, vol. 4629, pp. 196–205. Springer, Heidelberg (2007). doi:10.1007/978-3-540-74628-7_27
3. Aubur, D., Armantrout, R., Crystal, D., Dirda, M.: Oxford American Writer's Thesaurus. Oxford University Press, Oxford (2004)
4. Boldrini, E., Martínez-Barco, P.: EMOTIBLOG: a model to learn subjetive information detection in the new textual genres of the Web 2.0-multilingual and multi-genre approach. Ph.D. thesis (2012)
5. Cherry, C., Mohammad, S.M., De Bruijn, B.: Binary classifiers and latent sequence models for emotion detection in suicide notes. Biomed. Inf. Insights **5**(Suppl 1), 147–154 (2012)
6. Choudhury, M.D., Gamon, M., Counts, S.: Happy, nervous or surprised? Classification of human affective states in social media. In: Proceedings of the 6th International AAAI Conference on Weblogs and Social Media (2012)
7. Chowdhury, S., Chowdhury, W.: Performing sentiment analysis in bangla microblog posts. In: International Conference on Informatics, Electronics & Vision (ICIEV). IEEE (2014)
8. Cohen, J.: A coefficient of agreement for nominal scales. Educ. Psychol. Measure. **20**(1), 37 (1960)
9. Collins, M., Singer, Y.: Unsupervised models for named entity classification. In: Proceedings of the Joint SIGDAT Conference on Empirical Methods in Natural Language Processing and Very Large Corpora, pp. 100–110 (1999)
10. Dadvar, M., Trieschnigg, D., Ordelman, R., de Jong, F.: Improving cyberbullying detection with user context. In: Serdyukov, P., Braslavski, P., Kuznetsov, S.O., Kamps, J., Rüger, S., Agichtein, E., Segalovich, I., Yilmaz, E. (eds.) ECIR 2013. LNCS, vol. 7814, pp. 693–696. Springer, Heidelberg (2013). doi:10.1007/978-3-642-36973-5_62
11. Ekman, P.: An argument for basic emotions. Cognit. Emotion **6**, 169–200 (1992)

12. Gliozzo, A., Strapparava, C.: Semantic Domains in Computational Linguistics. Springer, Heidelberg (2009). doi:10.1007/978-3-540-68158-8
13. Hall, M., Frank, E., Holmes, G., Pfahringer, B., Reutemann, P., Witten, I.H.: The WEKA data mining software: an update. SIGKDD Explor. **11**(1), 10–18 (2009)
14. Lee, S., Lee, G.G.: A bootstrapping approach for geographic named entity annotation. In: Myaeng, S.H., Zhou, M., Wong, K.-F., Zhang, H.-J. (eds.) AIRS 2004. LNCS, vol. 3411, pp. 178–189. Springer, Heidelberg (2005). doi:10.1007/978-3-540-31871-2_16
15. Liew, J.S.Y., Turtle, H.R., Liddy, E.D.: EmoTweet-28: a fine-grained emotion corpus for sentiment analysis. In: Proceedings of the Tenth International Conference on Language Resources and Evaluation (LREC 2016) (2016)
16. Manning, C.D., Surdeanu, M., Bauer, J., Finkel, J., Bethard, S.J., McClosky, D.: The stanford CoreNLP natural language processing toolkit. In: Association for Computational Linguistics (ACL) System Demonstrations, pp. 55–60 (2014)
17. Miller, G.A.: WordNet: a lexical database for English. Commun. ACM **38**(11), 39–41 (1995)
18. Mohammad, S.: #Emotional tweets. In: Proceedings of the First Joint Conference on Lexical and Computational Semantics (2012)
19. Mohammad, S.M.: Sentiment analysis: detecting valence, emotions, and other affectual states from text. In: Emotion Measurement (2015)
20. Mohammad, S.M., Turney, P.D.: Crowdsourcing a word-emotion association lexicon. Comput. Lang. **29**(3), 436–465 (2013)
21. Montero, C.S., Suhonen, J.: Emotion analysis meets learning analytics: online learner profiling beyond numerical data. In: Proceedings of the 14th Koli Calling International Conference on Computing Education Research, pp. 165–169 (2014)
22. Neviarouskaya, A., Prendinger, H., Ishizuka, M.: Compositionality principle in recognition of fine-grained emotions from text. In: Proceedings of the Third International ICWSM Conference, pp. 278–281 (2009)
23. Pennington, J., Socher, R., Manning, C.D.: GloVe: global vectors for word representation. In: Empirical Methods in Natural Language Processing (EMNLP) (2014)
24. Platt, J.: Using analytic QP and sparseness to speed training of support vector machines. In: Proceedings of Advances in Neural Information Processing Systems, pp. 557–563 (1999)
25. Plutchik, R.: A general psycho evolutionary theory of emotion. In: Theories of Emotion, pp. 3–33 (1980)
26. Schwartz, H.A., Eichstaedt, J.C., Kern, M.L., Dziurzynski, L., Lucas, R.E., Agrawal, M., Park, G.J., Lakshmikanth, S.K., Jha, S., Seligman, M.E.P., Ungar, L.: Characterizing geographic variation in well-being using tweets. In: Proceedings of the International AAAI Conference on Weblogs and Social Media (2013)
27. Strapparava, C., Mihalcea, R.: Semeval-2007 task 14: affective text. In: Proceedings of the 4th International Workshop on Semantic Evaluations, pp. 70–74 (2007)
28. Wang, W., Chen, L., Thirunarayan, K., Sheth, A.P.: Harnessing twitter "big data" for automatic emotion identification. In: International Confernece on Social Computing (SocialCom) (2012)
29. Yarowsky, D.: Unsupervised word sense disambiguation rivaling supervised methods. In: Proceedings of the 33rd Annual Meeting on Association for Computational Linguistics (ACL 1995), pp. 189–196. Association for Computational Linguistics, Stroudsburg, PA, USA (1995)

Rapid Construction of a Web-Enabled Medical Speech to Sign Language Translator Using Recorded Video

Farhia Ahmed[2], Pierrette Bouillon[1], Chelle Destefano[3], Johanna Gerlach[1],
Angela Hooper[4], Manny Rayner[1],
Irene Strasly[1], Nikos Tsourakis[1(✉)],
and Catherine Weiss[5]

[1] University of Geneva, FTI/TIM, Geneva, Switzerland
{nikolaos.tsourakis,Emmanuel.Rayner}@unige.ch
[2] Geneva Society for the Deaf, Geneva, Switzerland
[3] Gypsysnail Arts, Adelaide, Australia
[4] NABS Interpreting Services, Adelaide, Australia
[5] School of Global, Urban and Social Studies, RMIT University,
Melbourne, Australia

Abstract. We describe an experiment in which sign-language output in Swiss French Sign Language (LSF-CH) and Australian Sign Language (Auslan) was added to a limited-domain medical speech translation system using a recorded video method. By constructing a suitable web tool to manage the recording procedure, the overhead involved in creating and manipulating the large set of files involved could be made easily manageable, allowing us to focus on the interesting and non-trivial problems which arise at the translation level. Initial experiences with the system suggest that the recorded videos, despite their unprofessional appearance, are readily comprehensible to Deaf informants, and that the method is promising as a simple short-term solution for this type of application.

Keywords: Speech translation · Medical translation · Sign language translation · Web

1 Introduction and Background

There has been surprisingly little work to date on speech to sign-language translation. The best-performing system reported in the literature still appears to be TESSA [3], which in 2002 was able to translate English speech into British Sign Language in a post office counter service domain, using coverage captured in 370 phrasal patterns. TESSA was evaluated in a realistic setting in a British post office, with three post office clerks on the hearing side of the dialogues and six Deaf subjects playing the role of customers, and performed creditably. Another substantial project is the one described in [16], which translated Spanish speech

© Springer International Publishing AG 2017
J.F. Quesada et al. (Eds.): FETLT 2016, LNAI 10341, pp. 122–134, 2017.
https://doi.org/10.1007/978-3-319-69365-1_10

into Spanish Sign Language; this, however, does not appear to have reached the stage of being able to achieve reasonable coverage even of a small domain, and despite being implemented several years after TESSA used a much less ambitious approach to sign language generation.

Speech-to-speech translation is now well-understood, and the reason why few speech-to-sign systems have been constructed is evidently the difficulty of producing signed output. It appears to have been taken for granted that the only way to produce this output is to use some kind of signing avatar. In the general case, where a wide range of productively specified output must be handled, this is evidently true. Signing avatar technology is still, however, at a stage of development which could perhaps be compared to that of TTS systems in the mid 80s. JASigning [6,8], which was developed over the course of three consecutive European Framework projects, is generally agreed to be by far the best general-purpose signing avatar currently available and represents the state of the art, but the quality of the output it produces is less than satisfactory. Although normally comprehensible to Deaf subjects, it is often criticized as "artificial" or "lacking in fluency", and there is a persistent feeling that even comprehensibility is not clearly sufficient for a safety-critical application like medicine.

In the long-term, it is evident that further development of systems like JASigning, which can create signed output from abstract descriptions, is the only way forward. Having used it ourselves for some nontrivial projects [4,15], it is equally obvious that, in its current form, this technology leaves much to be desired. Output quality is far from being the only problem. It takes a great deal of time to develop an application, particularly if there is no sign language lexicon resource available to supply machine-readable entries in HamNoSys.[1] HamNoSys lexica only exist for half a dozen of the world's estimated 200 sign languages — in particular, they do not exist for several of the largest ones, including ASL — and constructing HamNoSys entries from scratch requires on the order of an hour or more of effort per entry for all but the most expert sign language lexicographers.

In this paper, we investigate the feasibility of a low-tech short-term solution, recorded signed video, in the context of a medical speech translation application. The app, BabelDr [2,14], translates medical examination questions from French into a variety of target languages, with particular emphasis on those spoken by victims of the current European refugee crisis. The style is "flexible spoken phrasebook": the speaking medical professional can express themself fairly freely, but all utterances are mapped to a set of canonical question types, which are rendered into the target languages by professional translators. The patient responds nonverbally. In the highly constrained context of the medical speech translation task, recorded signed output appears to be a viable solution. With a suitably designed recording tool, the task of creating the videos is quick and efficient, and the quality of the output is much higher than for avatar-generated signed language. Modern disk and web technology mean that the overhead of storing and delivering the videos is not excessive.

---

[1] Hamburg Notation System for Sign Languages or HamNoSys [11] is the most commonly used formalism for describing the physical forms of signs.

In the rest of the paper, we expand on the above sketch. Section 2 describes the BabelDr application, Sect. 3 the issues involved in adding signed video output, and Sect. 4 issues arising at the level of translation. Section 5 briefly discusses evaluation, and Sect. 6 compares the two sign languages used. Section 7 concludes.

2   The BabelDr Medical Speech Translator

BabelDr is a joint project of Geneva University's Faculty of Translation and Interpretation (FTI/TIM) and Geneva University Hospital (HUG), active since July 2015 under funding from "La fondation privée des HUG". The goal is to develop methods that allow rapid prototyping of medium-vocabulary web-enabled medical speech translators, with particular emphasis on languages spoken by migrants. The application can be characterised as a flexible speech-enabled phrasebook. Semantic coverage consists of a prespecified set of utterance-types[2], but users can use a wide variety of surface forms when speaking to the system.

Each utterance-type is associated with a canonical source-language version, which is rendered into the target languages by suitably qualified translation experts. The central design goals are to ensure that

- translations are completely reliable,
- the bulk of the work can be performed directly by translation experts, with minimal or no involvement from language engineers,
- speech recognition performance is excellent for in-coverage data and adequate even for new users,
- new versions of the live app can be quickly deployed over the web, enabling rapid updating of coverage in response to requests from medical staff,
- new target languages can easily be added, enabling flexibility in the face of changing patient demographics.

A demonstrator system freely accessible on the web[3] translates French into Spanish, Italian, English, Arabic and Tigrinya.

2.1   Architecture and Development Process

The BabelDr app is implemented on top of the Lite Speech2Speech platform, a framework for development of spoken language translation systems which has been designed for use by developers whose main expertise is in translation rather than spoken language techology [13,14]. Rules are written in a form of Synchronized Context-Free Grammar (SCFG; [1]) adapted for the particularities of the multilingual speech translation task.

---

[2] The version used in the study reported here contained about 1,600 utterance-types. The current version is considerably larger.

[3] http://babeldr.unige.ch/demos-and-resources/.

```
Utterance
Source is (the|your) pain $$painType
Source does (the|your) pain feel $$painType
Target/english is the pain $$painType
Target/french la douleur est-elle $$painType
EndUtterance

TrLex $$painType source="deep" \
    english="deep"  french="profonde"
TrLex $$painType source="hard to localize" \
    english="hard to localize" french="difficile à localiser"
```

Fig. 1. Simple BabelDr rules to translate expressions like "is the pain deep" or "does the pain feel hard to localize" into French.

Examples of some simple rules are shown in Fig. 1.[4] The `source` portions of the rules define the English phrases which the source-language recogniser will cover; the `english` portions define a canonical version of the source, which at run-time is shown to the source-language user as a backtranslation; and the `french` portion defines the target-language translation.

As explained in [14], the normal development process splits up the rules into monolingual files linked by the canonical form. Thus for example the source-language developer only works with the `source` and `english` portions of the rules, and the French target-language developer only works with the `english` and `french` portions. The different parts of the rules are combined during compilation.

2.2 Web Deployment

The BabelDr system is deployed over the web using methods developed under the earlier CALL-SLT project [12]. Translation rules are compiled to produce recognition grammars that can be run on the commercial Nuance Recognizer 10 platform[5]; the grammars directly produce translation results for all the output languages, with no need for further processing. The compilation architecture is designed so that non-expert developers can upload new versions of the grammar files to the web-server over an FTP connection, then recompile and deploy the system using a single command.

The runtime web speech recognition architecture is described in [7]; users can connect to the app through any normal browser using a lightweight client.

---

[4] For presentational reasons, the rules have been simplified and shown as translating English into French. The real rules allow much greater syntactic variation and translate from French into five spoken languages.

[5] Since this paper was written, we have added functionality to perform robust matching against the grammar, using input from a large-vocabulary recogniser. This substantially improves speech understanding performance [17].

Table 1. BabelDr coverage: domains, number of utterances per domain, and typical examples.

Reception (52 utterance-types)
Je suis le docteur
(I am the doctor)
Abdominal pain (472 utterance-types)
Combien de fois par jour allez-vous à selles ?
(How many times a day are you going to the bathroom?)
Chest pain (449 utterance-types)
La douleur diminue-t-elle quand vous prenez de la nitro ?
(Is the pain less severe when you take nitroglycerin?)
Headache (434 utterance-types)
La douleur est-elle sur le devant de la tête ?
(Is the pain in the front of the head?)
Drug use (29 utterance-types)
Buvez-vous des boissons alcoolisées tous les jours ?
(Do you drink alcoholic beverages every day?)
Follow-up (145 utterance-types)
Avez-vous de l'argent pour payer les médicaments ?
(Do you have money to pay for the medication?)

2.3 Coverage

BabelDr is designed to help French-speaking medical professionals communicate with non-French-speaking patients in a hospital setting, primarily in the context of immigrants presenting themselves at the "Urgences" (A&E) department. At the moment, the coverage consists of about 1,600 semantic utterance-types which are divided up into the six subdomains "reception", "abdominal pain", "chest pain", "headache", "drug use" and "follow-up"[6]. Table 1 gives the distribution of utterance-types by domain and typical examples.

3   Adding Signed Video Output

In principle, it is clearly easy to add recorded signed output to an application like BabelDr: one simply records a video for each possible output and plays it at the appropriate moment. It is equally clear that there are many things that in practice could make the scheme unworkable. There may be too many videos to record; storing them may require unreasonable amounts of space; bandwidth problems could make the app too slow; the logistics of recording and uploading the videos could be too complex; finally, it may simply turn out to be difficult to translate the utterances into signed language. At the beginning of the exercise, it seemed quite possible to us that any of the above problems might pose an insuperable obstacle. We examine them in order.

---

[6] As of late 2017, this has grown to about 5,000 utterance-types and ten subdomains.

3.1 Too Many Videos

The current version of BabelDr covers about 1,600 possible utterances. Although a substantial number to translate and record, this seemed quite manageable to us if the task was organised in an efficient way and there were no other problems.

We decided to begin by recording videos for the "Reception", "Abdominal pain", "Drug use" and "Follow-up" domains, a total of 645 videos at the point when we began the exercise. Although this is less than half the total, the majority of the sentences in the "Chest pain" and "Headache" domains are structurally just minor variants of ones in the "Abdominal pain" domain, so we considered that it would be a realistic test of the idea.

Since most of our group is located in Geneva, Switzerland, we chose to record videos in Swiss French Sign Language (LSF-CH). Recording was carried out by one of the authors, a native signer of LSF-CH, in consultation with another, a sign language interpreter who is fluent in both LSF-CH and French. In order to provide comparison points, two of the Australian authors also translated the material into Auslan, starting with an English translation of the original French material. This was done using a slightly different methodology; once again, the two people concerned were a native signer of Auslan and a professional sign language interpreter, but this time the two people shared the task of doing the recording, each doing half the set.

A screenshot of the user interface for the version of BabelDr which includes recorded video output is shown in Fig. 2.[7]

3.2 Storage Space and Bandwidth

After experimenting with a few different recording formats, we determined that an MP4 video of a signed utterance in the medical examination domain is typically around 250 KB. A complete set of videos for the application thus requires only about 400 MB, which is evidently not going to create difficulties.

Initial experiments showed that signed videos in MP4 format were typically downloaded to the client in a small fraction of a second when using a normal high-speed connection in Western Europe, and did not noticeably affect latency.

3.3 Logistics of Recording and Uploading

For obvious reasons — in particular, the content frequently changes — it is important to streamline the recording and uploading process as much as possible. After some experimentation, we arrived at the following pipeline. As part of the compilation process, a file is created listing all the signed videos that need to be recorded. Each line contains text in the aural/oral language most closely associated with the signed language in question (for LSF-CH, this was French; for Auslan, English), together with relevant metadata.

---

[7] The app is freely accessible at https://speech2sign.unige.ch/en/applications/babeldr/.

Fig. 2. Screenshot of BabelDr recorded-video user interface. The doctor presses the button marked "Enregistrer" ("record") and speaks. The system displays the canonical source-language sentence (backtranslation) corresponding to the recognition result in the pane immediately above. If the doctor is satisfied that they have been correctly understood, they press the button marked "Traduire" ("translate") to produce a signed translation. The lower left pane shows examples of system coverage related to the most recently processed utterance, and the lower right pane the dialogue history.

The recording file is uploaded to a web tool which handles the actual recording and is allocated to the signer responsible for producing the recordings. When the signer logs in over the web, they are presented with their currently allocated items, formatted as a scrollable list. For each item, they are initially presented with the associated text; they click a button to record, and are subsequently able to review the video and if necessary rerecord it. Figure 3 shows the recording interface.

At any time, the developer who has posted the recording task can download the currently recorded content, in the form of a zipfile containing the videos and an updated metadata file. These only need to be copied to the relevant folder in the app content directory in order to update it, after which the app can be recompiled. The overhead involved in uploading the recording file at the beginning and downloading and installing the zipfile at the end is typically no more than a few minutes.

In summary, all the potentially difficult problems discussed so far turned out to be essentially trivial to deal with. The truly challenging questions, which we discuss in the next section, had to do with the translation process itself: how to translate French text into signed LSF-CH and Auslan, and be confident that the result adequately reflected the source content and was comprehensible to signers of the target languages.

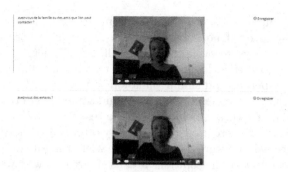

Fig. 3. Screenshot of the recording tool, showing two recorded videos. The area on the left of each video holds the text to be translated; the signer uses the button on the right to initiate and stop recording. Once a video exists for an item, it can be played by clicking it.

4   Translation Issues

Languages conceptualise the world differently. Translation always involves dealing with ambiguity, vagueness, register mismatches, lexical gaps and other well-documented issues, though the extent to which they cause practical problems varies a great deal from case to case [5]. It became apparent at an early stage that translation of medical examination questions from French into LSF-CH was challenging, but it was not obvious to us whether this said something general about sign language, or something specific about LSF-CH. For this reason, we decided also to translate the material into Auslan.

In order to keep the discussion focussed and concrete, we will concentrate on lexical gaps, which are the most important single issue. Based on discussions between the native LSF-CH signer author and the sign language interpreter author, we began by identifying 49 concepts which were perceived as difficult to translate into LSF-CH. By "difficult", we mean that the native signer and interpreter were in doubt as to the correct way to translate them, and the problem could not quickly be resolved by consultation of obvious sources such as online lexica and other signers.

The "difficult" concepts have a high frequency of occurrence in the domain; 216 of the 645 utterances (33%) contain at least one of them. Some, e.g. "anticoagulants", "beta-blocker", "gall bladder" and "MRI" are fairly technical, and it is not remarkable that they should cause problems. We were however struck by the fact that many of the "difficult" concepts, e.g. "stool", "groin", "constipated", "HIV positive", "incontinent" and "blood pressure" are everyday notions that a doctor would unreflectingly assume are familiar to the patient and straightforward to translate. If this is not true, it is reasonable to expect misunderstandings to arise. Our findings are broadly consistent with recent work by Pointurier-Pournin [10], which presents strong evidence suggesting that lexical gaps are problematic for hearing interpreters.

The practical question is what can be done to circumvent the difficulties in cases like these; even if no immediate translation of a word can be found, there are almost always recovery strategies that can be used. In descending order of preference, we tried looking in online resources, talking to Deaf peers, paraphrasis, fingerspelling and simple omission of the word. In the end, various combinations of these strategies allowed us to find some kind of translation for all 645 sentences. The first three (looking in online resources, talking to Deaf peers and paraphrasis), which were used about equally often, accounted for about 93% of the cases; the remainder were nearly all dealt with using finger-spelling. What is not clear is how effective the solutions are, as the reason why we marked these concepts as "difficult" in the first place was that the information available was inconsistent. In general, all the methods available had drawbacks, which we now discuss.

4.1   Online Resources

A fundamental problem is that LSF-CH, in common with most other sign languages, lacks standardisation and documentation, and exhibits large regional variation. The main online resource is a video dictionary with about 1,800 signs[8], but it does not list more than a selection of the more common signs currently in use, and the material is already significantly out of date. A second online dictionary[9] is being constructed by the Swiss Federation of the Deaf; it is much closer to being current, but concentrates on signs for everyday language and is still seriously incomplete. Although LSF-CH overlaps with French Sign Language (LSF) to the point where LSF-CH is sometimes called a dialect of the larger language, many lexical divergences exist, and there is no guarantee that LSF signs for specialised technical concepts will be considered acceptable or even comprehensible by LSF-CH signers. This means that LSF lexical resources like the Sematos dictionary[10] are of limited usefulness in the present context. In general, all the online resources date rapidly and often conflict both with current usage and with each other.

4.2   Consulting Deaf Peers

The two LSF-CH-fluent authors are well-connected to the LSF-CH community, and on many occasions asked Deaf peers for advice. Again, the problem was that recommendations were often inconsistent. This lack of consistency could be quite startling: we received different, incompatible recommendations for the sign to use when translating the concept "inflamation" from two experts who are both contributors to the same online lexical resource. A less dramatic, but fairly typical, example was the translation of the concept "bloated"; some informants suggested a sign made by moving the curved palm away from the stomach, some

---

[8] http://www.pisourd.ch/?theme=dicocomplet.

[9] http://signsuisse.sgb-fss.ch.

[10] http://www.sematos.eu/lsf.html.

disagreed and said that this sign in fact meant "pregnant", and some thought both meanings were available. In the end, the best we could do was to add extra signing meaning "when you eat a lot", but the drawbacks of this kind of solution are apparent.

4.3 Paraphrasis

Many difficult concepts can in principle be paraphrased using a small vocabulary. Often, though, unavailability of the correct technical term makes it difficult to refer to a concept in a concise and natural way. In theory, it might for example be possible to paraphrase "HIV positive" or "diabetic" using simpler signs. In practice, this felt like an unrealistic solution, and in both cases we chose to use the signs from the Pisourd online dictionary, despite initial doubts about their general acceptance by LSF-CH signers.

4.4 Fingerspelling and Omission

Fingerspelling is always a possible solution: one simply hopes that the patient will know the spoken language word, and spells it out. The obvious drawback is that the patient may not in fact know the word. In LSF-CH, where signers' knowledge of French is often poor, we were reluctant to use fingerspelling when other possibilities existed. If all else fails, the word can be omitted. This is evidently the least satisfactory solution.

5   Evaluation

Avatar-based sign language systems require careful evaluation, since it is difficult to estimate a priori how accurately an avatar renders the intended signed output. In a recorded video system, this type of evaluation is beside the point. Signers are used to recording, posting and watching videos of signing, and it is generally agreed that the standard of modern web video formats is sufficient. Initial ad hoc tests were enough to reassure us that this held true for our videos as well.

For the reasons given in the previous section, it is less obvious how comprehensible the videos are at the *conceptual* level. It is unfortunately not straightforward to perform a reliable evaluation at this level. Deaf subjects who have been shown the videos claim to understand nearly all of them; but it is well known that subjects tend to overstate their understanding, and asking test questions usually biases them by indirectly giving them part of the answer [9]. A more meaningful approach is to try to use the tool in a real or simulated communicative situation, as in the study from [3]. This, however, evaluates not so much the translation device as the entire communication setup, in particular the structure of the question coverage. We return briefly to this topic in the final section.

6   Comparison with Auslan

As already mentioned, we decided also to translate the material into Auslan in order to be able to compare with a second sign language. It is interesting to note that the two Auslan signers (a native Deaf signer and a qualified sign language interpreter) used far more fingerspelling; over three-quarters of the "difficult" concepts discussed in Sect. 4 were rendered into Auslan using finger-spelling, sometimes combined with paraphrasis. Both Auslan signers consider their strategy to be the natural way to translate the concepts. Anecdotally, this is consistent with the general perception that Auslan signers are better inte-grated into the surrounding hearing community than LSF-CH signers; LSF-CH signers avoid fingerspelling where possible, while Auslan signers embrace it.

7   Conclusions

It is not our purpose here to suggest that speech-to-sign translation using recorded video is a viable long-term solution. Evidently, this is at best implau-sible. But as a cheap short-term fix, it works surprisingly well, and makes it possible to build potentially useful limited domain translation apps now, at a low cost. Previous attempts to build speech-to-sign translators have been "tech-nology push": they have focussed on the problem of how to use an avatar to generate the output sign language, almost to the exclusion of everything else. This has hidden other problems, in particular those at the level of translation. By choosing a method which makes sign language generation trivial, we have been able to study the translation issues in more detail. Our findings suggest that these are not always simple, even for small domains like the one we have studied here, and will need to be addressed for any nontrivial speech-to-sign system.

For the specific case of medical speech to sign translation, our impression after carrying out this preliminary study is that there is at present a rather good case to be made for the recorded video solution. The negatives are obvious, but the positives seem in practice more important. Doctors consider the fact that the system can only produce a fixed set of possible outputs a desirable feature rather than a problem; it means that all translations can be checked ahead of time, removing the possibility of unpleasant surprises, and it is the solution we use for spoken as well as signed target languages. Even if the quality of the videos is unprofessional, Deaf people trust them more than avatar-generated signing, which often has trouble capturing important nuances. Costs are manageable: fees for recording the 1290 videos created in this study totalled slightly less than a thousand US dollars.

Our next goal will be to carry out an evaluation at the communication level. We are currently planning a study where doctors and Deaf subjects simulating patients will carry out role-playing exercises using the tool (a study of this type has already been carried out with Arabic-speaking subjects). We hope to report on results in due course.

Acknowledgements. The BabelDr project is funded by "La fondation privée des HUG" and carried out in collaboration with HUG. We would like to thank Nuance Inc. for generously allowing us to use their software for research purposes, and Hervé Spechbach and Sarah Ebling for many helpful comments.

References

1. Aho, A.V., Ullman, J.D.: Properties of syntax directed translations. J. Comput. Syst. Sci. **3**(3), 319–334 (1969)
2. Bouillon, P., Spechbach, H.: BabelDr: a web platform for rapid construction of phrasebook-style medical speech translation applications. In: Proceedings of EAMT 2016, Vilnius, Latvia (2016)
3. Cox, S., Lincoln, M., Tryggvason, J., Nakisa, M., Wells, M., Tutt, M., Abbott, S.: Tessa, a system to aid communication with deaf people. In: Proceedings of the Fifth International ACM Conference on Assistive Technologies, pp. 205–212. ACM (2002)
4. Ebling, S., Glauert, J.: Exploiting the full potential of JASigning to build an avatar signing train announcements. In: Proceedings of the Third International Symposium on Sign Language Translation and Avatar Technology (SLTAT), Chicago, USA, vol. 18, p. 19, October 2013
5. Eco, U.: Mouse or rat?: Translation as negotiation. Hachette, UK (2004)
6. Elliott, R., Glauert, J.R., Kennaway, J., Marshall, I., Safar, E.: Linguistic modelling and language-processing technologies for avatar-based sign language presentation. Univ. Access Inf. Soc. **6**(4), 375–391 (2008)
7. Fuchs, M., Tsourakis, N., Rayner, M.: A scalable architecture for web deployment of spoken dialogue systems. In: Proceedings of LREC 2012, Istanbul, Turkey (2012)
8. Jennings, V., Elliott, R., Kennaway, R., Glauert, J.: Requirements for a signing avatar. In: Proceedings of Workshop on Corpora and Sign Language Technologies (CSLT), LREC, pp. 33–136 (2010)
9. Kipp, M., Heloir, A., Nguyen, Q.: Sign Language avatars. animation and comprehensibility. In: Vilhjálmsson, H.H., Kopp, S., Marsella, S., Thórisson, K.R. (eds.) IVA 2011. LNCS, vol. 6895, pp. 113–126. Springer, Heidelberg (2011). doi:10.1007/978-3-642-23974-8_13
10. Pointurier-Pournin, S.: L'interprètation en Langue des Signes Française: contraintes, tactiques, efforts. Ph.D. thesis, Universitè de la Sorbonne nouvelle-Paris III (2014)
11. Prillwitz, S., für Deutsche Gebärdensprache und Kommunikation Gehörloser, H.Z.: HamNoSys: version 2.0; Hamburg Notation System for Sign Languages; an introductory guide. Signum-Verlag (1989)
12. Rayner, M., Baur, C., Chua, C., Bouillon, P., Tsourakis, N.: Helping non-expert users develop online spoken CALL courses. In: Proceedings of the Sixth SLaTE Workshop, Leipzig, Germany (2015)
13. Rayner, M.: Using the Regulus Lite Speech2Speech Platform, online documentation (2016). http://www.issco.unige.ch/en/research/projects/Speech2SpeechDoc/build/html/index.html
14. Rayner, M., Bouillon, P., Ebling, S., Strasly, I., Tsourakis, N.: A framework for rapid development of limited-domain speech-to-sign phrasal translators. In: Proceedings of the workshop on Future and Emerging Trends in Language Technology, Sevilla, Spain (2015)

15. Rayner, M., Bouillon, P., Gerlach, J., Strasly, I., Tsourakis, N.: An open web platform for rule-based speech-to-sign translation. In: Proceedings of ACL 2016, Berlin, Germany (2016)
16. San-Segundo, R., Montero, J.M., Macías-Guarasa, J., Córdoba, R., Ferreiros, J., Pardo, J.M.: Proposing a speech to gesture translation architecture for spanish deaf people. J. Vis. Lang. Comput. **19**(5), 523–538 (2008)
17. Rayner, M., Tsourakis, N., Gerlach, J.: Lightweight spoken utterance classification with CFG, tf-idf and dynamic programming. In: Camelin, N., Estève, Y., Martín-Vide, C. (eds.) SLSP 2017. LNCS (LNAI), vol. 10583, pp. 143–154. Springer, Le Mans, France (2017). doi:10.1007/978-3-319-68456-7_12

Incorporating Syllable Phonotactics to Improve Grapheme to Phoneme Translation

Stephen Ash[1](✉) and David Lin[2]

[1] University of Memphis, Memphis, TN, USA
sash@memphis.edu
[2] Baylor University, Waco, TX, USA
david_lin@baylor.edu

Abstract. Grapheme to Phoneme (G2P) translation is a critical step in many natural language tasks such as text-to-speech production and automatic speech recognition. Most approaches to the G2P problem ignore phonotactical constraints and syllable structure information, and they rely on simple letter window features to produce pronunciations of words. We present a G2P translator which incorporates syllable structure into the prediction pipeline during structured prediction and re-ranking. In addition, most dictionaries contain only word-to-pronunciation pairs, which is a problem when trying to use these dictionaries as training data in a structured prediction approach to G2P translation. We present a number of improvements to the process of producing high-quality alignments of these pairs for training data. Together these two contributions improve the G2P word error rate (WER) on the CMUDict dataset by ~8%, achieving a new state-of-the-art accuracy level among opensource solutions.

Keywords: Grapheme-to-phoneme conversion · Machine learning · Conditional random fields

1 Introduction

Grapheme to phoneme (G2P) translation is the task of converting an input sequence of *graphemes*, the set of symbols in a writing system, to an output sequence of *phonemes*, the perceptually distinct units of sound that make up words in a spoken language. The G2P problem has been studied thoroughly in the linguistics, natural language processing, and speech recognition communities. Few languages (e.g. Serbian) have a strict one-to-one correspondence between phonemes and graphemes. Therefore, the difficulty of systematic conversion comes from the level of ambiguity and irregularity in the orthography. Typical G2P systems for English use 27 graphemes as input (26 Roman alphabet letters and the apostrophe) and between 40 and 45 phonemes. In this manuscript, graphemes will be written between angle brackets as ⟨aloud⟩ and phonemes will be written using the Arpabet phonetic alphabet [9] between slashes as /AH L AW D/.

© Springer International Publishing AG 2017
J.F. Quesada et al. (Eds.): FETLT 2016, LNAI 10341, pp. 135–147, 2017.
https://doi.org/10.1007/978-3-319-69365-1_11

There are a number of problems that make grapheme to phoneme translation difficult (examples from English): (1) there is typically no one-to-one correspondence between graphemes and phonemes. For example, the c in ⟨cider⟩ sounds different from the c in ⟨cat⟩, which sounds similar to the k in ⟨kite⟩. (2) The number of letters that produce a single phoneme is not consistent. For example, the letter pair ch in ⟨change⟩ produces a single affricate phoneme. The mapping of pairs of letters is not consistent: e.g. the pair ph in ⟨phase⟩ compared to the ph in ⟨uphill⟩. (3) Usually one or a few graphemes produce a single phoneme, but there are exceptions where multiple phonemes are produced by a single grapheme: e.g. the x in ⟨six⟩ produces two phonemes: /S I CK S/.

(4) The output phoneme is not completely determined by local graphemes that are closest in sequence; there are some non-local effects. ⟨mad⟩ is pronounced /M AE D/, but adding a trailing e to make the word ⟨made⟩, changes the middle vowel, a, to the phoneme /EY/, and the e itself is unvoiced. Additionally, the trailing y changes the vowel phonemes in ⟨photograph⟩ to ⟨photography⟩.

(5) Existing dictionaries of words to pronunciations generally do not indicate which graphemes correspond to which phonemes. This complicates using dictionaries as training data in a supervised learning approach. This *alignment* of individual graphemes to phonemes is necessary if one is trying to use methods of structured prediction to produce sequences of phonemes from sequences of graphemes.

This paper describes a method of grapheme to phoneme translation using a pipeline of discriminative models that incorporate rich syllable information at multiple places in the process. The contributions in this paper are:

- We present an improved G2P pipeline using discriminative, probabilistic methods throughout, which include syllable structure in both the prediction of phonemes and the re-ranking of candidate pronunciations. Our implementation is available as part of the open-source G2P toolkit called **jG2P** available at http://bit.ly/83yysKL
- We suggest a number of improvements to the many-to-many alignment of words to pronunciations to create high quality training data to train the G2P pipeline.
- We release modified versions of the CMUDict v0.7 dataset with both graphemes and phonemes syllabified for use in other applications that require syllable structure.
- Among the open-source G2P solutions of which we are aware, our solution achieves the best word error rate (WER) on the CMUDict dataset, a common dataset used in bench-marking G2P systems.

2   Previous Work on G2P

The statistical version of the G2P problem is as follows: let G be the set of graphemes in the orthography (e.g. a, b, etc.). G^* is the Kleene star of G, which is the set of all possible grapheme strings. Similarly, let P be the set of phonemes (e.g. the diphthong /OY/, the fricative /V/, etc.). P^* is the set of all possible phonetic pronunciations. G and P usually include ϵ as a dummy symbol, which is used, for example, when graphemes are unvoiced. The probabilistic formulation of the G2P problem is the task of finding the best string of phonemes for the string of graphemes as in (1). g is a sequence of $g_{0..M}$ graphemes, and p is a sequence of $p_{0..N}$ phonemes.

$$\varphi(g) = \underset{p \in P^*}{\mathrm{argmax}}\, P(g, p) \qquad (1)$$

An *alignment* of graphemes to phonemes is a matching of substrings $g_{i:j}$ of g (or ϵ) to substrings $p_{k:l}$ of p (or ϵ). Typically the size of the substring of graphemes or phonemes is bounded. A n-m alignment limits the maximum size of the grapheme substring to length n and the maximum size of the phoneme substring to length m, as shown in Fig. 1.

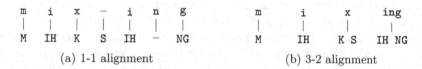

(a) 1-1 alignment   (b) 3-2 alignment

Fig. 1. 1-1 alignment vs 3-2 alignment of ⟨mixing⟩. An ϵ in the alignment is shown as – for clarity

A pairing of a grapheme substring to a phoneme substring can be treated as a single unit, a *graphone*, such as the substring ⟨ing⟩ paired to substring /IH NG/ in Fig. 1b. Therefore, the entire aligned grapheme and phoneme sequence can be represented by a sequence of graphones. [3] recognized that using graphones, one can factorize the probability in (1) similar to a language model, where the ith graphone is predicted by n previous graphones. [3] use a 9-gram language model with modified Kneser-Ney smoothing.

The first use of Conditional Random Fields (CRF) [11] for the problem of grapheme to phoneme translation comes from [16]. They use a 1-1 alignment model with ϵ only allowed on the grapheme side, and train a CRF using local grapheme window features. [1] created jG2P, which we build upon in this work. This system uses a pipeline of CRFs to perform alignment, pronunciation transcription, and re-ranking of candidate results.

[13] created an open-source G2P framework by encoding a graphone language model into a Weighted Finite State Transducer (WFST). This approach uses the Expectation-Maximization formulation described in [4] to produce a constrained alignment of the training data used to train the language model encoded in the transducer.

A number of hybrid methods have been proposed recently. [19] uses alignments produced by [14] to train an *insertion predictor* to predict where epsilons should be inserted into the grapheme sequence. Then they train a CRF to predict a phoneme using the previously predicted phoneme and a local window of graphemes. The best published WER on CMUDict at present is given by [15] using Long Short-term Memory Recurrent Neural Networks (LSTM) combined with a 5-gram graphone language model.

[5] demonstrates that adding phonological constraints to respect syllable structure improves the accuracy of the G2P task in multiple languages. [17] built a G2P system that uses a CRF with simple syllable features, such as begin and end syllable indicators, to predict phoneme sequences. They report that adding the syllable features reduced the Word Error Rate (WER) by 1.3% points.

3   Improvements to the G2P Pipeline

The phonology of human speech includes rich linguistic structure. Words are made up of syllables, which are made up of phonemes. Typical theory describes the syllable as made up of an optional *onset*, a *nucleus*, and an optional *coda*. Phonotactical constraints are the rules that determine which combinations of phonemes are allowed in each part of the syllable. These constraints differ from language to language. Most existing approaches to G2P translation only consider grapheme window features to predict phonemes. We recognize that predicting syllable structure may be a simpler task to model and learn than full phoneme prediction. Thus, we enhance the G2P pipeline to insert syllabification into the process.

Our grapheme-to-phoneme translation pipeline incorporating syllable prediction is shown in Fig. 2.

This figure illustrates a number of the pipeline's components: (1) the *aligner* is a CRF trained to predict alignment boundaries that partition the input grapheme string for use as input into a structured prediction component later in the pipeline. (2) The $syllabifier_g$ predicts syllable boundaries for a given input *grapheme* string (hence the g subscript). Using this information and the phonotactical constraints of the language, each grapheme is assigned a syllable role tag of **O**nset, **N**ucleus, or **C**oda (an ONC coding) to indicate its functional role in the syllable. (3) The *pronouncer* is a 1st-order CRF trained to predict phoneme substrings from grapheme substrings and other features. (4) The *graphone LM* is an 8-gram language model of graphones built with Kneser-Ney smoothing. This provides longer range sequence information that the re-ranker can utilize. (5) The $syllabifier_p$ predicts the end of syllable boundaries for a given input phoneme string (hence the p subscript). This provides syllable structure information about the predicted phoneme string to the re-ranker. (6) The re-ranker uses a discriminative model trained on a simple relevance loss function to reorder candidate translations using information from previous stages.

We built our enhancements into the jG2P open-source G2P system, which already contained some of the components in this pipeline. Our description here only focuses on the new components that we built. Existing components are covered in [1].

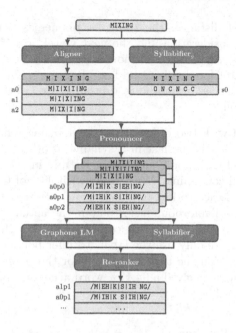

Fig. 2. The grapheme to phoneme translation pipeline with syllabification

3.1   Phoneme Syllabifier

There are a number of challenges in building components to do structured prediction of syllable boundaries. First, we want to use the CMUDict pronunciation dictionary [18] in our experiments, but it does not include syllable boundary information in the training examples. The CELEX2 database [2] contains ~140,000 example words and phoneme transcriptions with syllable boundaries. However, it uses a different phoneme alphabet from CMUDict; is sourced from British English spoken works and thus has different usages of vowel sounds; and it differs in some transcription conventions. For example, the last two syllables in ⟨homicidal⟩ are transcribed in CMUDict as /S AY D AH L/. CELEX2, by contrast, does not voice the last syllable nucleus and transcribes it as /S AY D L/.

We built a CRF to predict the syllable boundaries of the CELEX2 phoneme strings. We tried many permutations of feature functions, CRF orders, and topologies, but settled on a 1st-order linear chain CRF with the following feature functions:

1. Neighboring phonemes: ±3 phonemes before and after the current phoneme.
2. Phoneme class window: a window containing the classes of up to three phonemes before and after the current phoneme. The phoneme classes we used are: monothongs, dipthongs, r-colored vowels, stops, affricates, fricatives, nasals, liquids, and semi-vowels. Unsurprisingly, this feature proved to be useful in capturing the predictive characteristics in a way that generalized well.

3. Neighboring vowel distance: the count of phonemes between the current boundary under consideration and the next vowel or x if there is none. An analogous feature exists for the previous vowel.
4. First/Last: indicator for the first and last phoneme
5. Phoneme class: the class (monothong, dipthong, etc.) of the current phoneme under consideration

We experimented with two different output labeling schemes: (1) coding a 1 for each phoneme that is the last in a syllable, 0 otherwise; (2) coding each phoneme with a label O, N, or C indicating its role in the phoneme based on English phonotactical constraints. We trained with 90% of CELEX2 and tested on 10%. We compared each coding based on *word accuracy*: the % of test words where the predicted syllable boundaries match the actual syllable boundaries from CELEX. Note that in the second coding, even though we are predicting the O, N, or C labels, we only use the labels to infer boundaries in order to do a fair comparison between the two strategies. For the phoneme syllabifier, the binary boundary coding achieved a 94.17% word accuracy, and the ONC coding achieved a 98.33% word accuracy.

3.2   Grapheme Syllabifier

To build a grapheme syllabifier on CMUDict, first we needed to syllabify the phoneme strings in CMUDict, and then use those to infer the grapheme syllabification to build training data. We used the phoneme syllabifier that we built in Sect. 3.1 to predict phoneme boundaries on the CMUDict phoneme strings. CMUDict does not include syllable boundaries but does include stress markings on syllable nuclei, and thus we know the number of syllables in the CMUDict phonetic transcriptions. We used this as an approximate way to gauge the accuracy of applying our CELEX phonetic syllabifier on CMUDict. We define the word syllable count accuracy as the % of predicted words that agree in the count of syllables. Using the CELEX phoneme syllabifier with an ONC output coding, we get a word syllable count accuracy of 99.00% on CMUDict. Interestingly, using the boundary output coding achieves slightly better 99.55% accuracy. Thus, we used the boundary coding version. For each CMUDict word, we generated the top-5 syllabifications and chose the best candidate that agreed in the number of expected syllables.

Next, we used the aligner described in Sect. 3.3 to infer the best 4×3 alignment of graphemes to phonemes. This alignment best describes how adjacent graphemes contribute to one (or more) phonemes. Initially, we imposed a constraint on the alignment to enforce that no alignments cross syllable boundaries in order to simplify systematically inferring boundaries. However, some graphemes in English produce multiple phoneme sounds that cross a syllable boundary. For example, ignoring syllable boundaries, the 2-2 alignment of ⟨casually⟩ is shown in Fig. 3. The u grapheme in ⟨casually⟩ produces /AH W/. The /W/ phoneme is the onset of the third syllable of the word. We abandoned this constraint to the alignment model and instead used the strategy of marking

Fig. 3. 2-2 alignment of ⟨casually⟩

the first grapheme as a syllable boundary when any phoneme in the correspondence crosses a syllable boundary. This results in ⟨casually⟩ being syllabified as ⟨ca.su.a.lly⟩ with an aligned ONC coding O|N|O|N|N|O O|N.

With this now labeled training data, we built a first-order CRF to predict syllable boundaries for grapheme strings. The feature functions used for this CRF are similar to the *aligner* feature functions described in [1]: surrounding graphemes and window features of the *shape* of letters, i.e. whether they are consonants, vowels, or punctuation. We trained on 90% of the CMUDict dataset and tested on 10%. We measured accuracy in two ways: (1) Word Accuracy is the % of words where the predicted syllabification of the graphemes matches expectation exactly (using the inferred syllabification described previously). (2) Word Syllable Count Accuracy is the % of words where the count of syllables in the predicted syllabification matches the count of syllables present in the original CMUDict dataset (based on syllable stress markings). The grapheme syllabifier achieved a Word Accuracy of 91.38% and a Word Syllable Count Accuracy of 94.78%. As a point of comparison, the popular Perl script Lingua-EN-Syllable [7], a simple rule-based approach to counting syllables, achieves a Word Syllable Count Accuracy of 82.84% on the same test dataset.

3.3   Grapheme to Phoneme Alignment of Training Data

The unequal number of symbols in G and P and the many-to-many correspondence of graphemes to phonemes are challenging aspects of the G2P problem. When using a statistical formulation of the G2P problem, there are two aspects to alignment that need to be addressed: (1) at test-time when only presented with g, the system must reconstruct the alignment of g in order to apply structured prediction; (2) training data is often recorded as a word and its pronunciation, $\langle g, p \rangle$. Thus, the training data does not have a delineated correspondence to use in learning.

jG2P addresses the test-time alignment challenge using a separate component depicted in Fig. 2 as the *aligner*. To create aligned training examples, we use an approach similar to that described in [13]: we calculate all possible m by n pairings of grapheme substrings to phoneme substrings, where m is the max length of graphemes in the pair and n is the max length of phonemes in the pair. We model the probability distribution of these pairs and use Expectation Maximization to learn the probability of each graphone.

We improve this m-by-n alignment in a number of ways: (1) we add a penalty term to the joint probability distribution of m-by-n pairs to capture a number of semantic constraints. (2) We add a simple rule-based *acronym pronouncer* to filter out acronyms and other simple patterns that would otherwise add noise to the learned joint distribution.

[10] proposes adding a *city block* penalty to the multi-gram maximum likelihood formulation. We extend this by adding an *epsilon* penalty, *unlikely phoneme combination* penalty, and a *graphone whitelist*. The general penalty is applied as $q'_{g,p} = pow(q_{g,p}, s)$, where $q_{g,p}$ is the maximum likelihood estimate of a grapheme substring g aligned with a phoneme substring p, and s is the penalty term. The penalized q is used during inference to affect the overall sequence probability. Obviously, when $s = 1$ no penalty is applied, but as s increases, the overall sequence probability decreases.

The city block penalty calculates s as the length of the grapheme substring plus the length of the phoneme substring. The intuition for this penalty is that substrings of length n are replacing (at most) n unigram strings. Since the overall sequence probability is calculated as the product of all of the components, longer substrings are artificially preferred due to the fewer multiplications of probabilities. By exponentiating the original probability by the length, it normalizes out this advantage. Using the city block penalty allows us to tractably use a maximum grapheme substring of size 4 and a maximum phoneme size of 3 (i.e. a 4-3 alignment), which improves overall alignment quality. In our experience, without the city block penalty, trying to use a maximum size of grapheme or phoneme substring more than 2 results in poor performance.

Using 4-3 alignments captures most of the natural, local phenomena in English; e.g. the ⟨ough⟩ aligned to /AO/ in ⟨thought⟩. By capturing the real correspondences in the multi-gram alignment, we rely on epsilon transitions less. There are legitimate cases for epsilons, such as unvoiced graphemes (e.g. trailing, silent e), but in our experience with multi-gram alignments, they are present most frequently as the consequence of an artificially short maximum substring size. While doing an error analysis of the city block penalty without special treatment for epsilons, we observed a number of alignments where a multi-gram alignment should've been used instead of an ε alignment. To combat this, we created an *epsilon penalty*. Any graphone with an ε received a penalty factor $s = 2$.

Additionally, in our error analysis, we found some irregular multi-phoneme alignments that we wanted to penalize. We created an *unlikely phoneme combination* heuristic by further penalizing any multi-phoneme substrings that contained both *hard* and *soft* phonemes. We define a hard phoneme as any stop, affricate, fricative (excluding /HH/), nasal, or liquid. We define a soft phoneme as any vowel or semi-vowel. We also exclude any graphones that are *spoken* letters. For example, the graphone k-/K EY/ *pronounces* the letter k. As a graphone, this would be penalized by the heuristic, but some word constructions use pronounced letters, for example ⟨kmart⟩ and ⟨xscribe⟩. Thus, we recognize these special cases, and do not penalize pronounced words in this heuristic.

Lastly, the *graphone whitelist* heuristic is just a simple hand-crafted list of graphones that should not be penalized. In our error analysis, we found a few 2-2 graphones, such as ⟨W H⟩-/HH W/, that were not being picked by the Viterbi walk over the joint distribution. Adding a simple whitelist heuristic is a simple way to avoid the conflicting heuristics.

Figure 4 shows the pseudo-code for the final penalizer; g is the grapheme substring, p is the phoneme substring in the graphone, and q is the maximum likelihood estimate of the graphone probability. This penalizer is applied at optimization time during the Expectation step in the forward-backward algorithm and at test time during the Viterbi walk.

PENALIZER(g, p, q)

1    $s = \text{length}(g) + \text{length}(p)$
2   **if** $(g == \epsilon \text{ or } p == \epsilon)$
3          $s = 2.0$
4   **if** $(\text{IS-NOT-PRONOUNCED-LETTER}(g, p)$
      and $\text{CONTAINS-HARD-AND-SOFT}(p))$
5          $s = s * 1.4$
6   **if** $(\text{IS-WHITELISTED}(g, p))$
7          $s = 1.0$
8   **return** $\text{pow}(q, s)$

Fig. 4. Penalizer pseudo-code incorporating heuristics for English phonotactical constraints

3.4   Incorporating Syllable Structure into Phoneme Prediction

The third stage in jG2P's pipeline is the structured prediction of phoneme substrings from grapheme substrings. A first-order CRF is trained using the aligned examples. We take advantage of the feature engineering flexibility of CRFs and include features that utilize the predicted structure from the syllabifier$_g$. In addition to the letter window and shape window features already present in jG2P, we add new feature functions:

1. Grapheme ONC Code: the grapheme + ONC code indicating if the current grapheme is in the onset, nucleus, or coda of the current syllable.
2. Neighboring ONC Codes: the ONC codes for graphemes ± 2 characters around the current grapheme.
3. Syllable Index: encodes if the grapheme appears in the first, second, etc. syllable.
4. Neighboring Syllable Vowel Support: for each vowel grapheme that appears in the nucleus of a syllable, we emit a feature value that encodes information about the syllable immediately before and after the current syllable. The feature value is the graphemes that make up the nucleus + the first two characters of the onset + the first character of the coda (if any). In this way, the neighboring nucleus can influence the voicing of a syllable.

3.5   Reranking Candidate Phoneme Sequences

The *re-ranker* calculates a total ordering over all candidate phoneme sequences that were produced through the pipeline. We use the existing re-ranker from jG2P, which includes features for the alignment probability, the pronouncer probability, the score from an 8-gram graphone language model, and other features described in [1]. We add one new feature function: the difference between the predicted count of syllables from syllabifier$_g$ and syllabifier$_p$ (run on the candidate phoneme sequence).

4   Experimental Setup and Results

To evaluate the results of our G2P pipeline, we use the CMUDict dataset (v0.7b) of words to pronunciations [18]. This dataset contains ~134k entries of words and pronunciations with many noisy examples. Similar to [13], we test all unique grapheme input sequences and, in the case of multiple, acceptable pronunciations, count a win if the predicted phoneme sequence matches *any* of the accepted phoneme strings.

jG2P uses the MaxEnt classifier and CRF implementations from the open-source library: Mallet [12]. The complete system is trained using a Google Compute Cloud instance with 32 CPUs and 28 GB of RAM. Training the entire pipeline takes 5.5 h, which is currently a total cost under $2.00 USD.

Table 1. Comparison of jG2P * with recent state-of-the-art results. Results with † are known open-source implementations

System	PER (%)	WER (%)
Novak [13]†	5.90	24.80
Wang [17]	5.73	24.89
Kheang [8]	5.60	29.40
Wu [19]	**5.50**	23.40
Rao [15]	9.10	**21.30**
Ash [1]†	6.00	25.20
jG2P *† Sect. 3	5.69	24.08

The two most frequently used metrics for measuring G2P performance are phoneme error rate (PER) and word error rate (WER). PER is the % of phonemes predicted incorrectly, and WER is the % of predicted phoneme strings with at least one incorrect phoneme. Therefore, for both WER and PER, lower scores are better. Table 1 compares the results of our improved jG2P implementation, labeled jG2P*, to a few recent publications. All of these publications use the CMUDict dataset, but in some cases we cannot verify if the author used the exact same train/test split of data.

To evaluate the relative impact of our improvements, we ran the system in three different configurations: (1) jG2P without our improvements, (2) jG2P with only the alignment improvements (no syllable features), (3) jG2P with only syllable features (no alignment improvements), and (4) jG2P with all improvements described in Sect. 3. The results of this comparative run are shown in Table 2.

Table 2. Comparison of overall performance with different features turned off

System	PER (%)	WER (%)
without improvements	6.09	25.15
with only alignment Sect. 3.3	5.93	24.66
with only syllable Sect. 3.2	6.13	24.99
with all improvements	**5.69**	**24.08**

5   Discussion

The results in the previous section demonstrate that incorporating syllable structure and improving the alignment of training data leads to a modest improvement in translation accuracy. The CMUDict dataset is a good benchmark, because it is known to contain many irregularities and is viewed as 'hard' [6]. Phonetisaurus [13] reports a similar WER and PER but uses an older version of the CMUDict dataset with a different cross-validation split of data. Running Phonetisaurus on our exact split of data achieves a 26.4% WER. Our implementation achieves 24.1%, an 8.5% improvement. To determine if the difference is meaningful, we ran five random splits of the data and compared the results. A paired, two-tailed Student-t hypothesis test gives a p-value = .01762, indicating a statistically significant difference ($p < .05$) in the average error rates. Our improvements do not beat the best published WER of 21.3% [15]. However, to the best of our knowledge, their implementation is not available as an open-source toolkit. We cannot compare their result to ours across multiple random splits.

Our approach to incorporating syllable structure is different than the previous setup described in [17]. They construct a WFST as the union of a lattice created by a graphone language model and a lattice from a CRF model, using a weighted average of the two model scores as edge weights. Our approach avoids the hyper-parameter to control the weighted average and incorporates richer syllable features leading to improved results as shown in Table 1.

The pipeline produces high quality top-k results due to the re-ranker component. While only 75.8% of the correct answers are predicted in the top ranked spot in the results, that increases to 92.1% if you consider the top-5 results as acceptable for a match. High quality top-k results are important for many applications, such as phonetic similarity search of personal names.

We recognize that a pipeline solution such as ours will suffer from propagating errors in early stages. To combat this problem, we produce multiple candidates at each step and flow each down the pipeline individually. In the final stage, the re-ranker re-orders all candidates using information from previous stages. This simplifies each component, allowing us to use efficient convex optimization methods to train.

In feature engineering, we tried many variations of feature functions, incorporating syllable information. We rejected a number of feature functions such as encoding the relative position of the grapheme in the syllable as in [17]. We also rejected a feature function that encoded the position of the current syllable in the word (e.g. first, last, before-last).

We experimented with a few different approaches to coding syllable prediction. As described in Sect. 3.1, training the phoneme syllabifier on CELEX2 to emit O,N,C labels improved performance of that component. This makes sense on phoneme strings as the linear chain CRF can take advantage of this predicted structure. For the grapheme syllabifier, using an O,N,C coding decreased performance significantly for a few reasons: (1) all of the ambiguities that make vowel grapheme to vowel phoneme prediction hard also make precise identification of the syllable nucleus hard. (2) reconstructing syllable breaks from O,N,C codes on graphemes is ambiguous when there are consecutive vowels with N-ucleus codes. These vowels might contribute to the same vowel phoneme or might be voiced as two syllables with no coda/onset between them (e.g. the /IY EY/ in ⟨alleviate⟩). To avoid these problems, we use a binary coding to indicate syllable boundaries from the grapheme syllabifier.

6   Conclusion

In this paper, we improve grapheme to phoneme translation by incorporating syllable structure information into a sophisticated pipeline solution and improving the alignment of training data for use in machine learning solutions to G2P. Our improvements are available at http://bit.ly/83yysKL as part of the open-source library, jG2P. Our solution does not beat the best published state of the art but does provide the best Word Accuracy among the available open-source G2P toolkits.

References

1. Ash, S., Lin, D.: Grapheme to phoneme translation using conditional random fields with re-ranking. In: Sojka, P., Horák, A., Kopeček, I., Pala, K. (eds.) TSD 2016. LNCS, vol. 9924, pp. 314–325. Springer, Cham (2016). doi:10.1007/978-3-319-45510-5_36
2. Baayen, R.H., Piepenbrock, R., Gulikers, L.: Celex2. Linguistic Data Consortium, Philadelphia (1996)
3. Bisani, M., Ney, H.: Joint-sequence models for grapheme-to-phoneme conversion. Speech Commun. 50(5), 434–451 (2008)

4. Deligne, S., Yvon, F., Bimbot, F.: Variable-length sequence matching for phonetic transcription using joint multigrams. In: 4th European Conference on Speech Communication and Technology (1995)
5. Demberg, V., Schmid, H., Möhler, G.: Phonological constraints and morphological preprocessing for grapheme-to-phoneme conversion. In: Association for Computational Linguistics, vol. 45, p. 96 (2007)
6. Eger, S.: Do we need bigram alignment models? On the effect of alignment quality on transduction accuracy in G2P. In: Proceedings of EMNLP, vol. 18, pp. 127–136 (2015)
7. Greg Fast. Lingua-en-syllable (1999). http://search.cpan.org/gregfast/Lingua-EN-Syllable-0.251
8. Kheang, S., Katsurada, K., Iribe, Y., Nitta, T.: Solving the phoneme conflict in grapheme-to-phoneme conversion using a two-stage neural network-based approach. IEICE Trans. Inform. Syst. **97**(4), 901–910 (2014)
9. Dennis, H.: Klatt. Review of the arpa speech understanding project. J. Acoust. Soc. Am. **62**(6), 1345–1366 (1977)
10. Kubo, K., Kawanami, H., Saruwatari, H., Shikano, K.: Unconstrained many-to-many alignment for automatic pronunciation annotation. In: Proceedings of the APSIPA, pp. 1–4 (2011)
11. Lafferty, J., McCallum, A., Pereira, F.: Conditional random fields: Probabilistic models for segmenting and labeling sequence data, pp. 282–289 (2001)
12. McCallum, A.K.: Mallet: A machine learning for language toolkit (2002)
13. Novak, J.R., Minematsu, N., Hirose, K.: WFST-based grapheme-to-phoneme conversion: open source tools for alignment, model-building and decoding. In: 10th International Workshop on Finite State Methods and Natural Language Processing, p. 45 (2012)
14. Novak, J.R., Minematsu, N., Hirose, K., Hori, C., Kashioka, H., Dixon, P.R.: Improving WFST-based G2P conversion with alignment constraints and RNNLM n-best rescoring. In: Interspeech (2012)
15. Rao, K., Peng, F., Sak, H., Beaufays, F.: Grapheme-to-phoneme conversion using long short-term memory recurrent neural networks. In: IEEE International Conference on Acoustics, Speech, and Signal Processing (ICASSP) (2015)
16. Wang, D., King, S.: Letter-to-sound pronunciation prediction using conditional random fields. IEEE Sig. Process. Lett. **18**(2), 122–125 (2011)
17. Wang, X., Sim, K.C.: Integrating conditional random fields and joint multi-gram model with syllabic features for grapheme-to-phone conversion. In: Interspeech, pp. 2321–2325 (2013)
18. Weide, R.: The CMU pronunciation dictionary, release 0.7a (2014)
19. Wu, K., Allauzen, C., Hall, K., Riley, M., Roark, B.: Encoding linear models as weighted finite-state transducers. In: Interspeech (2014)

Hybrid Conceptual and Statistical Measure for Semantic Textual Similarity Evaluation

Alejandro Tarafa Guzmán and Ademar Ferreira[✉]

Polytechnic School of the University of São Paulo, Av. Prof. Luciano Gualberto,
3/380, São Paulo, SP 05508-900, Brazil
alejandro.tarafa@usp.br, ademar@lac.usp.br
http://www.poli.usp.br/

Abstract. We propose in this paper an improved methodology to evaluate semantic textual similarity between two sentences. Our model associates semantic and statistical information by means of a chunking parser in such a way that the combination is inherently integrated to the overall system. Evaluation results with SemEval 2016 sentence data sets are encouraging.

Keywords: Semantic textual similarity · Chunking parser · Semantic similarity · N-gram similarity · WordNet

1 Introduction

Semantic similarity evaluates the degree of semantic equivalence between two sentences. In natural language processing (NLP) applications, such as information retrieval and summarization, determining if two text fragments have similar meaning is of great importance. Ideally, we would like that a computational algorithm might perform such a similarity evaluation automatically and as closely as possible to that of a human. Corresponding tasks in NLP are referred to as semantic textual similarity (STS) tasks [2].

Methods used to resolve STS tasks normally either use semantic knowledge, as incorporated, for example, in WordNet, or statistics and text corpora, like in n-gram based methods. With respect to corpus-based techniques, Hulth, however, [9], and [8], have asserted that computational linguistics would profit from introducing usage of language properties in natural language processing, instead of using purely statistical methods. In consonance with this principle, features like linguistic knowledge and chunking are used in this work as a means to positively influence STS tasks. We propose in this paper a methodology to associate both types of information, semantic and statistical, in such a way that the combination is inherently integrated to the overall system. In this way, our aim is to investigate whether chunking, which introduces structured linguistic knowledge, combined with statistical similarity approaches, will provide a better framework for the evaluation of Sematic Textual Similarity.

© Springer International Publishing AG 2017
J.F. Quesada et al. (Eds.): FETLT 2016, LNAI 10341, pp. 148–157, 2017.
https://doi.org/10.1007/978-3-319-69365-1_12

A key feature of our model is inspired by Abney [1], who has remarked that, humans effectively use parsing by chunks in their use of language, This idea can be utilized to better resolve NLP tasks such as STS evaluation. In fact, while reading aloud a passage for the first time, we might hesitate on how to divide it to stress the right prosodic or patterns for intonation purposes. This hesitation only means that we are searching out, "on-line", the correct parsing of that sentence onto appropriate chunks. This intuition is included in our model as extraction of partial syntactic structures, the types of phrases, contained in the sentences. We use these noun, verbal, etc. phrases as the units of intermediate semantic analysis.

In the next section a brief overview is given on recent related work on STS studies. The details of our evaluation system are presented in Sect. 3, and Sect. 4 presents experimental results. Section 5 is a brief discussion of the results, and a conclusion is given in the last section.

2   Related Work

In this section we review related work on STS evaluation measures relevant to the approach in this paper. These measures estimate the degree of semantic similarity between two textual segments, also said text snippets, like sentences or paragraphs. Previous studies on STS evaluation methods concentrated mostly on either large texts or individual words. The later tendency of examining the similarity between short text passages has been mainly motivated by applications such as Question Answering and Information Retrieval, to data available on the Web. In these instances what is at stake is the similarity at semantic level. Since the matching of words is not enough for solving this problem, the structure of the text passage must be accounted for [11]. Correspondingly, the way of considering similarity in STS evaluation measures has attempted to evolve from lexical matching or word semantic similarity to similarity at the text (sentence) semantic level. The achievements on this struggle are promising but there is still a long way to satisfaction.

Up to 2006, there were very few publications on STS measures for very short texts [10], while there were several methods for evaluating semantic similarity of words. Ideally, we would search for a model that could automatically evaluate the similarity between two texts at semantic level. This is, however, a difficult problem, since it should deal not only with the words, but also with the inter-structure between both texts [7].

Composing lexical matching metrics with other techniques became the route chosen by several authors since then. In practice, this takes the form of a combination of word-to-word similarity metrics into a text-to-text semantic similarity metric, as in the algorithm proposed by [7]. They combine a knowledge-based measure, for semantics, calculated using a thesaurus like WordNet, with a corpus-based measure, that uses statistical distributional information from large corpora, to determine the inverse document frequency associated with a word. Despite some improvement over lexical only matching metrics, their method still uses a bag-of-words approach, and as such, does not take into account structural and syntactical information to evaluate semantic similarity.

In this same trend, Buscaldi et al. [5] combined a n-gram based technique with a conceptual similarity measure, based on WordNet, to compose the final score by the geometric mean between the two results to measure the similarity between text fragments. Due to the use of n-grams, that afford some structural similarity insight, their combined method offered some improvement on STS evaluation, as indicated by one of their rankings in the SemEval 2012 contest [2].

The advent of the SemEval competitions on STS tasks, starting in 2012, can be considered a watershed to the task of semantic textual similarity evaluation. To evaluate STS systems, SemEval 2012 [2], and also the following years up to 2016, have proposed pilot contests in which participants should examine the degree of semantic equivalence between two sentences. Several systems were proposed to SemEval and evaluated against test sets, using the Pearson correlation coefficient in relation to a gold standard human semantic evaluation. Participating systems have taken a variety of approaches to solve STS. However, we can say that all these techniques might be classified in two basic trends, already present in SemEval 2012. One of them uses a linguistically principled way, relying on various semantic and distributional properties of texts, and the other one is based on machine learning regression models that combine large sets of features. Our model belongs to the first category. For examples of works in these categories presented to SemEval 2016, see [3]. Interestingly, use of deep learning-based and feature-based models have become current thanks to the availability of sentence data sets of SemEval together with corresponding gold standard evaluations for training.

3   Description and Operation of the System

3.1   Overview of the Model

The system we use to evaluate the semantic similarity between two sentences is illustrated in Fig. 1. It is composed of a semantic subsystem and a n-gram subsystem, interconnected through a sentence approximation module, which is central to our method and is responsible for its novelty, as will be elaborated further on.

In summarization and information retrieval, noun phrases (NPs) are a fundamental concept. If rightly extracted, NPs allow a first understanding of a sentence or text [6], similarly to a human when reading it. In this work we use a probabilistic partial parser, called a chunker (Fig. 1), to identify the linguistic structures in the sequence of tokens categorized in the parts-of-speech tagging phase. Extracted parts of the tagged sequences, according to a grammar, constitute the NPs. Verbal phrases (VPs) as well as PVs, phrasal verbs (idiomatic expressions), are also extracted. The concepts (words) within such structures are then evaluated semantically using WordNet. If any two words from each sentence are semantically similar, one of these words is approximated, that is, replaced by the other, resulting in equal words in the two sentences. These modified sentences will then show an increased number of exact matches, favoring a better n-gram similarity evaluation. This is in brief the novel principle used by our semantic similarity evaluation system.

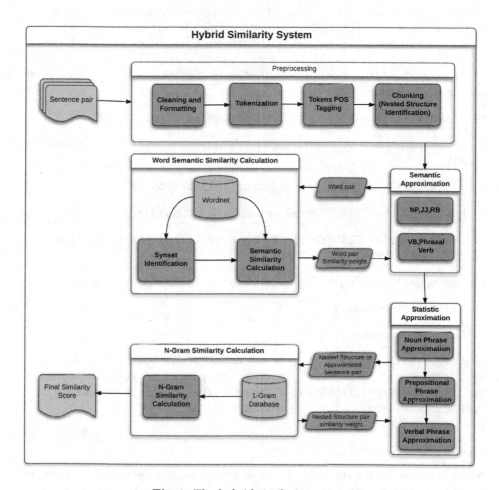

Fig. 1. The hybrid similarity system

3.2   System Implementation and Operation Fig. 1

The chunker. The input to the system is a sentence pair. Tokenization and part-of-speech tagging are implemented by using the Python NLTK - Natural Language Toolkit library[1], in which we have included the Stanford tagger[2] [12].

---

[1] http://www.nltk.org.
[2] http://nlp.stanford.edu/software/tagger.shtml.

A chunk parser analyzes the sequence of categorized tokens and identifies the syntactic structures defined in a grammar. The corresponding word pairs of nouns, adjectives, adverbs, verbs and phrasal verbs in the two sentences are passed to the semantic or conceptual similarity module. According to Abney [1], "a simple context-free grammar is quite adequate to describe the structure of chunks". Correspondingly, in this preliminary study, our chunker uses a simple grammar defined in NLTK. This grammar, which is certainly incomplete, but serves our purpose, is represented by the following regular expressions bellow.

Noun phrases: A determiner or an adjective or any type of noun, which must appear at least once:

```
NP: {<PDT|DT|JJ|NN.*>+}   # Chunk sequences of DT, JJ, NN.
```

Prepositional phrases: A preposition or subordinating conjunction followed by an NP:

```
PP: {<IN><NP>}  # Chunk prepositions followed by NP.
```

Verbal phrases: Any verb, followed by an NP or PP or a clause:

```
VP: {<VB.*><NP|PP|CLAUSE>+$}  # Chunk verbs and their arguments
CLAUSE: {<NP><VP>}  # Chunk NP, VP
```

Phrasal verb: Any verb, possibly followed by a NP, followed by an adverb:

```
PV: {<VB.*><NP>?<RB>?}
```

Complete grammar:

```
NP: {<PDT|DT|JJ|NN.*>+}        # Chunk sequences of DT, JJ, NN
PP: {<IN><NP>}                 # Chunk prepositions followed by NP
VP: {<VB.*><NP|PP|CLAUSE>+$}   # Chunk verbs and their arguments
CLAUSE: {<NP><VP>}             # Chunk NP, VP
PV: {<VB.*><NP>?<RB>?}
```

(Simple grammar used)

Semantic similarity module. The semantic similarity between two concepts is a relative measure that evaluates how close in meaning they are in the hierarchy of synsets (hierarchical synonym lists) in WordNet. In this module two synsets S1 and S2 are obtained from WordNet, in association with two words w1 and w2, syntactically categorized, received from the Approximation module. The semantic similarity between w1 and w2 is the maximum similarity value as calculated by an algorithm using the synsets S1 and S2. Our calculation uses the semantic measure defined by [13].

If the corresponding NP or VP phrase has only one word, in this case a noun or a verb respectively, then the semantic similarity measure is directly used for approximation purpose. This means that if the obtained similarity between w1 and w2 is greater than a threshold (we used 0.8), then w1 will replace w2 (or vice versa). The transitive property is used: If a word w1 is similar to a word w2 and w2 is similar to w3, then w1 is similar to w3 for replacement purpose. The case of phrases with two or more words is considered statistically, as will be described.

Notice that, while WordNet only considers words lexically and individually, our use of it achieves a higher quality of semantic similarity evaluation, since words evaluated as maximally similar turn out to belong to corresponding NP and VP phrases in both sentences, preserving chunking pertinence, as to similarity consideration.

The n-gram similarity module. The n-gram similarity is based on the principle that two sentences are semantically similar if they share a sequence of non-empty terms, and the longest this sequence, the greater the similarity. The algorithm we used to calculate the n-gram similarity is the same as the one proposed by Buscaldi [4,5], that is, the Clustered Keywords Positional Distance (CKPD) model. The similarity of the n-grams in different types of phrases is evaluated in the n-grams similarity calculation module, starting with noun phrases, then prepositional, and verbal phrases. In case of similarity greater than 0.7, corresponding phrases are approximated, with the larger one replacing the smaller one. This is in order to maximize the statistical measure, evaluated in terms of symbols by the n-gram module used. The transitivity property also applies.

If phrases extracted by the chunker have two or more words in either sentence, then corresponding bi-grams, tri-grams, etc. will be evaluated statistically for purposes of approximation. After all n-grams have been evaluated and all phrases approximated, the two original sentences, now maximally approximated, are finally n-gram- evaluated for the global semantic textual similarity (see Fig. 1).

3.3   Example of STS Evaluation

To better visualize the operation of the whole process of our model, we present the STS evaluation of a pair of simple sentences, A and B, taken from SemEval 2013 HDL data set No. 729.

Sentences A and B:

A: Newark mayor rescues neighbor from burning house

B: Newark mayor saves neighbor from fire

Sentence tokenization and tagging:

A: [(u'newark', u'NN'), (u'mayor', u'NN'), (u'rescues', u'VBZ'), (u'neighbor', u'NN'), (u'from', u'IN'), (u'burning', u'NN'), (u'house', u'NN')]

B: [(u'newark', u'NN'), (u'mayor', u'NN'), (u'saves', u'VBZ'), (u'neighbor', u'NN'), (u'from', u'IN'), (u'fire', u'NN')]

Syntactic trees (Figs. 2 and 3)

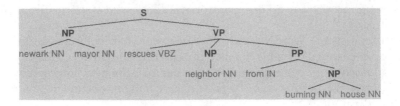

Fig. 2. Syntactic tree corresponding to sentence A

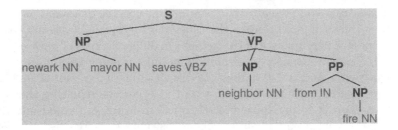

Fig. 3. Syntactic tree corresponding to sentence B

Corresponding NPs, VPs, PPs:

A:

1. NPs:
   - newark_NN mayor_NN
   - neighbor_NN
   - burning_NN house_NN
2. PPs:
   - from_IN burning_NN house_NN
3. VPs:
   - rescues_VBZ neighbor_NN from_IN burning_NN house_NN

B:

1. NPs:
   - newark_NN mayor_NN
   - neighbor_NN
   - fire_NN
2. PPs:
   - from_IN fire_NN
3. VPs:
   - saves_VBZ neighbor_NN from_IN fire_NN

A replacement example, with similarity degree (semantic threshold: 0.8, N-Grams threshold: 0.6):

Semantic similarity:

1. NPs:
   - Replace noun, fire_NN by burning_NN *similarity 0.94*
   - NP: fire_NN *-turns-*➤ burning_NN
   - PP: from_IN fire_NN *-turns-*➤ from burning_NN
2. VPs:
   - Replace verb, save_VBZ by rescues_VBZ *similarity 0.8*
   - saves_VBZ neighbor_NN from_IN burning_NN *-turns-*➤ rescues_VBZ neighbor_NN from_IN burning_NN

Ngrams similarity:

1. PPs:
   - Replace PP, from_IN burning_NN house_NN by from_IN burning_NN *similarity 0.67*
2. VPs:
   - Replace VP, rescues_VBZ neighbor_NN from_IN burning_NN by rescues_VBZ neighbor_NN from_IN burning_NN(note that after replacement the PP the VPs are identical) *similarity 1.0*

Approximated sentences:

A: newark mayor rescues neighbor from burning

B: newark mayor rescues neighbor from burning

Final similarity evaluation: 1.0

Notice that this example is just for illustrative purpose. The results of the STS evaluation are significant only if applied to a large number of sentences, as will be the case in the experimental results section.

4   Preliminary Experimental Results

In order to test our STS evaluation system, we have run it with the sets of sentences from SemEval 2016 Task 1, and compared our results with those obtained by some of the competitors (see Table 1). Our objective here is not competition, but just to assess the current possibilities of our model in comparison to state-of-the-art systems.

Observing the rankings in the SemEval 2016 Task 1 (Agirre2016) we see that our result for the post-editing dataset, 0.82277, is better than the results of the second and fifth places, respectively 0.82085 for the UWB team, and, 0.80939 for the UMB team [3]. Besides, we remark that our result on the answer - answer dataset was higher than the one obtained by the Ricoh team, best placed on the post-editing data. However, our score for the question - question evaluation set, the most difficult one according to the organizers of SemEval 2016, is bellow average. But all systems have struggled on this data set [3].

Table 1. Pearson coefficient results obtained by our model on datasets from SemEval 2016.

Results for SemEval 2016 Task 1:				
Ans.-Ans.	HDL	Plagiarism	Postediting	Ques-Ques
0,54755	0,61691	0,73621	0,82277	0.32652

5   Discussion

The fact that all teams classified variously on different datasets only shows that there is much to learn before a general good system is obtained. We believe our system obtained some good preliminary results, in the above comparison, because of its higher quality in terms of combining, in an integrated way through a chunking parser, linguistic knowledge of syntactic structures with the statistical evaluation of n-gram measure. Since our system is not optimized as to preprocessing, we believe better results are achievable when this will be done. Regarding the values used for thresholds in the similarity evaluations, we observe that the numerical values used are a priori first guesses, to run the model on the datasets. More appropriate values could be determined by experimental calibration, somewhat dependent on the dataset. Also, the values for thresholds could be used to favor similarity (recall), or precision, to better avoid mismatches.

6   Conclusion and Future Work

We have observed that the scores obtained by our system are dependent on the sentence data set, as it should be expected, but in general they keep a fair correlation with the gold standard evaluation. This encourages us on proceeding to ameliorate our STS evaluation system. As future work to improve our system, we envisage using a grammar with more rules, in order to consider phrases with more complex syntactic structures.

Acknowledgment. The authors would like to thank the reviewers for their comments and suggestions on the first draft.

References

1. Abney, S., Abney, S.P.: Parsing by chunks. In: Berwick, R.C., et al. (eds.) Principle-Based Parsing: Computation and Psycholinguistics, pp. 257–278. Kluwer Academic Publishers (1991)
2. Agirre, E., Cer, D., Diab, M., González - Agirre, A.: SemEval 2012 Task 6: a pilot on semantic textual similarity. In: 1st Joint Conference on Lexical and Computational Semantics, pp. 385–393. ACL, Montreal (2012)
3. Agirre, E., Banea, C., Cer, D., Diab, M., Gonzalez-Agirre, A., Mihalcea, R., Rigau, G., Wiebe, J.: SemEval-2016 Task 1: semantic textual similarity, monolingual and cross-lingual evaluation. In: 10th International Workshop on Semantic Evaluation, pp. 509–523. ACL, San Diego (2016)

4. Buscaldi, D., Rosso, P., Gomez-Soriano, J.M., Sanchis, E.: Answering questions with an n-gram based passage retrieval engine. J. Intel. Inf. Syst. **34**, 113–134 (2010)
5. Buscaldi, D., Tournier, R., Aussenac-Gilles, N., Mothe, J.: IRIT: textual similarity combining conceptual similarity with an N-gram comparison method. In: 1st Joint Conference on Lexical and Computational Semantics, pp. 552–556. ACL, Montreal (2012)
6. Chen, K.-H., Chen, H.-H.: Extracting noun phrases from large-scale texts: a hybrid approach and its automatic evaluation. In: 32nd Annual Meeting of the Association for Computational Linguistics, pp. 234–241. ACL, Las Cruces (1994)
7. Corley, C., Mihalcea, R.: Measuring the semantic similarity of texts. In: Workshop on Empirical Modeling of Semantic Equivalence and Entailment, pp. 13–18. ACL, Ann Harbor (2005)
8. Hulth, A., Megyesi, B.B.: A study on automatically extracted keywords in text categorization. In: 21st International Conference on Computational Linguistics, pp. 537–544. ACL, Sydney (2006)
9. Hulth, A.: Improved automatic keyword extraction given more linguistic knowledge. In: EMNLP Conference on Empirical Methods in Natural Language processing, pp. 216–223. ACL, Stroudsburg (2003)
10. Li, Y., McLean, D., Bandar, Z.A., O'Shea, J.D., Crockett, K.: Sentence similarity based on semantic nets and corpus statistics. IEEE Trans. Knowl. Data Eng. **18**, 1138–1150 (2006)
11. Mihalcea, R., Corley, C., Strapparava, C.: Corpus-based and knowledge-based measures of text semantic similarity. In: Proceedings of the American Association for Artificial Intelligence, pp. 775–780. Boston (2006)
12. Toutanova, K., Klein, D., Manning, C., Morgan, W., Rafferty, A., Galley, M.: Stanford log-linear part-of-speech tagger (2000)
13. Wu, Z., Palmer, M.: Verbs semantics and lexical selection. In: 32nd Annual Meeting of the Association for Computational Linguistics, pp. 133–138. ACL, Stroudsburg (1994)

General Representation Model
for Text Similarity

Fernando Giner[(✉)] and Enrique Amigó[(✉)]

National Distance University, UNED, C/Juan del Rosal 16, Madrid, Spain
fginer3@alumno.uned.es, enrique@lsi.uned.es
http://www.nlp.uned.es

Abstract. Text similarity is a central issue in multiple information access tasks. General speaking, most of existing similarity models focus on a particular kind of text features such as words, n-grams, or linguistic features or distributional semantics units. In this paper, we introduce a general theoretical model for integrating multiple sources in the text feature representation called **F**eature **P**rojection **I**nformation model. The proposed model allows us to integrate traditional features such as words with other sources such as the output of classifiers over different categories or distributional semantics information. The theoretical analysis shows that traditional approaches can be seen as particularizations of the model. Our first empirical results support the idea that additional features in the representation step outperform the predictive power of similarity measures.

Keywords: Enrichment · Features · Similarity · Text representation

1 Introduction

Computing textual similarity is a central issue in information access tasks such as Information Retrieval, Document Clustering, Textual Entailment and so on. Similarity measures require a representation step in which texts are characterized as a set of features such as words, stems, semantic senses, n-grams, named entities, etc. Sharing words is an evidence of similarity. However, we can consider other text features. For instance, sharing a certain kind of named entities, or belonging to the same category according to a classifier (i.e. *motor*, *news* or a certain polarity value) or to the same cluster according to a certain clustering system are also evidences of similarity.

However, in most cases, similarity measures are applied over a single kind of features. The first reason is that it would be necessary to fix the relative weight of heterogeneous features. For instance, what is the relevance of sharing the same document category regarding sharing a certain word or n-gram? Another reason is that adding information increase the noise. That is, the most relevant features can be eclipsed by non informative features.

In this paper, we define a general theoretical framework called **F**eature **P**rojection **I**nformation model (FPI) that integrates heterogeneous features in the

© Springer International Publishing AG 2017
J.F. Quesada et al. (Eds.): FETLT 2016, LNAI 10341, pp. 158–169, 2017.
https://doi.org/10.1007/978-3-319-69365-1_13

representation step. The model is grounded on the concepts of *abstract feature*, *feature projection* and *information quantity*. From a theoretical point of view, an important strength is that depending on the abstract feature in consideration, the projection and statistical assumptions, FPI derives into different traditional representation models.

In our experiments, we check empirically the hypothesis that applying FPI, adding heterogeneous features increases the effectiveness of the similarity computation. This result can open the door to integrate diverse features in a coherent text representation for similarity computation. We evaluate FPI by integrating words and text classification outputs associated to different category sets into the same representation scheme. The applied corpus is the Replab [1] data set, in which tweets potentially related with certain companies are annotated for reputational analysis purposes.

2   Related Work

A useful survey on text similarity measures can be found in [4]. We summarize here the most relevant research lines in this area. In most traditional similarity models, texts are represented as bag of words (BoW), or n-grams. The similarity is computed according to metric space distances (i.e. cosine, euclidean distance) or set based measures (i.e. Jaccard, Dice, etc.). In order to reward informative (specific) words or n-grams, the representation step can include a weighting process such as *Inverse Document Frequency* (IDF) or Information Quantity ($-log(P(word))$). Linguistic units at higher levels such as Named Entities, chunks, phrases or syntactic structures have been also applied for representing texts when estimating similarity [3,7].

The lack of these representation models is that they are not enough when texts use different words to say the same things. Briefly, we can categorize the solutions for this into: (i) ontology based approaches, in which words are replaced by nodes in certain concept data base such as Wordnet or Wikipedia, and (ii) distributional semantics based approaches like Latent Semantic Indexing [2] or word embeddings in which original words are replaced by related words according to coocurrence statistics in a corpus [12].

On the other hand, there exist supervised approaches for similarity, Liu et al. [9] categorized these approaches in two sets. In the first one, distance metrics are learned from the training data associated with explicit class labels. This is the case of Linear Discriminant Analysis or Neighbourhood Components Analysis, among others. The second category corresponds with weakly supervised learning approaches which try to learn distance metrics with pairwise constraints, or known as side information. This includes Relevant Component Analysis, Discriminative Component Analysis or Information-Theoretic Metric Learning. A common characteristic of all these approaches is that the training similarity data must reflect directly the similarity criterion that we want to estimate. That is, they do not allow to integrate similarity training data focused on different text aspects.

In summary, the challenge tackled in this article is that, although all these methods add complementary information about texts, they are applied independently. As far as we know there not exists a general theoretical framework to integrate all this information in a robust manner for text representation and similarity computation.

3   The Feature Projection Information Model (FPI)

Briefly, the FPI model consists of characterizing texts as the projection of abstract features. For instance, the appearance of words, the coocurrence with other words in a text corpora or the system output of a text classifier are examples of abstract feature projections. The main barrier when aggregating characteristics from different nature is the weighting process. We need to know to what extent a projection must have effect in the similarity computation. According to the Tversky's observation in cognitive scenarios [13], specific features have more effect than general features; for instance, it is well known that the goodness of IDF weighting approaches come from the fact that overlap in rare words has an special effect when comparing or characterizing texts. The specificity of features can be formalized in terms of *Information Quantity* $(-log(P(feature)))$. According to this, we weight the projection from heterogeneous features in terms of Information Quantity. In addition to state the relative weight of features, the Information Quantity allows us to fix a threshold that discards noisy information from heterogeneous features.

Formally, we first decompose a text in basic units that will be called *Linguistic Units*:

Definition 1. *A linguistic unit, u, is the atomic piece in which texts can be decomposed, that is, a text, T, is defined as a set of linguistic units*

$$T = \{u_1..u_n\}.$$

In this model, the text characterization or representation is the process of measuring the relatedness between abstract features and linguistic units.

Definition 2. *An abstract feature, σ, is a characteristic which can be associated with a single text. We will denote the set of abstract features by $\mathcal{F}$.*

For instance, words, n-grams, named entities or word senses can be related to a certain extent with the text to be represented. We can also specify abstract features related to supervised data; for instance, we could have a corpus of texts talking about *motor* which could help us to infer the presence of the abstract feature *Motor* in a certain text.

In addition, we need some mechanism to estimate the proximity or appearance of an abstract feature in a text, this is the *projection*.

Definition 3. *Given an abstract feature, $\sigma \in \mathcal{F}$, a projection function of the feature, f_σ, is a function which estimates the presence of the abstract feature in texts.*

$$f_\sigma : \Omega \longrightarrow \mathbb{R}$$
$$\mathcal{T} \rightsquigarrow f_\sigma(\mathcal{T})$$

This projection can be modeled in different ways. For instance it could be the occurrence or the frequency of a word in a text, or the likelihood returned by a classification system for a single text and class.

The projection function gives us a *score* or a value for each text, $\mathcal{T} \in \Omega$, and each feature, σ. This allows us to consider the probability of finding a text with a projection larger than a certain value. This is the criterion in the model to normalize the weight of feature projections:

Definition 4. *The weight of a projection function of an abstract feature, σ, in a text, $\mathcal{T}$, is the Information Quantity of finding another text with a projection larger than $f_\sigma(\mathcal{T})$ in a text corpus Ω.*

$$\mathcal{I}(f_\sigma(\mathcal{T})) = log \left(\frac{1}{P_{\mathcal{T}' \in \Omega}(f_\sigma(\mathcal{T}') \geq f_\sigma(\mathcal{T}))} \right).$$

Assuming independence across linguistic units in $\mathcal{T}$, we can formalize the projection of an abstract feature into a text as:

$$\mathcal{I}(f_\sigma(\mathcal{T})) \;\; = \;\; \sum_{u \in \mathcal{T}} \mathcal{I}(f_\sigma(u)) \;\; = \;\; \sum_{u \in \mathcal{T}} log \left(\frac{1}{P_{u' \in \Omega}(f_\sigma(u') \geq f_\sigma(u))} \right). \quad (1)$$

Some abstract features only add noise in the similarity computation, for instance, stopwords or classes with low weight in the text. The model allows us to apply a common Information Quantity threshold in order to discard low informative features in a text.

If we assume independence across features, then we can compute the Information Quantity of a single text as:

$$\mathcal{I}(\mathcal{T}) = \sum_{\sigma \in \mathcal{F}} \mathcal{I}(f_\sigma(\mathcal{T})). \quad (2)$$

In order to apply traditional similarity measures, we need to define the intersection and union of texts. In concordance with previous work [5] we compute the Information Quantity of the union and intersection of texts in terms of minimum and maximum values[1]:

---

[1] Notice that minimum and maximum operators are the standard joining and intersection operators for multisets.

Definition 5. *The information quantity of the intersection and the union of two texts, $\mathcal{T}$ and $\mathcal{T}'$, in an abstract feature, σ, is the minimum and maximum projection for both texts, respectively:*

$$\mathcal{I}\big(f_\sigma\left(\mathcal{T}\cap\mathcal{T}'\right)\big) = min\Big(\mathcal{I}\big(f_\sigma(\mathcal{T})\big),\mathcal{I}\big(f_\sigma(\mathcal{T}')\big)\Big).$$

$$\mathcal{I}\big(f_\sigma\left(\mathcal{T}\cup\mathcal{T}'\right)\big) = max\Big(\mathcal{I}\big(f_\sigma(\mathcal{T})\big),\mathcal{I}\big(f_\sigma(\mathcal{T}')\big)\Big).$$

We can extend this to define the intersection and the union over every feature in a natural way, as the intersection and the union of each feature in each text.

$$\mathcal{I}\left(\mathcal{T}\cap\mathcal{T}'\right) = \sum_{\sigma\in\mathcal{F}}\mathcal{I}\big(f_\sigma(\mathcal{T}\cap\mathcal{T}')\big) \ \wedge \ \mathcal{I}\left(\mathcal{T}\cup\mathcal{T}'\right) = \sum_{\sigma\in\mathcal{F}}\mathcal{I}\big(f_\sigma(\mathcal{T}\cup\mathcal{T}')\big).$$

In brief, the proposed representation model consists of: (i) computing the projection of each feature in the text, (ii) computing the Information Quantity of each projection, (iii) discarding projections under a certain information quantity level, and (iv) applying a traditional similarity measure by using the information quantity of single feature projections, union or intersection operators.

4 Interpreting Traditional Representation Models

4.1 Bag of Words and the Vector Space Model

The BoW representation scheme with *Term frequency* (TF) as feature salience fits into our model when assuming that: (i) both linguistic units and abstract features are words, $\mathcal{F} = \{w \in \Omega\}$, (ii) linguistic units are independent, $\mathcal{I}\big(f_\sigma(\mathcal{T})\big) = \sum_{u\in\mathcal{T}}\mathcal{I}\big(f_\sigma(u)\big)$, (iii) the projection of an abstract feature (vocabulary word) into a linguistic unit (text word) is the matching function, $f_\sigma(\mathcal{T}) = 1$, if $\sigma \in \mathcal{T}$, and (iv) every word is equiprobable in the whole corpus, $P(w) = k$, $\forall w \in \Omega$. Under these assumptions, the weight of the projection is proportional to its frequency:

$$\mathcal{I}\big(f_w(\mathcal{T})\big) = \sum_{u\in\mathcal{T}}\mathcal{I}\big(f_w(u)\big) = \sum_{u\in\mathcal{T}}log\left(\frac{1}{P_{u'\in\Omega}\big(f_w(u')\geq f_w(u)\big)}\right)$$

$$= \sum_{\substack{u\in\mathcal{T}\\u=w}}log\left(\frac{1}{P_{u'\in\Omega}\big(f_w(u')\geq 1\big)}\right) + \sum_{\substack{u\in\mathcal{T}\\u\neq w}}log\left(\frac{1}{P_{u'\in\Omega}\big(f_w(u')\geq 0\big)}\right)$$

$$= \sum_{\substack{u\in\mathcal{T}\\u=w}}log\left(\frac{1}{P_{u'\in\Omega}\big(f_w(u')\geq 1\big)}\right) + 0 = \sum_{\substack{u\in\mathcal{T}\\u=w}}k = tf(w,\mathcal{T})\cdot k. \quad (3)$$

Therefore, we have a representation of the texts by its features (frequency of a word) and we can compute the Euclidean distance with:

$$Dist_{Euclid}(\mathcal{T},\mathcal{T}') = \sqrt{\sum_{w\in\mathcal{F}}\Big(\mathcal{I}\big(f_w(\mathcal{T})\big) - \mathcal{I}\big(f_w(\mathcal{T}')\big)\Big)^2}.$$

We can also express other geometric and set based measures such as cosine, Dice, etc. The Jaccard measure can be written as in [5]:

$$Dist_{jacc}(T, T') = \frac{\sum_w \mathcal{I}(f_w(T \cap_w T'))}{\sum_w \mathcal{I}(f_w(T \cup_w T'))} = \frac{\sum_w min(tf(w, T), tf(w, T'))}{\sum_w max(tf(w, T), tf(w, T'))}.$$

4.2   Informativeness Based Representation Models

Some well known and effective models such as *Term Frequency - Inverse Document Frequency* (TF.IDF) or the Lin distance [8] consider that less likely features have more weight in the representation. These models fit into our theoretical framework by taking the same assumptions than in previous models but considering that words are not equiprobable in the whole corpus and documents are similarly long in the collection. Under these assumptions, the feature projection weight derives into the traditional TF.IDF:

$$\mathcal{I}(f_w(T)) = \sum_{\substack{u \in T \\ u = w}} log\left(\frac{1}{P_{u' \in \Omega}(f_w(u') \geq 1)}\right) = tf(w, T) \cdot log \frac{1}{P_{u' \in \Omega}(w = u')} =$$

$$= tf(w, T) \cdot log \frac{1}{P_{w \in \Omega}(w)} \propto tf(w, T) \cdot log \frac{1}{P_{T' \in \Omega}(w \in T')}. \quad (4)$$

In [8], the Lin similarity between two texts, T and T', is measured by the ratio between the amount of information needed to state the commonality of T and T' (intersection) and the information needed to fully describe what T and T' are (sum). According to our model, the Lin distance can be expressed as:

$$Lin(T, T') = \frac{\mathcal{I}(common(T, T'))}{\mathcal{I}(description(T, T'))} - \frac{\mathcal{I}(T \cap T')}{\mathcal{I}(T) + \mathcal{I}(T')}$$

$$= \frac{\sum_w \mathcal{I}(f_w(T \cap T'))}{\sum_w \mathcal{I}(f_w(T)) + \sum_w \mathcal{I}(f_w(T'))}$$

$$= \frac{\sum_{w \in T \cap T'} log(P(w)^{-1})}{\sum_{w \in T} log(P(w)^{-1}) + \sum_{w \in T'} log(P(w)^{-1})}.$$

4.3   Supervised Classification Models

We can exploit our model to include in the text representation the automatic annotation of supervised classification systems. For instance, in addition to words or n-grams, we can add in the representation to what extent a text is associated to a certain category according to a classification system. Most of classification systems assign a certain confidence for each predefined category. Therefore, it is enough to consider each category as an abstract feature and each projection over the text as the confidence level assigned by the system to the category. That is, being $f_\sigma(T)$ the likelihood assigned for a certain category by a classification system:

$$\mathcal{I}\big(f_\sigma(T)\big) = log\left(\frac{1}{P_{T' \in \Omega}\big(f_\sigma(T') \geq f_\sigma(T)\big)}\right).$$

The interesting point is that under this model, we can add features from different classification categories and systems into the same representation.

4.4 Distributional Semantics

We can interpret and integrate more complex approaches into our model such as distributional semantics models, which has produced effective results when estimating similarity [6, 10, 11]. In general, those methods represents word in a high-dimensional space, inferred form statistics of coocurrences in a corpus. Some examples are latent semantic analysis (LSA), variants of the topic model or the recently popular word embeddings resource. In order to integrate this information into FPI model, it is enough to consider each dimension as a feature, and each word as a linguistic unit. The projection is the corresponding feature value.

5 Evaluation

We want to check empirically the hypothesis that, under a certain Information Quantity threshold, adding features from heterogeneous sources improves the accuracy of the similarity estimation. As a proof of concept, we will use a tweet corpus in order to predict if two tweets are similar enough to belong to the same topic.

5.1 Dataset

We chose the RepLab dataset [1], which uses Twitter data in English and Spanish (more than $142,000$ tweets). The RepLab2013 corpus consists of a collection of tweets which were downloaded asking for the name of some companies or entities (e.g. *BMW*, *Bank of America*, *Oxford University*, . . .). The corpus includes 61 entities, for each entity, at least 700 and $1,500$ tweets were collected for the training and test sets respectively. The corpus also comprises additional background tweets for each entity (up to $50,000$ tweets).

The tweets of each entity, in the training and test datasets, were manually annotated regarding to topics. Some of these topics are organizational (e.g. *"customer feedback"*) while others correspond with a particular event (e.g. *"Bank of America Chicago Marathon"*). It is important to note that the topics in the training data set do not necessarily correspond with the topics in the test data set. Therefore, applying classification techniques in isolation is not enough. Furthermore, the training topics contain, in most of cases, just a few tweets.

Additionally, each tweet was manually categorized with respect to standard reputation dimensions, they were the same for all the entities (e.g. *Performance, Leadership, Innovation*, etc.).

5.2 Task and Similarity Models

For evaluation purposes, we will consider the topic annotations as gold-standard. The similarity estimation task will consist of predicting whether two tweets are referring to the same topic.

In this experiment, we use as similarity measure the ratio between the intersection and the union of texts, where texts are represented as a set of feature projections:

$$Sim(\mathcal{T}, \mathcal{T}') = \frac{\mathcal{I}(\mathcal{T} \cap \mathcal{T}')}{\mathcal{I}(\mathcal{T} \cup \mathcal{T}')} = \frac{\sum_\sigma \mathcal{I}(f_\sigma(\mathcal{T} \cap \mathcal{T}'))}{\sum_\sigma \mathcal{I}(f_\sigma(\mathcal{T} \cup \mathcal{T}'))}.$$

The intersection and union of texts are computed as in Definition 5. The different features, $\sigma \in \mathcal{F}$, are aggregated as in (2), $\mathcal{I}(\mathcal{T}) = \sum_{\sigma \in \mathcal{F}} \mathcal{I}(f_\sigma(\mathcal{T}))$. The information quantity of feature projection across linguistic units are aggregated according to (1) in Definition 4, $\mathcal{I}(f_\sigma(\mathcal{T})) = \sum_{w \in \mathcal{T}} f_\sigma(w)$.

The pending variable is the definition of features, its projections and information quantity over each word, $\mathcal{I}(f_\sigma(w))$. In this respect, we will compare in this experiment the following approaches. The first one is the bag of words model. That is, assuming words as abstract features and linguistic units, independence across linguistic units and features, and equiprobability of words in the whole corpus. The resulting feature projection of a word, w, into a text, $\mathcal{T}$, is $\mathcal{I}(f_w(\mathcal{T})) = tf(w, \mathcal{T}) \cdot k$, as in (3). Notice that the resulting similarity measure is equivalent to the traditional Jaccard. We will denote this approach as *FPI-Jaccard*.

The second approach is applying the Lin's distance representation model, as in (4). In this case, we assume that each abstract feature or word has a certain probability in the whole corpus (not necessarily the same for each word). In order to estimate this probability we consider the training, background and test corpora. We will denote this approach as *FPI-Lin*.

$$\mathcal{I}(f_w(\mathcal{T})) = tf(w, \mathcal{T}) \cdot log \frac{1}{P_{\mathcal{T}' \in \Omega}(w \in \mathcal{T}')}.$$

The main advantage of our model is that we can integrate new features to the word based feature set. In the third approach, we consider the training data of topics. For this, we assume that each topic in the training data is an abstract feature, linguistic units are independent, and the projection of each feature in each linguistic feature is estimated as a conditional probability, $P(\sigma|u)$, in a similar way than in the Naive Bayes classification method, we will denote this approach as *FPI+Topics*.

We derive the projection of a training topic (abstract feature) in a word (linguistic unit) in the following way. Being σ a certain topic in the training data set:

$$f_\sigma(w) = P(\sigma|w) = \frac{P(w|\sigma) \cdot P(\sigma)}{P(w)} \simeq \frac{\frac{freq_\sigma(w)}{|\sigma|} \cdot \frac{|\sigma|}{|\Omega|}}{\frac{freq(w)}{|\Omega|}} = \frac{freq_\sigma(w)}{freq(w)}.$$

where $freq_\sigma(w)$ represents the amount of occurrences of w in the topic, σ, (that is, in the set of tweets of the training dataset which belong to the topic), and $freq(w)$ represents the amount of occurrences of w in the whole corpus, Ω. The Information Quantity is computed as in Definition 4, considering every word in the whole corpus, Ω, as probability sample set.

$$\mathcal{I}(f_\sigma(w)) = -log\Big(P_{w' \in \Omega}\big(f_\sigma(w') \geq f_\sigma(w)\big)\Big).$$

The main advantage of FPI is that it allows us to integrate information from different text classification systems applied over different categories. In addition to topic training data, we consider the classification of texts into reputational dimension categories. The idea is that belonging to the same dimensional category should be an additional evidence of similarity. For this, we consider also the projection of reputational dimensions into texts in the same way than in the case of topic training data, we will denote this approach as *FPI+Dimensions*.

Then, we compute the Information Quantity of every projection according to Definition 4. In order to avoid noise, we apply different Information Quantity thresholds for the classifiers and we discard feature projection under the threshold.

Finally, we will implement an approach which aggregates all the information sources, we will denote this approach as *FPI+Topics+Dimensions*.

5.3   Evaluation Benchmark

Firstly, we generate a random sample of $1,000$ tweet pairs from each entity test data set. Among them, there are 500 tweet pairs, whose elements belong to the same topic (not necessarily the same); and the others 500 pairs are pairs whose elements belong to different clusters. In order to evaluate similarity measures, we apply *Precision at k*. That is, the ratio of tweet pairs sharing topic within the k closest instances according to the similarity measure, denoted by $Rank_k^{Sim}$:

$$Prec_k(Sim) = P\Big(topic(T) = topic(T')|(T, T') \in Rank^{Sim}(k)\Big).$$

In other words, for each approach, we increasingly order the $1,000$ distances computed between the tweets pairs, then we calculate the *Precision at k* with the ratio between the number of tweet pairs belonging to the same cluster in the first k distances and the number of similarity instances, i.e., k. Finally, we compute the average *Precision at k* across entity data sets.

5.4   Results

Table 1 shows the first results. In this table, measures have been evaluated according to Precision at 200 (the accuracy of the top 20% of similarity instances). Each row represents a feature configuration. Each column represents a certain Information Quantity threshold. Given that in this experiment we only apply thresholds for classification systems based features, the values in *FPI-Jaccard* and *FPI-Lin*'s approaches (rows first and second) are fixed. The purpose of this is to visualize the capability of the model to add additional features (classifiers) without adding noise. As the table includes the thresholds 0.0, 2.0, 5.0, 10.0, 15.0, 20.0, and the empirically optimal threshold 11.0.

Table 1. Precission at 200 for all the evaluated approches.

Inf. Quantity Thresold / Approach	0.0	2.0	5.0	10.0	11.0	15.0	20.0
FPI-Jaccard				0.8324			
FPI-Lin				0.8798			
FPI+Topics	0.8798	0.8177	0.8806	0.8462	**0.8833**	0.8804	0.8798
FPI+Dimensions	0.8798	0.7717	0.7959	0.8920	**0.8956**	0.8801	0.8798
FPI+Topics+Dimen.	0.8798	0.7704	0.7959	0.8906	**0.8961**	0.8806	0.8798

The first observation is that *FPI-Lin*'s outperforms *FPI-Jaccard*. That is, applying information quantity and assuming different probabilities for words increases the effectiveness of the similarity estimation. This result is coherent with multiple works that corroborate the effectiveness of considering projection functions as IDF in the text representation step.

The second observation is that the results of adding additional supervised features (topics and dimensions) is highly sensitive to the information quantity threshold. Under a low threshold, the model adds noise from the additional features, decreasing substantially the evaluation results. With an extremely high threshold, the additional features have not effect. However a very relevant result is that **the optimal threshold is the same when adding dimensions, topics or both**. In addition, we have observed in other experiments that the optimal threshold for k at 200 the applying thresholds to the Lin distance is also 11. This suggests that the optimal threshold is consistent across features. That is, this variable depends more to the nature of the collection and similarity ground truth than to the particular features.

As an additional experiment, Fig. 1 show the performance across k levels in precision with a fixed information quantity threshold of 11. As the figure shows, the performance increase of additional features is visible at medium k levels (from $k = 100$ to $k = 500$). The reason is that classification methods do not contribute when there is a high similarity according to words. However, the indirect evidence

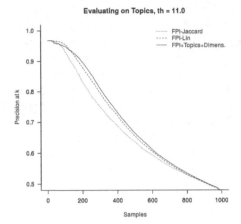

Fig. 1. Precision at k curves, with threshold = 11.0. Approaches: *FPI-Jaccard* and *FPI-Lin*, and *FPI-Topics+Dimensions*

of similarity are more effective in medium similarity levels. That is, when word overlap is not enough to capture the similarity between texts.

The third (and most important) observation is that, in concordance with our hypothesis, with an optimal Information Quantity threshold adding features increases progressively the performance of the similarity estimation. We have seen that considering topic training data increases the effectiveness of similarity estimation. However, it is more important to note that considering dimensions increases even to a greater extent the similarity effectiveness, although similarity is evaluated over topics rather than dimensions. The reason is that the categorization of tweets by dimensions contains more information about each category than the categorization by topics. This suggests that considering heterogeneous features improves the similarity estimation even when these features do not focus directly on the similarity evaluation target. But the most important contribution of FPI is that we can combine both features, achieving even higher effectiveness.

6   Conclusions

In this paper, we have introduced a general model for text representation. At theoretical level, some strengths are: (i) It allows us to integrate information from heterogeneous sources in the texts representation step, including lexical features and supervised system outputs. (ii) The model derives into traditional approaches such as TF, TF.IDF, set based similarity measures or Lin's distance depending of the assumptions about abstract features, projections and statistical dependency across linguistic units, and (iii) the model gives a robust and simply way to avoid noise when adding additional features.

From a practical point of view, the first experiments showed in this paper suggest the veracity of the hypothesis that, given an optimal Information Quantity threshold, adding new features from heterogeneous sources outperforms the similarity prediction. Moreover, the results suggest that the information quantity threshold tends to be robust across different kinds of features.

In addition, this seminal work opens the door for multiple experiments and theoretical analysis. Some open question for future work are: (i) To interpretate more recent approaches such as distributional semantic models in the generic theoretical framework. An interesting question is to what extent they integrate the concept of Information Quantity. (ii) New experiments integrating more complex features (i.e. distributional semantics) into the feature set. (iii) Repeating the experiments over new text similarity benchmarks, or (iv) confirming the robustness of Information Quantity thresholds across new features and similarity scenarios.

Acknowledgments. This research was supported by the Spanish Ministry of Science and Innovation (Vox-Populi project TIN2013-47090C3-1-P).

References

1. Amigó, E., de Albornoz, J.C., Chugur, I., Corujo, A., Gonzalo, J., Martín-Wanton, T., Meij, E., de Rijke, M., Spina, D.: Overview of replab 2013: evaluating online reputation monitoring systems. In: Proceedings of Information Access Evaluation. Multilinguality, Multimodality, and Visualization - 4th International Conference of the CLEF Initiative (CLEF 2013) (2013)
2. Deerwester, S., Dumais, S.T., Furnas, G.W., Landauer, T.K., Harshman, R.: Indexing by latent semantic analysis. J. Am. Soc. Inf. Sci. **41**(6), 391–407 (1990)
3. Giménez, J., Màrquez, L.: Linguistic measures for automatic machine translation evaluation. Mach. Transl. **24**(3–4), 209–240 (2010)
4. Gomaa, W.H., Fahmy, A.A.: Article: a survey of text similarity approaches. Int. J. Comput. Appl. **68**(13), 13–18 (2013)
5. Grefenstette, G.: Explorations in automatic thesaurus discovery, vol. 278. Springer Science & Business Media (2012)
6. Han, L., Kashyap, A.I., Finin, T., Mayfield, J., Weese, J.: UMBC EBIQUITY-CORE: semantic textual similarity systems. In: Proceedings of the Second Joint Conference on Lexical and Computational Semantics. Association for Computational Linguistics, June 2013
7. Hovy, E., Lin, C.-Y., Zhou, L.: Evaluating DUC 2005 using basic elements. In: Proceedings of DUC, vol. 2005. Citeseer (2005)
8. Lin, D.: An information-theoretic definition of similarity. In: ICML, vol. 98, pp. 296–304 (1998)
9. Liu, W., Tian, X., Tao, D., Liu J.: Constrained metric learning via distance gap maximization. In: Proceedings of the Twenty-Fourth AAAI Conference on Artificial Intelligence, AAAI 2010, pp. 518–524. AAAI Press (2010)
10. Malik, R., Subramaniam, L.V., Kaushik, S.: Automatically selecting answer templates to respond to customer emails. In: Veloso, M.M. (ed.) IJCAI, pp. 1659–1664 (2007)
11. Mihalcea, R., Corley, C., Strapparava, C.: Corpus-based and knowledge-based measures of text semantic similarity. In: Proceedings of the American Association for Artificial Intelligence (AAAI 2006), Boston, Massachusetts, July 2006
12. Mikolov, T., Sutskever, I., Chen, K., Corrado, G., Dean, J.: Distributed representations of words and phrases and their compositionality. CoRR, abs/1310.4546 (2013)
13. Tversky, A.: Features of similarity. Psychol. Rev. **84**, 327–352 (1977)

Extending Feature Decay Algorithms
Using Alignment Entropy

Alberto Poncelas[(✉)], Andy Way, and Antonio Toral

ADAPT Centre, School of Computing, Dublin City University, Dublin, Ireland
{alberto.poncelas,andy.way,antonio.toral}@adaptcentre.ie

Abstract. In machine-learning applications, data selection is of crucial importance if good runtime performance is to be achieved. Feature Decay Algorithms (FDA) have demonstrated excellent performance in a number of tasks. While the decay function is at the heart of the success of FDA, its parameters are initialised with the same weights. In this paper, we investigate the effect on Machine Translation of assigning more appropriate weights to words using word-alignment entropy. In experiments on German to English, we show the effect of calculating these weights using two popular alignment methods, GIZA++ and FastAlign, using both automatic and human evaluations. We demonstrate that our novel FDA model is a promising research direction.

Keywords: Data selection · Machine translation · Mathematical foundations

1 Introduction

Machine-learning approaches dominate in many fields. Many researchers have demonstrated that for a range of tasks, the more training data available, the better the system performance. In the field of Statistical Machine Translation (SMT), this was underlined in one of the first papers on phrase-based SMT [1], where improvements in BLEU score [2] of approximately 1 point were seen for a range of European language pairs each time the amount of training data from Europarl [3] was doubled.

However, others have shown that it is not always the case that having more data is necessarily better. [4] demonstrated that SMT performance decreases when additional training data is used to build the underlying models. Furthermore, a range of work beginning with [5] has shown that competitive SMT performance can still be achieved with fractions of the original training data if the characteristics of the test data can be examined and the optimal training data selected for the translation of that test set. The specific technique used is Feature Decay Algorithms (FDA), which have demonstrated excellent performance in a number of tasks by maximizing the diversity of the test set features while simultaneously increasing target coverage by using smaller yet more relevant amounts of training data. While the decay function is at the heart of the

© Springer International Publishing AG 2017
J.F. Quesada et al. (Eds.): FETLT 2016, LNAI 10341, pp. 170–182, 2017.
https://doi.org/10.1007/978-3-319-69365-1_14

success of FDA, its parameters are initialised with the same weights. In this paper, we investigate the effect on MT of assigning more appropriate weights to words using word-alignment entropy.

In SMT at least, it is clear that data selection is of crucial importance if we are to avoid the "garbage in, garbage out" syndrome. If optimal runtime performance is to be achieved, then the quality of the training data needs to be as good as it can be for the task at hand. Techniques have been developed in SMT which result in huge speed-ups in runtime performance. One such method is the FastAlign word-alignment model [6], which has been shown to deliver speedups of up to tenfold with no discernible drop-off in performance, compared to using GIZA++ [7], the most popular tool used in SMT for word alignment. As might be expected, these speedups have proved attractive to industry, and have been deployed in translation pipelines to good effect [8].

Nonetheless, MT engine training is a task that (generally) only needs to be done once, so in our view quality clearly trumps speed. Accordingly, in this paper we also set out to test whether there is any drop-off in performance by using FastAlign for the calculation of word-alignment entropy in FDA compared to using GIZA++. In experiments on German to English, we show the effect of calculating these weights using these two popular alignment methods, and examine the results using both automatic and human evaluations.

The remainder of this paper is organised as follows. In Sect. 2, we describe the related work on which our own research is based, with a special focus on FDA and word alignment. In Sect. 3, we detail our methodology which extends FDA using word-alignment entropy. Section 4 describes the experiments conducted, with the results discussed in Sect. 5. In Sect. 6, we conclude, and list a number of avenues for further work in this area.

2 Related Work

There are several methods for data selection [9]. Those most closely related to this work iteratively select one or more sentences from a candidate pool, updating at each step a set of sentences obtained in previous iterations (the "selected pool"). Those functions that select the next sentences depending on the selection pool are called "context-dependent" functions. The most related work to ours is the context-dependent function known as FDA [5, 10]. We provide an overview of FDA in Sect. 2.1, and outline the alignment models in Sect. 2.2.

2.1 Feature Decay Algorithms

FDA [5, 10] is a method that tries to maximize the variability of n-grams in the training set by decreasing their value as they are added to the selected pool. In order to do that, the n-grams in the test set (the document we want to translate) are extracted as features with an initial value. These features are then extracted from the training set. Each sentence has an importance score of being selected which is the normalized sum of the value of its features. At each step the sentence with the highest score is selected. Then the values of the features of the selected sentence are decreased as in (1):

$$decay(f) = init(f)\frac{d^{C_L(f)}}{(1 + C_L(f))^c} \qquad (1)$$

L is the selected pool, d is the feature score polynomial decay factor, while c is the feature score exponential decay factor. $C_L(f)$ is the count of the feature f in L, which makes the most frequent features decay faster, thereby allowing an increase in variability of n-grams in the training data. The initialization function is defined in (2):

$$init(f) = log(|U|/C_U(f))^i|f|^l \qquad (2)$$

where $|U|$ is the size of the training data, $C_U(f)$ is the count of the feature f in the training data and $|f|$ is the number of tokens of f.

2.2 Word-Alignment Models

IBM models [11] introduced the idea of adding alignment variables to the conditional probability $p(f_1...f_m|e_1...e_l)$ of a sentence $f_1 \ldots f_m$ in the target language being the translation of a sentence $e_1 \ldots e_l$ in the source. Concretely, (3) describes the conditional probability of IBM model 2:

$$p(f_1...f_m, a_1...a_m|e_1...e_l, m, l) \qquad (3)$$

where the alignment variables $a_1 \ldots a_m$ map each foreign word f_i with $i \in \{1 \ldots m\}$ to an e_j with $j \in \{1 \ldots l\}$.

GIZA++ [7] is the most widely used language-independent toolkit for calculating word alignments from bilingual corpora according to the IBM models. The FastAlign alignment model [6] is a variation of IBM model 2 that introduces a diagonal tension λ parameter that measures the overall correspondence of word order and an efficient re-estimation of the parameters that makes it around 10 times faster than GIZA++ while still obtaining comparable quality.

3   Applying Alignment Entropy in FDA

The FDA algorithm has already demonstrated its competitiveness by achieving excellent results in several Workshops on SMT from 2013–2015, on both MT and quality estimation tasks. Nonetheless, there appears to be scope to improve FDA still further by using word-alignment entropies. [5] show that the feature decay rate has a very strong effect on the final translation quality whereas the initial feature values, inclusion of higher order features, or sentence length normalizations do not.

3.1   Where Should Alignment Entropy Be Applied?

In FDA, in formula (1), the parameters c (the feature score exponential decay factor) and d (the feature score polynomial decay factor) of the decay function are the same for every feature by default.

We propose instead that each feature should have different decay ratios. We contend that source n-grams that are regularly aligned to the same n-grams in the target language should have a higher decay ratio, since we require fewer occurrences to 'guess' the translation. For instance, a word in German like "Deutschland" should have a more rapid decay as we would expect it to be aligned to the English word "Germany" in most cases when translating from German to English. In contrast, other German words like "zu" or "von" could be aligned to many different English words depending on the context of the sentence, and so the uncertainty of alignment is higher.

We want, therefore, to assign different values of d in (1) which by default is 0.5. In the implementation, the calculations of the decay function are made in the logarithmic scale, so if the value of d is in the range (0–1) higher values will result in slower decay.

According to [5], the choice of the *init* function does not affect the result as much as the decay function does, so we do not change it. Furthermore, in our experiments, we are varying only the value of d because in previous experiments variations in the value of the parameter c did not lead to as good results as those where the value of d was varied.

A method for measuring the difficulty of an n-gram to be aligned is using alignment entropy. Entropy measures uncertainty, as defined in (4):

$$entropy(x) = - \sum_i p(x_i) * log(p(x_i)) \qquad (4)$$

3.2   Computing Alignment Entropy in FDA

In order to calculate the alignment entropy of a source word, we need to know the probability of its being aligned to words in the target language. Using FastAlign or GIZA++, it is possible to obtain the alignment probabilities of unigrams, which can be used to calculate the translation entropies. In this paper the experiments have been conducted calculating only the unigram entropies; if this proves to be a promising direction, we can always extend this method to higher-order n-grams. Furthermore, introducing alignment entropy to n-grams one order at a time will help us understand its benefits; if we were to perform this technique on (say) unigrams to 5-grams, it could not be guaranteed that we would understand exactly where the benefits of such an approach were to be attributed.

Let A_s be the set of words that are potential translations of the source word s, and $p(s,t)$ be the probability of s being aligned with the word t. Accordingly, the new decay ratio d will be given by the decay score computed in (5):

$$score(s) = \frac{\sum_{t \in A_s} p(s,t) * log(p(s,t))}{log(|A_s|)} \qquad (5)$$

In order to have the decay score in the (0–1) range, we normalize the entropy of alignment of each word by dividing by $log(|A_s|)$, the maximum possible entropy.

For unfound words (i.e. whose alignment probability cannot be retrieved via FastAlign or GIZA++), we cannot calculate their alignment entropy in (5), so we assign them the average alignment entropy value of the rest of the (found) words.

In what follows, we use $score(w)$ to indicate the alignment entropy (or "decay score") of a word w. This is the value that will be used as the d parameter in the decay function in (1).

4   Experiments

Our experiments have two goals: (i) to explore and compare the performance of GIZA++ and FastAlign when using their alignment probabilities for calculating the decay scores used in FDA; and (ii) to improve the results obtained by the default FDA using unigrams as features. In order to explore both objectives, we designed three experiments:

– Baseline: data selection performed via FDA, using default decay scores.
– FastAlign experiment: data selection performed via FDA using the probabilities obtained with FastAlign to score the words.
– GIZA++ experiment: data selection performed via FDA using the probabilities obtained with GIZA++ to score the words.

FDA selects unigrams, bigrams and trigrams as features by default. However, given that in this work we begin calculating decay scores only for unigrams, we decided to perform the three experiments using only unigram features.

We train SMT systems on the selected data with the Moses toolkit [12] with default settings and using GIZA++ for word alignment. We also perform four tuning executions of each experiment using MERT [13], so that the reported scores are based on the average of the runs, and significance tests are more robust [14].

4.1   Data Sets

Based on the work described in [10] for WMT-15, we perform a similar experiment. However, our approach has significant differences since we use unigrams as a feature in this work. The data sets used in the experiments are as follows: (i) *Test data*: The test document provided in the WMT 2015 German-to-English translation task; (ii) *Training data*: The training data provided in the WMT 2015 translation task setting a maximum sentence length of 126 words; (iii) *Selected data*: We select 66.4 million words in total (source- and target-language sides); (iv) *Language Model*: 3-gram and 8-gram Language Models (LMs) built using the target-language side of the selected data via the KenLM toolkit [15]; (v) *Tuning data*: 5K randomly sampled sentences from development sets provided in the WMT Translation Tasks from the years 2010 to 2014.

5   Results

After obtaining the results, we conduct a comparison of the performance of the two decay score models, and also compare both experiments with the baseline.

5.1   Comparison of FastAlign and GIZA++

The Effect of Found vs. Unfound Words. In Table 1, we present a summary of the scores obtained by using GIZA++ and FastAlign. We observe that we obtain higher decay scores in both experiments compared to the default 0.5 value of the baseline system. This demonstrates that the FDA algorithm may indeed be very sensitive to changes in the parameter d in (1), as we suspected.

For the purpose of readability, we also present the numbers in Table 1 in graphical format in Fig. 1. There are essentially two observations: (i) for FastAlign, there are two spikes in the plot: the high one around the mean of 0.94 (because of the high number of unfound words), and a smaller one around 1.0,

Table 1. Statistics of the scores obtained using GIZA++ and FastAlign, with a comparison with the baseline system. Found-words are those words for which their alignment probability has been obtained. Mean and stdev indicate the mean and standard deviation of the scores of all the words in the test set.

	baseline	FastAlign	GIZA++
found-words	–	54.4%	87.6%
mean	0.5	0.9401	0.7198
stdev	0.0	0.0510	0.2439

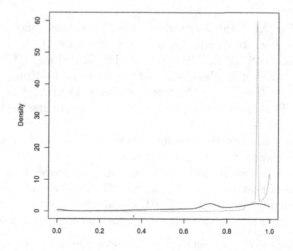

Fig. 1. Density plot of the decay scores of FastAlign (grey) and GIZA++ (black) experiments.

indicating FastAlign's tendency to give high scores; and (ii) for GIZA++, there is a small bump around the mean (0.71), but the decay scores are almost equally distributed.

Note also that the percentage of words found by GIZA++ is higher than the percentage of FastAlign: only 12.4% of the words are unfound by GIZA++, whereas 45.6% are unfound by FastAlign, almost four times as many.

In addition, the scores obtained using GIZA++ have a higher standard deviation. Recall that the decay score of the unfound words was assigned as the average of the decay score of the found words. Since the FastAlign experiment shows a higher percentage of unfound words, the standard deviation is lower. In Fig. 1, we can see the effect of this, with most FastAlign words being clustered around the mean. Even though the means of all three systems are quite different, this very low standard deviation for FastAlign is noteworthy.

Table 2. Results of the average of the scores after 4 tuning executions for the baseline, FastAlign and GIZA++ experiments with LM order 3 and 8. The results in bold for GIZA++ indicate a statistically significant improvement (at level p=0.01) compared to FastAlign.

	baseline		FastAlign		GIZA++	
	LM = 3	LM = 8	LM = 3	LM = 8	LM = 3	LM = 8
BLEU	0.2291	0.2299	0.2237	0.2232	0.2282	**0.2279**
NIST	6.9475	6.9667	6.8911	6.8728	6.9327	6.9496
TER	0.5970	0.5957	0.5988	0.6001	0.5984	0.5973
METEOR	0.2833	0.2840	0.2818	0.2811	**0.2827**	**0.2836**
CHRF3	50.06	50.09	49.54	49.46	49.83	50.02
CHRF1	50.66	50.76	50.39	50.29	50.59	50.65

Implications for MT Performance. We also present the performance of the MT systems after tuning in Table 2 using a range of different evaluation metrics: BLEU [2], NIST [16], TER [17], METEOR [18] and CHRF [19]. These scores give an estimation of the quality of the translated output compared to a translated reference. The higher the score, the better the translation is estimated to be, except for TER, which being an error measure, indicates better translation output by lower scores.

We also provide comparative results with two different LMs: one with n-gram order 3 and the other with n-gram order 8.

As we can see, the entropies calculated with the probabilities of GIZA++ outperform those of FastAlign, for all metrics. The improvements over FastAlign are statistically significant for METEOR, as calculated with Bootstrap Resampling [20].[1] The influence of the larger n-gram order can be seen to good effect,

---

[1] Note that we were unable to calculate statistical significance for the CHRF metric. Note too that prior to tuning, statistically significant improvements were seen for GIZA++ over FastAlign for BLEU, NIST, TER and METEOR.

too, with better results occurring with the larger LM for both the baseline and GIZA++ experiments, but interestingly not for FastAlign. Note too that the BLEU score for GIZA++ with the 8-gram LM – despite being statistically significantly better than the FastAlign score – is a little lower than with the trigram LM.

5.2   Comparison with the Baseline

Automatic Evaluation. As we saw in the previous section, the results computing word-alignment entropy with GIZA++ surpass those when FastAlign was used. However, it can be seen from Table 2 that the GIZA++ system *never* improves over the baseline engine.[2] However, none of the results of the baseline system are statistically significantly better than those of the GIZA++ engine.

As expected, results after tuning result in better performance; BLEU score improves by about 2%. However, the TER scores are worse after tuning for all three systems. The system parameters were optimized using BLEU score. Note that [21] observed that performing tuning using a particular metric may not lead to optimal scores on the test set for that metric, so something similar may be going on here.

In addition, recall that the results in Table 2 report the mean of the four tuning executions. It is instructive to investigate the difference in scores obtained from each of these runs, as seen in Table 3. It can be seen very clearly that for most metrics, the GIZA++ system can outperform the baseline; for METEOR, results are better in two of the four runs.[3] Of course, while we would not selectively pick the set-up with the best run for our purposes, we nonetheless take some encouragement from these results, as they demonstrate that our method does have the promise to outperform the baseline set-up.

Human Evaluation. As the results from the automatic evaluation were somewhat mixed, we decided to conduct a human evaluation of the outputs of the system with the trigram LM. Automatic scores offer some insight into system performance, but sometimes good output is penalised by the automatic metrics owing to the output being significantly different from the 'gold standard' reference translation.

---

[2] In experiments before tuning (excluded here for reasons of space), the METEOR and CHRF scores of the output of the system executed with GIZA++ did outperform the baseline system before tuning.

[3] Why is it the case that better scores are more likely with the METEOR evaluation metric? This measure evaluates a hypothesis against a reference calculating sentence-level similarity scores. In so doing it searches for all the possible matches of the words between the two sentences. The words can match (i) if they are the same, (ii) if they have the same stem, (iii) if they are synonyms, or (iv) if they are found as a match in a paraphrase table. Therefore, this metric takes into consideration not only the n-grams, but also the semantic of the words. As the human evaluation shows, many semantically equivalent translations are output by our GIZA++ system, which are penalised by most automatic metrics, but not by METEOR.

Table 3. Results of the average of the scores as well as those of the 4 tuning executions for the baseline and GIZA++ experiments with LM of order 3 and 8. The results in bold show improvements over the baseline for individual runs.

LM 3		
	Mean	Scores for 4 tuning runs
baseline		
BLEU	0.2291	0.2291, 0.2291, 0.2289, 0.2291
NIST	6.9475	6.9441, 6.9441, 6.9575, 6.9441
TER	0.5970	0.5968, 0.5968, 0.5976, 0.5968
METEOR	0.2833	0.2832, 0.2832, 0.2833, 0.2832
CHRF3	50.064	50.133, 50.133, 49.858, 50.133
CHRF1	50.662	50.668, 50.668, 50.644, 50.668
GIZA++		
BLEU	0.2282	**0.2321**, 0.2269, 0.225, 0.2287
NIST	6.9327	**7.003**, 6.9297, 6.8536, 6.9443
TER	0.5984	**0.5935**, 0.5991, 0.6037, 0.5974
METEOR	0.2827	**0.2848**, 0.2824, 0.2793, **0.2844**
CHRF3	49.827	50.019, 49.737, 49.352, **50.200**
CHRF1	50.591	50.928, 50.528, 50.22, **50.690**
LM 8		
	Mean	Scores for 4 tuning runs
baseline		
BLEU	0.2299	0.2306, 0.2308, 0.2290, 0.2291
NIST	6.9667	6.9799, 6.9863, 6.9565, 6.9441
TER	0.5957	0.5944, 0.5929, 0.5988, 0.5968
METEOR	0.2840	0.2845, 0.2846, 0.2838, 0.2832
CHRF3	50.089	50.005, 50.078, 50.140, 50.133
CHRF1	50.759	50.815, 50.863, 50.687, 50.668
GIZA++		
BLEU	0.2279	0.2304, 0.2223, 0.2305, 0.2283
NIST	6.9496	6.9850, 6.8628, **6.9901**, 6.9604
TER	0.5973	0.5934, 0.6047, 0.5937, 0.5974
METEOR	0.2836	0.2843, 0.2807, **0.2854**, 0.2841
CHRF3	50.024	49.976, 49.846, **50.293**, 49.979
CHRF1	50.649	50.840, 50.146, **50.903**, 50.706

Table 4. Example translations obtained from the baseline and GIZA++ systems (*before tuning*). In this table, the BLEU scores of the baseline translations exceed those of the GIZA++ system by 0.3 points or more.

Reference	baseline	GIZA++
It is **hard** to accept that life goes on, even if you do not want it	It is **hard** to accept that life goes on, even if you do not want	It is **difficult** to accept that life goes on, even if we do not want to
I **want** to help so much	I **want** to help	I **would like** to help
No compensation **is paid**	There will be no compensation **is paid**	There will be no compensation **being paid**

Table 4 provides some instances where the GIZA++ outputs are considered worse by more than 0.3 BLEU points than the respective outputs of the baseline. However, in the first sentence, we see that the GIZA++ system produces *difficult* compared to the baseline's *hard*, which is perfectly acceptable. Furthermore, we argue that the way the GIZA++ translation ends is better even than the reference translation.

In the second example, the GIZA++ engine outputs *would like* instead of *want*, which again is a perfectly acceptable translation. In the third case, the system output by GIZA++ is an acceptable English sentence, unlike the string produced by the baseline, which is nonetheless a better match of the reference supplied. Note that all these examples contain words with similar semantics to the reference, which may explain the higher METEOR scores obtained by the GIZA++ system compared to the other metrics (cf. footnote 3).

Table 5. Comparing the outputs of the best baseline and GIZA++ systems (*after tuning*). The GIZA++ sentences are adjudged by BLEU to be better than the baseline outputs by more than 0.3 points.

Reference	baseline	GIZA++
But in the end they all die	But in the end will die them all	But in the end they all die
We 'll go on to Richmond and hope we can do better there	We drive to Richmond and we hope that it can do better	We drive to Richmond and hope that we can do better there

By contrast, Table 5 provides two examples where the GIZA++ sentences are adjudged by BLEU to be better than the baseline outputs by more than 0.3 points. In the first example, the GIZA++ output mirrors the reference exactly, while the baseline output suffers from poor word order. The second example improves over the baseline in terms of pronominal ellipsis, pronoun selection and correctly inserting the adverb *there*.

Finally, we performed a ranking experiment of the outputs of the baseline and the GIZA++ systems on a random sample of 100 outputs. We found that 48% of the sentences were similar in quality, in 24% of the cases the baseline was better and in 28% GIZA++ was better.

Data Set Analysis. In the GIZA++ experiment we obtain fewer occurrences of proper names in the training set, e.g. the baseline data contains the word *Sydney* 600 times, but this word occurs only 333 times in the GIZA++ experiment. This is to be expected as such words typically have lower translation entropies. In contrast, we obtain more occurrences of other words, e.g. *schwer* ('difficult/heavy') occurs 5 times with GIZA++ compared to 4 in the baseline, while *gehen* ('to go') occurs 21 times with GIZA++ compared to 17 in the baseline. This increases the chances of obtaining synonyms, of course, which might explain the results in Tables 4 and 5.

Note too that there are more Out-of-Vocabulary items in the training set of the GIZA++ experiment (4284) compared to the baseline training set (4175). In Fig. 1, we observed that the distribution of the entropies is highly skewed, which causes a large amount of words to have a slow decay. This can be disadvantageous, as too many occurrences of a particular set of the vocabulary might be required before arriving at the threshold where other words can be selected.

6   Conclusions and Future Work

This work has an ambitious goal, namely to try to improve the performance of FDA, a method which has obtained a number of first-place results on a range of tasks at WMT evaluations over several years.

We observed that certain decay parameters crucial to the excellent showing of FDA in these competitions received default values. We conducted a range of experiments to see the effect of replacing these default values with a word-specific alignment-entropy score. We demonstrated that alignment entropies computed with FastAlign led to inferior performance with respect to those calculated via GIZA++. Any speed-quality trade-off by using FastAlign appears detrimental to this task.

Nonetheless, it proved difficult to outperform the baseline SMT scores. However, inspecting the individual MERT runs showed that the GIZA++ system had the potential to outperform the baseline. Furthermore, human evaluations demonstrated (i) that GIZA++ outputs were being unreasonably penalised in the automatic evaluations, and (ii) that GIZA++ outputs could be generated with clearly better quality than those of the baseline.

Accordingly, we deem these experimental findings to be promising enough to warrant an extension to higher-order n-grams. We also intend to conduct experiments on different language pairs and data sets. Finally, we propose to discover whether combining the outputs of the default FDA and our new model may improve the overall results.

Acknowledgements. This research is supported by the ADAPT Centre for Digital Content Technology, funded under the SFI Research Centres Programme (Grant 13/RC/2106) and co-funded under the European Regional Development Fund, and the European Union Seventh Framework Programme FP7/2007-2013 under grant agreement PIAP-GA-2012-324414 (AbuMaTran).

References

1. Koehn, P., Och, F., Marcu, D.: Statistical phrase-based translation. In: Proceedings of Conference combining Human Language Technology Conference series and the North American Chapter of the Association for Computational Linguistics Conference serie. (edmonton, Canada), pp. 48–54 (2003)
2. Papineni, K., Roukos, S., Ward, T., Zhu, W.-J.: Bleu: a method for automatic evaluation of machine translation. In: Proceedings of the 40th ACL, Philadelphia, PA, USA, pp. 311–318 (2002)
3. Koehn, P.: Europarl: a parallel corpus for statistical machine translation. In: MT Summit X Conference Proceedings: The Tenth Machine Translation Summit, Phuket, Thailand, pp. 79–86 (2005)
4. Ozdowska, S., Way, A.: Optimal bilingual data for French-English PB-SMT. In: Proceedings of the 13th Annual Meeting of the European Association for Machine Translation, Barcelona, Spain, pp. 96–103 (2009)
5. Biçici, E., Yuret, D.: Instance selection for machine translation using feature decay algorithms. In: Proceedings of the Sixth Workshop on Statistical Machine Translatio, Edinburgh, Scotland, pp. 272–283 (2011)
6. Dyer, C., Chahuneau, V., Smith, N.: A simple, fast, and effective reparameterization of IBM model 2. In: Proceedings of Human Language Technologies: Conference of the North American Chapter of the Association of Computational Linguistics, Proceedings, Atlanta, Georgia, USA, pp. 644–648 (2013)
7. Och, F., Ney, H.: A systematic comparison of various statistical alignment models. Comput. Linguist. **29**(1), 19 51 (2003)
8. Shterionov, D., Du, J., Palminteri, M.A., Casanellas, L., ODowd, T., Way, A.: Improving KantanMT training efficiency with FastAlign. In: Proceedings of AMTA 2016, Austin, TX, pp. 222–231 (2016)
9. Eetemadi, S., Lewis, W., Toutanova, K., Radha, H.: Survey of data-selection methods in statistical machine translation. Mach. Transl. **29**(3–4), 189–223 (2015)
10. Biçici, E., Liu, Q., Way, A.: ParFDA for fast deployment of accurate statistical machine translation systems, benchmarks, and statistics. In: Proceedings of the Tenth Workshop on Statistical Machine Translation, Lisbon, Portugal, pp. 74–78 (2015)
11. Brown, P.F., Della Pietra, S.A., Della Pietra, V.J., Mercer, R.L.: The mathematics of statistical machine translation: parameter estimation. Comput. Linguist. **19**, 263–311 (1993)
12. Koehn, P., Hoang, H., Birch, A., Callison-Burch, C., Federico, M., Bertoldi, N., Cowan, B., Shen, W., Moran, C., Zens, R., Dyer, C., Bojar, O., Constantin, A., Herbst, E.: Moses: open source toolkit for SMT. In: Proceedings of 45th Annual Meeting of the ACL on Interactive Poster & Demonstration Sessions, (Prague, Czech Republic), pp. 177–180 (2007)
13. Och, F.: Minimum error rate training in statistical machine translation. In: ACL-2003: 41st Annual Meeting of the Association for Computational Linguistics, Proceedings, Sapporo, Japan, pp. 160–167 (2003)

14. Clark, J.H., Dyer, C., Lavie, A., Smith, N.A.: Better hypothesis testing for statistical machine translation: controlling for optimizer instability. In: Proceedings of the 49th Annual Meeting of the Association for Computational Linguistics: Human Language Technologies, vol. 2, Short Papers, Portland, Oregon, pp. 176–181 (2011)
15. Heafield, K.: KenLM: faster and smaller language model queries. In: Proceedings of the Sixth Workshop on Statistical Machine Translation, Edinburgh, Scotland, pp. 187–197 (2011)
16. Doddington, G.: Automatic evaluation of machine translation quality using n-gram co-occurrence statistics. In: Proceedings of the Second International Conference on Human Language Technology Research, San Diego, CA, pp. 138–145 (2002)
17. Snover, M., Dorr, B., Schwartz, R., Micciulla, L., Makhoul, J.: A study of translation edit rate with targeted human annotation. In: Proceedings of the 7th Conference of the Association for Machine Translation in the Americas, Cambridge, Massachusetts, USA, pp. 223–231 (2006)
18. Banerjee, S., Lavie, A.: Meteor: an automatic metric for MT evaluation with improved correlation with human judgments. In: Proceedings of the ACL Workshop on Intrinsic and Extrinsic Evaluation Measures for Machine Translation and/or Summarization, Ann Arbor, Michigan, pp. 65–72 (2005)
19. Popovic, M.: chrF: character n-gram F-score for automatic MT evaluation. In: Proceedings of the Tenth Workshop on Statistical Machine Translation, Lisbon, Portugal, pp. 392–395 (2015)
20. Koehn, P.: Statistical significance tests for machine translation evaluation. In: Proceedings of EMNLP 2004, Barcelona, Spain, pp. 388–395 (2004)
21. He, Y., Way, A.: Improving the objective function in minimum error rate training. In: Proceedings of the Twelfth Machine Translation Summit, Ottawa, Canada, pp. 238–245 (2009)

Towards a Topic Discovery and Tracking System with Application to News Items

Daniel Brüggermann, Yannik Hermey, Carsten Orth, Darius Schneider, Stefan Selzer, and Gerasimos Spanakis$^{(\boxtimes)}$

Department of Data Science and Knowledge Engineering, Maastricht University, Maastricht 6200MD, Netherlands
{d.bruggermann,y.hermey,c.orth, d.schneider, s.selzer,jerry.spanakis}@maastrichtuniversity.nl

Abstract. Rapid proliferation of the World Wide Web led to an enormous increase in the availability of textual corpora. In this paper, the problem of topic detection and tracking is considered with application to news items. The proposed approach explores two algorithms (Non-Negative Matrix Factorization and a dynamic version of Latent Dirichlet Allocation (DLDA)) over discrete time steps and makes it possible to identify topics within storylines as they appear and track them through time. Moreover, emphasis is given to the visualization and interaction with the results through the implementation of a graphical tool (regardless the approach). Experimental analysis on Reuters RCV1 corpus and the Reuters 2015 archive reveals that explored approaches can be effectively used as tools for identifying topic appearances and their evolutions while at the same time allowing for an efficient visualization.

Keywords: Topic detection · Topic tracking · Non-negative matrix factorization · Dynamic latent dirichlet allocation

1 Introduction

With the rapid progress of computer technology in recent years, there has been an enormous increase in the availability of electronic information on the Internet. However, these vast amounts of data (emails, news sources, forums, etc.) are practically impossible to be harnessed by any human user in their primitive forms. The problem will only deteriorate without the development of approaches to deal with this information overload.

Different stakeholders (companies, individuals, policy makers, etc.) would be interested to harness the amount of free text data available in the web in order to make timely decisions, monitor information and support further actions. Topic detection and tracking in large textual streams (e.g. news items over long time spans) can assist in these efforts as it will reveal trends and evolutions in the underlying storylines. There are many techniques about topic extraction like

Authors contributed equally to the manuscript, thus appear in alphabetical order.

© Springer International Publishing AG 2017
J.F. Quesada et al. (Eds.): FETLT 2016, LNAI 10341, pp. 183–197, 2017.
https://doi.org/10.1007/978-3-319-69365-1_15

Nonnegative Matrix Factorization (NMF) [18] or Latent Dirichlet Allocation (LDA) [5] but there are not many extensions to dynamic data handling. Time dependent modeling of documents can be computationally expensive and complex [2] and despite the fact that such approaches can be effective, none of these effectively handles the visualization issue which can make results more intuitive. Thus, there is much space for developing more effective approaches in terms of both computation and visualization of the results.

This research work aims at exploring how machine learning techniques can be utilized in order to detect topics (and subsequently trends or storylines) from a news items flow through time. Results are visualized and evaluated using the (fully annotated and freely available) RCV1 Reuters corpus (810.000 documents) and the actual Reuters 2015 Reuters archive (obtained by the authors). Section 2 presents an overview of current research work in the area. The NMF based approach is described in Sect. 3 and the DLDA approach in Sect. 4. Section 5 presents the experimental results and finally, Sect. 6 concludes the paper.

2   Related Work

Topic detection and tracking is a long studied task [8] and many approaches have already been attempted. Non-negative matrix factorization is used in the field of text mining to factorize and thereby decrease the dimension of a large matrix [11]. There exist only few approaches so far that applied NMF for dynamically changing text data, i.e. when detecting and tracking topics over time. Although the original data size can be too large for matrix factorization, there already exist variants of the algorithm using an dynamic approach, processing data in chunks [21]. [6] use an online NMF algorithm that applies the factorization to the data of each time step and then updates the matrix bases from the previous calculations accordingly by some metric. However, both these algorithms are not able to detect emerging topics. [17] defines an evolving set and an emerging set of topics within the NMF algorithm and appends the matrices accordingly in both dimensions whenever a new time step is considered. Topics are only detected when they emerge rapidly, and removing topics that are not relevant anymore is not discussed (the matrices increase gradually). [19] introduces a sliding window over the time steps. First, NMF is applied on a certain time step, and then the discovered topics are assigned to the topic model defined by the previous time steps, if possible. If they do not fit into the model, they are added to the emerging set of topics, which are added to the model as soon as there are enough documents that cover this new topic. Within the emerging set, the texts are categorized into new topics using hierarchical clustering.

All these works have several drawbacks. First, they mostly focus on sources like social media [14,24], thus the magnitude of their data is several orders smaller than ours. Moreover, temporal dimension introduces further complexity due to the need for additional distributions or function that characterize this dynamic change [10].

Latent Dirichlet Allocation (LDA) [5] is a generative probabilistic mixture model for topic detection. In such a model, words define a vocabulary and topics are represented by a probabilistic distribution of words from this vocabulary. Each word may be part of several topic representations. LDA assumes that each document from a collection of documents is generated from a probabilistic distribution of topics.

LDA has been extended in order to handle documents over long periods and many variations exist. Other approaches have been proposed as well [3] but scalability is an issue and visualization is not feasible. A milestone in the area was the work of [22] since they associated a beta distribution over time with each topic to capture its popularity. There are also nonparametric models developed either using Gaussian mixture distributions [1] or utilizing Markovian assumptions [7]. These models are very effective but it is very difficult to choose a good distribution over time that allows both flexible changes and effective inferences. Disadvantage of these methods is that they either exhibit limited forms of temporal variation, or require computationally expensive inference methods.

There are extensions of the LDA model towards topic tracking over time such as [23]. But according to [20], these methods deal with constant topics and the timestamps are used for better discovery. Opposed to that, our approach utilizes a dynamic model of LDA [4] that after examining the generated distributions for changes that denote turning points or arcs. Finally, results are visualized using a stacked graph modeling and can be explored in an intuitive way by relating one topic to another.

3   The Proposed NMF-Based Pipeline

Instead of modifying the NMF algorithm, this section elaborates on an algorithm that applies NMF on time steps with arbitrary granularity, and then uses a metric to evaluate the similarity between topics generated for these time steps. This way, topics can also fade away if they do not have a representative at a certain time step, and new topics can emerge if a topic is not similar enough to any existing topic. The similarity metric is intuitively easy to understand and less complex than the related work. Moreover, results can be visualized at any step. The process of NMF over time is described in Fig. 1 and is described by the following phases:

- Phase 1:
  - Define the time step unit (day, week, etc.) and extract texts from this equivalent time step.
  - Define the number of topics to be generated in each time step (a very low number might lead to a mix of multiple topics with insufficient separation whereas a very high number might create topics too specific and increase computational time)
- Phase 2:
  - Run NMF algorithm for each time step s ($[T_s \times D_s] \approx [T_s \times H_s][H_s \times D_s]$) which decomposes the term-document matrix ($T \times D$) to discover the hidden dimensions or topics (H)

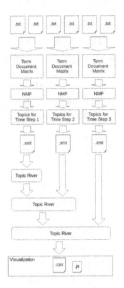

Fig. 1. Work flow of the NMF Code. Example with 6 text files and 3 time steps.

- Convert the term-topic (H_s^T) and topic-document (H_s^D) matrices to ranked topic instances which store the term and document list (ranking is done by the values of the equivalent matrices)
- Normalize values over all terms/documents in order to compare NMF results from discrete time steps (vocabulary and number of documents can change per time step)

- Phase 3:
  - Use a metric to identify if a time step's topic matches any topic from the preceding time steps: A topic is defined by its terms, and following Zipf's law [15], only a low number of terms have significant relevance to a topic. Thus, comparing the top-N-ranked terms (where N is set to 20 but can be adjusted by the user) of two topics, and defining a threshold ϵ for the similarity to be enough to define one of the topic as successor of the other, creates a *topic wave* over time (ϵ was set to 0.5 but can be adjusted by the user). Comparison between any topics $H1$ and $H2$ in any two timesteps s_1 and s_2 is possible through the H_s^T vectors and can be computed as:

    $dist(H1, H2) = \sum_i \sqrt{(H1_{s1,i}^T - H2_{s2,i}^T)}$ where i denotes the common terms between the two topics examined.

    A new topic wave begins at this time step if no previous topic is similar enough (thus if $dist > \epsilon$). Topic waves fade away if no topic is found at a time step that is similar enough to the topic wave's most relevant terms. It has to be noticed that a topic wave can reappear; topics of a time step are always compared against all existing waves, not just the ones that appeared in the last time step. This intuitively makes sense, e.g. for recurrent topics like the FIFA World Cup, that are barely relevant outside of their time frame.

- Topic waves from all time steps generate a *topic river* which then can be used to visualize the result. The relevance of all topic waves at a given time step sum up to 100%, and the sum of all topic waves over all time steps defines the topic river.
- Repeat Phases 2 and 3 for the equivalent number of time steps

4   The Proposed DLDA Approach

4.1   Dynamic Latent Dirichlet Allocation (DLDA)

The Dynamic LDA model is adopted and used on topics aggregated in time epochs and a state space model handles transitions of the topics from one epoch to another. A gaussian probabilistic model to obtain the posterior probabilities on the evolving topics along the time line is added as additional dimension. Figure 2 shows a graphical representation of the dynamic topic model.

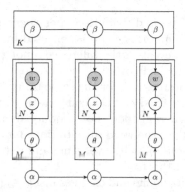

Fig. 2. Plate diagram representing the dynamic topic model (for three time slices) as a Bayesian network. The model for each time slice corresponds to the original LDA process (z denotes the word distribution, θ denotes the topic distribution, N is the total number of words per document, M is the total number of documents and K is the total number of topics. Additionally, each topic's parameters α and β evolve over time [4])

DLDA (as well as LDA) needs to know the number of topics in advance. That depends on the user and the number of stories that we could like to be detected. For example, the RCV1 corpus has 103 actually used annotated topics, plus a large amount of unlabeled documents, so the parameter for the extraction is set to 104 topics. This corresponds to the 103 annotated topics and one additional "ERROR" topic for the unlabeled documents. Moreover, the timestep has to be determined at this point. This again can be set to any time unit. For example,

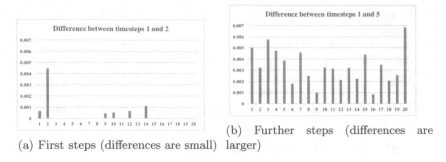

(a) First steps (differences are small)

(b) Further steps (differences are larger)

Fig. 3. Example differences in word distributions for a topic using top-20 words

the RCV1 corpus used here (July and August of 1996) contains 42 days which makes exactly 6 weeks of time. The dynamic topic model is accordingly applied to 6 time steps corresponding to the 6 weeks of the data set.

4.2   Topic Emergence and Storyline Detection

DLDA produces a list of topic distributions per time step. Topics appear not to evolve in a great degree and this trend is reflected by the word distributions. Inspecting them in detail reveals little difference among the word distributions for the time steps of each topic. Figure 3 shows the word distribution score differences for two different timesteps and for the same topic. The number of topics in the dynamic topic model is fixed and the computation infers the topics through a probabilistic distribution. This does not produce dynamic topics (appearing or disappearing) but instead, the word distributions for one topic could be used to capture gradual changes gradually over time and detect a new turning point (or arc) in the storyline of this topic.

To identify such turning points and changes inside the word distributions, the second step of the two folded approach consists of applying a similarity measure to identify time steps, where the word distributions change enough to identify a new arc within current topic. Cosine similarity is used in this case to measure differences in the distributions from time step to time step. This means that when a change in the topic distribution is not that big to create a new topic, then it is checked whether it could be that a sub-topic or a change under the same topic can be assessed.

If a significant change is identified using this similarity measure, then significant events within the topics (or storylines) are noticed. These changes in the storylines can be detected and visualized by a topic river like the one in Fig. 4. Peaks (like for example the yellow peak at the 3rd time-step) reveal important changes in the storyline development and thus can be used to monitor the storyline.

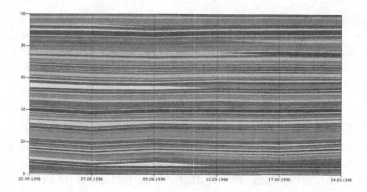

Fig. 4. Topic rivers for August and September 1996 for emerging topics: x-axis represents time units (weeks) and y-axis represents normalized topic prevalence (sums to 100) (Color figure online)

Moreover, storyline aggregation can be performed using the same similarity measure as before. Points of aggregation, where previously separate topics should become one, are computed this way. As DLDA once more does a good job in clustering, the distance between different topics is rather high.

5   Experiments

5.1   Datasets and Preprocessing

The Reuters Corpus RCV1 is used as a benchmark dataset [12]. It consists of roughly 800.000 news articles from the time of August 1996 to August 1997. The topic assignments for the articles make use of 103 out of 126 originally provided topics. These topics form a tree hierarchy, thus documents typically have multiple labels. Moreover, an actual copy from Reuters 2015 archive (roughly 330.000 news articles) was extracted[1] using a webcrawler containing the URL, time, headline, description, contents and tags.

Both algorithms (NMF and DLDA) can be very computationally expensive in terms of time and memory. The size of the vocabulary should be reduced to handle memory issues, preferably without loss of quality. The steps followed for preprocessing are: stemming (using Porter's Stemmer [16]), stopword removal, americanization (reducing words to american spelled ones utilizing code from Stanford Core NLP's tool [13]), lemmatization (also based on Stanford Core NLP tool), low occurence removal (deleting terms used by less than five documents). This process leads to a significant reduction in the vocabulary, i.e. from 308.854 district tokens we are left with a final vocabulary of 131.202 unique words.

Both algorithms rely on the selection of number of topics and the time unit. In our case week is selected as time unit and number of topics was either compared

---

[1] http://www.reuters.com/resources/archive/us/.

to the original Reuters categorization or to an arbitrary number (e.g. 30). In any case, selection of these parameters relies on the use case of the system (a smaller number of topics will lead to more changes in the topic distributions) but developing automated approaches for these parameters is one of the future work directions.

5.2   Implementation and Visualization Details

All topics of a time step are stored in a Java class and serialized as an XML file. This way, the most time-intensive part of the algorithm can be separated from generating visualization data. The XML files can be loaded into the program as soon as all desired data files are processed. Data is visualized using the .NET framework visualization library[2] in a form of a normalized stacked area graph: For each topic there is a value (Y-axis) for each time step (X-axis) that represents the prevalence of that topic. These values are normalized for each time unit and then displayed in a graph, where similar topics are next to each other. Graph is interactive in terms of offering a zoom function, tooltips to analyze topics in a certain range and a connection to view relevant documents.

5.3   NMF Results

With the NMF algorithm, we were able to calculate topics from the annotated Reuters Corpus of the year 20.08.1996–19.08.1997. We chose "week" as a time unit (7 days of text data). We also calculated topics for the whole year of 2015 (around 336.000 articles), which is not annotated, but represents more recent data which can be easier checked manually for coverage of all recent events from that year. We generated 30 topics for week-wise intervals and visualized the results using the implemented charting tool and results are presented in Fig. 5.

Table 1 shows different prominent topics of 2015, that were reflected in topics generated by our algorithm. Table 2 shows an example for a (short) topic wave, present in four time steps. The first two topics in January follow the terror attack in Paris on the magazine staff of *Charlie Hebdo* at January 7th. The third topic is in February and covers a terror attack of the terror group Houthis, located in Yemen. Finally, the last topic represents a terror attack on tourists in Tunesia in June 2015. The similarity between the topics within the topic wave can thus be confirmed by the actual events.

An overview of all topics, reveals that the most relevant topics usually are of business-related nature, made up of general financial terms like "stock market", "import" and "share", and not very specific to the corresponding time period. This appears to be an attribute of the test data, the Reuters Corpus, that has a dedicated section of articles that contain financial content, thus creating high TF-IDF values for these terms that are often used in this small section of documents. The same problem on a smaller scale exists for weather forecasts.

---

[2] https://msdn.microsoft.com/en-us/library/dd456632.aspx.

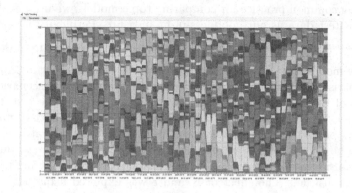

Fig. 5. Visualization of 30 topics from year 2015: x-axis represents time units (weeks) and y-axis represents normalized topic prevalence (sums to 100)

Table 1. Topics and their most relevant terms in 2015 (topic labels are manually selected)

Greece Financial Crisis	Charlie Hebdo Attacks	FiFA Corruption	Ukraine Crisis	VW Emission Scandal
greeks	attacker	fifa	ukraine	vws
greece	paris	soccer	russia	piech
syriza	charlie	cups	russians	winterkorn
tsipras	hebdo	blatter	sanctions	ceos
euros	police	corruption	moscow	porsche

Table 2. Evolution of a topic: terror attacks in Paris, Jemen, Tunesia

Jan 08	Jan 15	Feb 12	Jun 25
attacker	police	attacker	tunisia
paris	charlie	houthis	attacker
hebdo	french	police	tourists
police	attacker	boko	tunisians
french	hebdo	haram	hotels
islamic	paris	killed	tourism
france	muslims	islamic	beaches
killed	cartoons	yemen	islamists
muslims	islamists	militant	killed
kouachis	killed	libya	sousse

Following common practice for comparing topic models, we use perplexity of the held-out test data as our goodness-of-fit measure. Perplexity is defined as: $exp\left(-\frac{\sum_{d=1}^{D}\sum_{i=1}^{N_d}\log p(w_{d,i}|M)}{\sum_{d=1}^{D}N_d}\right)$ where $w_{d,i}$ represents the i-th term in document d, M is the model and N_d is the number of words in document d. In order to allow comparisons, all models were trained using a real-world scenario (using news items of the first 8 months of 2015 as training set and the last 4 months as testing set). As the number of topics is increased beyond that minimum, overfitting appears to set in, as was also observed in other literature work [9]. Results can be found in Fig. 6 where also the effect of parameter N (number of top-words considered for comparison between topics) is presented and the choice of $N = 20$ is justified. The effect of N and ϵ was explored using a grid search approach for different values: low value of ϵ leads to many new topics appearing at each time step which might reduce perplexity but results are not robust whereas high value of ϵ leads to stable topic rivers where not many new topics appear and that increases perplexity. ϵ value of 0.5 (combined with $N = 20$) was found to produce the best results.

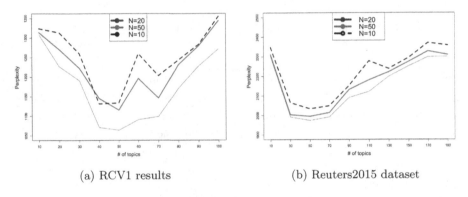

(a) RCV1 results   (b) Reuters2015 dataset

Fig. 6. Perplexity results for NMF-based algorithm

In order to evaluate the retrieval performance, a matching between the topics extracted by NMF and the RCV1 categories is attempted. Both NMF and RCV1 provide multi-labeled instances (each document is "assigned" to multiple topics), which leads to difficulties in assessing performance in a comparative way but treating each label for each document as a separate instance overcomes this issue. Then, precision and recall for each pair of NMF and RCV1-annotated topics are computed. The F-score is 0.496, derived from a precision of 0.521 and recall of 0.473, denoting that 103 topics over time does not lead to satisfactory results (as also suggested from Fig. 6). Further reducing the number of topics, leads to an increase in F-score of around 20% considering a merging of similar RCV1 annotated categories which gives promising directions for the proposed method.

5.4   LDA Results for Story Detection

Due to time limitations, the dynamic topic model was applied to only two months of the RCV1 corpus (Summer 1996). It was able to partially identify and reveals events of late summer 1996. Table 3 shows some of the identified events. The top 10 words of the topics' word distributions already give a precise overview of the topics' contents.

Table 3. Extracted topics reveal events from August and September 1996

Child abuse in Belgium	Tropical storm Edouard	Peace talks in Palestina	Kurdish war in Iraq
child	storm	israel	iraq
police	hurricane	peace	iraqi
woman	north	israeli	iran
death	wind	netanyahu	kurdish
family	west	minister	turkey
girl	mph	palestinian	northern
murder	mile	arafat	arbil
dutroux	coast	talk	baghdad
body	move	government	force
sex	flood	west	united

These topics describe events over a the period of two months and their change during the examined time frame (2 months) can be further explored in order to derive useful information for their evolution. Table 4 shows the differences in the top 20 words of the word distributions for one example topic (about Iraq). Inspecting the top articles for this topic reveals an evolution of the story behind the topic, as the main articles in the first weeks talk about the threat imposed by Iraqi forces and air strike battles, while the last weeks talk about concrete U.S. troop deployment in Kuwait. Table 5 presents the headlines of the corresponding articles for verification. Exploring the differences in the topic distributions between these weeks can help identify this change in the events. While the first weeks the similarity between the distribution is almost identical (less than 0.01 difference), difference between week 3 and week 4 is significant (more than 0.02) and thus reflects this "turning point" within the same topic.

Moreover, visualization works in a way that similar topics are on top of each other in the graph. Exploration of nearby topics can reveal further events within similar storylines. Following the same process as for NMF, we evaluated the performance against RCV1 predefined categories and that gave an F-score of 0.288, derived from a precision of 0.432 and recall of 0.216. Low scores (both for NMF and DLDA) are explained due to the fact that RCV1 corpus contains many unlabeled documents and that the nature of two tasks (classification versus topic detection) is different.

Table 4. Word distribution top word differences for Iraq topic

week 1	week 4	week 5
iraq	iraq	iraq
missile	missile	gulf
attack	gulf	kuwait
saudi	iraqi	military
iraqi	military	missile
military	kuwait	iraqi
gulf	attack	united
force	united	force
united	force	saudi
war	zone	zone
defense	saddam	troops
air	defense	war
kuwait	war	attack
zone	saudi	defense
arab	air	washington
official	strike	arab
arabia	southern	official
strike	official	air
saddam	troops	saddam
southern	washington	arabia

Table 5. Article headlines for top documents of Iraq topic

week 1–3	week 4	week 5–6
Perry cites two incidents in Iraq no-fly zone	Iraq fires at U.S. jets, U.S. bombers move closer	U.S. boosts Kuwait defence by deploying Patriots
U.S. warns it will protect pilots over Iraq	U.S. gets Kuwaiti approval for troops deployment	U.S. ground troops set to fly to Gulf
Defiant Saddam urges his warplanes to resist U.S	Kuwait agrees new troop U.S. deployment	U.S. carrier enters Gulf, troops land in Kuwait
Saddam urges his warplanes and gunners to resist	Iraq says fired missiles at US and allied planes	U.S. sends last of 3,000 ground troops to Gulf
U.S. launches new attack on Iraq - officials	Iraq fires at U.S. jets, U.S. bombers move closer	U.S. declines to rule out Iraq strikes

Finally, an example of some topics of summer 1996 and their presence (in terms of percentage of documents that the equivalent topic distribution is non-zero) is shown in Fig. 7. One can identify topics that are recurring and present turning points (like the "Russia-1") which has two major hits or topics that have

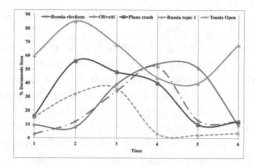

Fig. 7. Emerging topics and turning points example

more bursty presence (like the "Olivetti" case in Italy or the "Tennis Open"). It should also be noticed the effect of topics that cover different stories under the same arc (e.g. the "plane crash" topics is already present in the news (referring mostly to TWA800 flight accident but it becomes more prevalent once a new plane crash in Russia (Vnukovo2801 flight) occurs, which also boosts the "Russia-1" since they are overlapping). These experiments reveal the ability of the system to identify turning points in storylines and track their presence and evolution.

6   Discussion and Conclusion

This paper presented two algorithmic approaches to the topic detection and tracking from news items corpora. The first approach applied NMF on separate time steps of the data and then connected using a similarity metric. By using extensive cleaning of the vocabulary during pre-processing, a fast data processing algorithm was developed and the proposed pipeline is more simplified than literature work but still effective. The generated topics can easily be identified by their most relevant terms and associated with events happening in the corresponding time period. The second approach utilized a dynamic version of LDA and was able to identify some of the main events happening at the summer of 1996 (e.g. the Kurdish civil war or the horrible crimes in Belgium). In order to identify details and possible turning points of a topic, a second step of comparing the word distributions inside each topic at each time step is added. Similarly, topics can also be aggregated revealing trends and arcs under the same storyline. Moreover, "burstiness" of topics can be detected and used for identifying new or recurring events.

Summarizing the two approaches, the DLDA method produces topics, that are on a more generalized level. A high frequency of topic evolution can not be seen here but the algorithm can detect turning points within the developing stories. On the other hand, the NMF approach is significantly faster and can effectively detect new stories, track them until they disappear (and detect them again if they re-appear). Changes in the topics appear to be fast enough regardless the threshold set for detecting changes showing the evolution here is large.

Further evaluation of two approaches against each other is needed in order to identify these differences in a microscopical level.

Results reveal the possibilities of monitoring storylines and their evolution through time and the opportunities for detecting turning points or identifying several sub-stories. Visualization of the results and the interaction with the stacked graph provide a framework for better monitoring the storylines. Besides the detailed comparison of the two algorithms, future work involves developing approaches that will validate the results and allow for more comprehensive and sophisticated topic descriptions. Moreover, automated approaches for determining the number of topics and the time unit will be explored. This will give the opportunity to create stories or summaries based on the topic waves created by the system.

References

1. Ahmed, A., Xing, E.P.: Timeline: a dynamic hierarchical dirichlet process model for recovering birth/death and evolution of topics in text stream. arXiv preprint arXiv:1203.3463 (2012)
2. Allan, J., Carbonell, J.G., Doddington, G., Yamron, J., Yang, Y.: Topic detection and tracking pilot study final report (1998)
3. Banerjee, A., Basu, S.: Topic models over text streams: a study of batch and online unsupervised learning. In: SDM, vol. 7, pp. 437–442. SIAM (2007)
4. Blei, D.M., Lafferty, J.D.: Dynamic topic models. In: Proceedings of the 23rd International Conference on Machine Learning, ICML 2006, pp. 113–120. ACM, New York (2006)
5. Blei, D.M., Ng, A.Y., Jordan, M.I.: Latent dirichlet allocation. J. Mach. Learn. Res. **3**, 993–1022 (2003)
6. Cao, B., Shen, D., Sun, J.-T., Wang, X., Yang, Q., Chen, Z.: Detect and track latent factors with online nonnegative matrix factorization. In: IJCAI, pp. 2689–2694 (2007)
7. Dubey, A., Hefny, A., Williamson, S., Xing, E.P.: A nonparametric mixture model for topic modeling over time. In: SDM, pp. 530–538. SIAM (2013)
8. Fiscus, J.G. Doddington, G.R.: Topic detection and tracking evaluation overview. In: Topic Detection and Tracking, pp. 17–31. Kluwer Academic Publishers, Norwell (2002)
9. Griffiths, T.L., Steyvers, M.: Finding scientific topics. Proc. Nat. Acad. Sci. **101**(suppl 1), 5228–5235 (2004)
10. Hong, L., Dom, B., Gurumurthy, S., Tsioutsiouliklis, K.: A time-dependent topic model for multiple text streams. In: Proceedings of the 17th ACM SIGKDD International Conference on Knowledge Discovery and Data Mining, pp. 832–840. ACM (2011)
11. Lee, D.D., Seung, H.S.: Learning the parts of objects by non-negative matrix factorization. Nature **401**, 788–791 (1999)
12. Lewis, D.D., Yang, Y., Rose, T.G., Li, F.: RCV1: a new benchmark collection for text categorization research. J. Mach. Learn. Res. **5**, 361–397 (2004)
13. Manning, C.D., Surdeanu, M., Bauer, J., Finkel, J., Bethard, S.J., McClosky, D.: The stanford CoreNLP natural language processing toolkit. In: Association for Computational Linguistics (ACL) System Demonstrations, pp. 55–60 (2014)

14. Paul, M., Girju, R.: Cross-cultural analysis of blogs and forums with mixed-collection topic models. In: Proceedings of the 2009 Conference on Empirical Methods in Natural Language Processing, vol. 3, pp. 1408–1417. Association for Computational Linguistics (2009)
15. Piantadosi, S.T.: Zipfs word frequency law in natural language: a critical review and future directions. Psychon. Bull. Rev. **21**(5), 1112–1130 (2014)
16. Porter, M.F.: An algorithm for suffix stripping. Program **14**(3), 130–137 (1980)
17. Saha, A., Sindhwani, V.: Learning evolving and emerging topics in social media: a dynamic NMF approach with temporal regularization. In: Proceedings of the fifth ACM International conference on Web Search and Data Mining, pp. 693–702 (2012)
18. Sra, S., Dhillon, I.S.: Generalized nonnegative matrix approximations with bregman divergences. In: Advances in Neural Information Processing Systems, pp. 283–290 (2005)
19. Tannenbaum, M., Fischer, A., Scholtes, J.C.: Dynamic topic detection and tracking using non-negative matrix factorization. In: Proceedings of the 27th Benelux Artificial Intelligence Conference (BNAIC). BNAIC (2015)
20. Wang, C., Blei, D.M., Heckerman, D.: Continuous time dynamic topic models. In: McAllester, D.A., Myllymki, P. (eds.), UAI, pp. 579–586. AUAI Press (2008)
21. Wang, F., Li, P., Christian König, A.: Efficient document clustering via online nonnegative matrix factorizations. In: SDM, vol. 11, pp. 908–919. SIAM (2011)
22. Wang, X., McCallum, A.: Topics over time: a non-markov continuous-time model of topical trends. In: Proceedings of the 12th ACM SIGKDD International Conference on Knowledge Discovery and Data Mining, pp. 424–433. ACM (2006)
23. Wei, X., Sun, J., Wang, X.: Dynamic mixture models for multiple time-series. In: Veloso, M.M. (ed.) IJCAI, pp. 2909–2914 (2007)
24. Yang, J., Leskovec, J.: Patterns of temporal variation in online media. In: Proceedings of the Fourth ACM International Conference on Web Search and Data Mining, pp. 177–186. ACM (2011)

Author Index

Printed in the United States
By Bookmasters